HOW REAL
Is the Federal Deficit?

HOW REAL
Is the Federal Deficit?

Robert Eisner

THE FREE PRESS
A Division of Macmillan, Inc.
NEW YORK

Collier Macmillan Publishers
LONDON

The Free Press
A Division of Macmillan, Inc.
866 Third Avenue, New York, N.Y. 10022

Collier Macmillan Canada, Inc.

Printed in the United States of America

printing number
1   2   3   4   5   6   7   8   9   10

Library of Congress Cataloging-in-Publication Data

Eisner, Robert.
    How real is the federal deficit?

    Bibliography: p.
    Includes index.
    1. Budget deficits—United States.   I. Title.
HJ2051.E37   1986   339.5′23′0973   86-1076
ISBN 0-02-909430-5

You and I, as individuals, can, by borrowing, live beyond our means, but only for a limited period of time. Why then do we think that collectively, as a nation, we are not bound by that same limitation? For decades we have piled deficit upon deficit, mortgaging our future and our children's future for the temporary convenience of the present. To continue this long trend is to guarantee tremendous social, cultural, political and economic upheavals.
—Ronald Reagan, Inaugural Address, January 20, 1981

For every buyer there must be a seller, and for every lender a borrower. One man's expenditure is another's receipt. My debts are your asset, my deficit your surplus.
—James Tobin, Nobel Laureate in Economics, in *National Economic Policy*, 1966

Blessed are the young, for they shall inherit the national debt.
—Herbert Hoover

Contents

Tables and Figures

Figures

Preface

Popular perceptions of governmental deficits reflect more in the way of personal predilections and political posturing than scientific insight. But economists are human, and we too have been influenced by private and political passions. Misled or ill-armed by our own figures and data, we have too often misapplied theoretical economic analysis, or abandoned it.

While this work builds on the Keynesian model of the determinants of income and employment, it infuses that model with the traditional neoclassical emphasis on the role of real wealth and abhorrence of "money illusion." It is aimed at economists and noneconomists of all schools and political persuasions.

The pages that follow support old theory with new data, or with new, corrected measures of old data. They will give comfort to those who, if only in the closet, have continued to identify themselves with established formulations. They should give pause to those who have marched to new drummers.

Robert Eisner
December 1985

Acknowledgments

A series of grants from the National Science Foundation have offered critical support to the research on which this book is based.* Initial estimates of real budget deficits were prepared for the Council of Economic Advisers in 1981 and were incorporated in the *Economic Report of the President February 1982.*

A great deal of my research on this subject has been done in collaboration with Paul J. Pieper. I am most indebted to him for his contributions to our joint work as well as to this current effort. And I am grateful to the *American Economic Review, The Public Interest,* the *Journal of Macroeconomics,* and the North-Holland Publishing Company for permission to incorporate parts of my own papers and the articles that I have co-authored with Professor Pieper. Sang-In Hwang has been an indefatigable and extraordinary research assistant along the entire path from computer to

*In particular, NSF grants SES-7717555 and SES-8200324 for the development of expanded measures of national income (the "Total Incomes System of Accounts") and, currently, grant SES-8409793 to examine "Inflation and the Adjustment and Impact of Fiscal Variables." The National Science Foundation is, of course, in no way responsible for the particular contents of this book or the views I express therein.

tables to text. I am also indebted for assistance along the way from Steve Zimmer, George Houlihan, and John Keating. Molly Fabian has done her usual superb job in typing the manuscript and myriad tables.

I have received most useful, detailed comments from Alan Blinder and useful comments as well from Gardner Ackley, Michael J. Boskin, Mary Eccles, Edith C. Eisner, Robert Heilbroner, Paul McCracken, Joseph Pechman, Frank S. Russek, Mary Alice Shulman, Lester Thurow, James Tobin, and Murray Weidenbaum. Credit for help or comments with regard to earlier papers and articles is due to Lawrence Kotlikoff; Elizabeth Fogler and John Musgrave; John J. Seater, W. Michael Cox, and Eric Hirschhorn; Otto Eckstein, H. S. Houthakker, and Allen Sinai; and Moses Abramovitz, E. Cary Brown, Paul Evans, Benjamin Friedman, Robert J. Gordon, Bert G. Hickman, Frank de Leeuw, Frederick Mishkin, Dale T. Mortensen, and George Neumann; and to anonymous referees. I am especially indebted to copy editor Ann Hirst and Edith Lewis of The Free Press for their fine and painstaking work in editing final copy.

And my thanks finally to Grant Ujifusa of The Free Press for convincing me of the value of presenting my formulations and findings in this forum, and helping me do it.

1

Debt and Deficits: Curse, or Blessing in Disguise?

THERE HAS ALWAYS BEEN a certain amount of hysteria surrounding the federal debt and deficits. Politicians and pundits compete in their proclamations of future disaster and the attribution of its causes.

Meanwhile, for most of the American public, debt and deficits are like sin: morally wrong, difficult to avoid, but not easy to keep track of. Our federal deficits have each year been adding huge, $200 billion chunks to the "national debt." The sheer magnitude of that debt, currently approaching $2 trillion, suggests to some the danger of national bankruptcy.

Yet, election after election, from the early days of Franklin Roosevelt's presidency on, Republicans have traditionally cried out against budget deficits with little apparent success, either substantively or politically. Walter Mondale tried to reverse field and lead Democrats in a similar crusade in 1984. His failure is well-remembered recent history.

A few short years before, the Carter Administration, faced with seemingly explosive inflation, reacted sharply to the then supposedly large federal deficits believed responsible. It tight-ened fiscal policy and encouraged tight money as well. Carter thus further weakened a sluggish economy and contributed to his own demise.

Those Carter policies, we shall show, were based on false intelligence, misread by friend and foe alike. They were unnecessary and misguided. *In fact, we did not have real federal budget deficits from 1977 to 1980.*

The new Reagan Administration in 1981, in the name of combatting inflation, continued the Carter policies. But it did so with sufficient dedication and efficiency to bring on the worst recession since the Great Depression of the 1930s. Business investment and profits plummeted, and unemployment rose to a post–World War II record of 10.7 percent of the labor force. We counted almost ten million Americans unsuccessfully looking for jobs, and millions more too discouraged to look further, or only "partially employed for economic reasons."

And then came an economic miracle. We began to run really huge budget deficits, and the economy recovered sharply. A new "Reaganomics" and hitherto unheralded preachers of a "supply-side" gospel claimed credit.

But what really happened? Did the recovery take place despite the great move to very large deficits, as traditional budget balancers might insist? Were the deficits essentially irrelevant, as monetarists tell us? Or is there something else to the story—something basic and fundamental?

The real story is that federal budget deficits *can* have great consequences for the economy. Startling as this may seem, these may be good as well as bad. And deficits can be too small as well as too large. We cannot begin to know the consequences of deficits until we measure them correctly.[1]

And because we have not measured deficits correctly, we have confused economic analysts, turned economic theory on its head, and committed grievous errors in economic policy. If we continue to act this way, we court future disaster.

When World War II brought us an early bout with inflation, a popular song had it that "A dollar ain't a dollar any more." The refrain in recent years could be put another way, that "A deficit ain't a deficit any more."

Why? Because inflation plays many tricks, and one of its biggest has been largely overlooked in the mounting rhetoric over budget deficits. *That trick, simply enough, is that as inflation wipes out the value of money, it also wipes out the value of debt.* As it does that, it profoundly alters the significance of conventional ways of measuring the deficit.

Accordingly, meaningful correction for inflation can cause a dramatic shift in understanding. Deficits which have appeared to be enormous can turn out to be moderate. Moderate deficits may even be converted into surpluses!

Mismeasuring deficits, we have confused economic policy and theory alike. We think we have deficits when we do not, and take counteractions that cause recessions. We further see consequences of what we call deficits belying the predictions of economic theory, and question and repudiate our theory.

Inflation, however, is not the only source of our confusion about the deficit. The federal government has a strange accounting system. It differs not only from that of private business, but also from that of state and local governments. Every large corporation, just like the State of California under Ronald Reagan, distinguishes between current and capital expenditures. Every individual sensibly managing his own finances must so distinguish. Our official measures of the federal deficit do not.

Why make the distinction? Because it makes a difference whether a family's outgo exceeds its income—a deficit—because of gambling losses in Las Vegas or the purchase of a new home. Business investment in excess of retained earnings is applauded as contributing to economic growth. But by federal government accounting practice, AT&T, General Motors, IBM, and many other companies would be guilty of "deficit financing." And so, indeed, would most of our state and local governments, which by their own accounting generally show balanced budgets or tidy surpluses.

The reason for all of these anomalies? The federal government, alone, does not differentiate between capital and current expenditures.

There is much more to the story that too often escapes public understanding. For example, for every borrower there must be a lender. In other words, the federal deficit is someone else's surplus. If the government can be viewed as getting poorer by going into debt, then the individuals, businesses, and state and local governments that acquire the debt are getting richer. This

has profound effects on private spending and saving and on the
health of the economy. But again, to know the effects, we have
to make our measures correct.

As the federal government runs deficits, it presumably increases its debt. But construction and analysis of federal balance
sheets yield some anomalous findings. With all the deficits, the
general trend of real federal debt—the debt adjusted for inflation—has been downward. On a per capita basis it has indeed
gone down very sharply over most of the last forty years. And
the government's net worth, the difference between its assets—
financial and real—and its liabilities, has moved from red to black.

All of this illuminates a fiscal landscape substantially different
from that portrayed by today's headlines. The struggles of
Administration and Congress, the battles of former budget chief
David Stockman and chief economic advisor Martin Feldstein appear in a different light. And so too do the clashing positions of
presidential hopefuls, Senate Majority Leader Robert Dole and
Congressman Jack Kemp.

Corrected measures of debt and deficits also demand major
revision of recent economic history. The indictment of twenty
years of economic mismanagement leveled by this Administration
at its predecessors proves wide of the mark, but other crucial
policy errors come to light. The initial economic failures and subsequent recovery of Ronald Reagan's first term get new explanations, at considerable variance from official interpretation.

Revising our view of the past, we gain new insights into what
to do about the future. Corrected perceptions of our true budgetary posture suggest the need for policies sharply different from
those most loudly advocated in Washington and on Wall Street.

As a basis for a new approach, we develop corrected measures
of government debt and deficits. Conventional, official accounting deals in nominal and par values, regardless of what securities
are really worth. We correct this accounting for changes in market
values of assets and liabilities due to changing interest rates and
changes in real values due to inflation. We thus derive real market
measures relevant to the course of the economy.

We can then see the implications of a consistent set of federal
accounting rules, distinguishing between expenditures for current consumption and those that entail investment in the nation's
future. This leads beyond capital budgeting to a broad view of

all public assets and liabilities, long-term as well as short-term, financial and real, tangible and intangible.

Such new measurement lays the groundwork for new analysis. After reviewing the state of economic thinking on the effects of debt and deficits upon the economy, we can look at the facts. A statistical study confirms that deficits are very important, more important than our old, faulty measures indicated. And as a consequence of all this, our analysis has import for much of the disarray in modern macroeconomic theory. Correct measures of debt and deficits clear a path through the thickets of confusion shaped by the varying claims of monetarists, supply-siders and the apostles of market-clearing rational expectations. In so doing, they open the way to a new "Keynesian-neoclassical synthesis."

To know how deficits matter we not only have to measure them correctly. We also have to understand their real role in the economy.

Of fundamental importance to this understanding is the notion that the federal debt, however frequently viewed as a burden to the government or to future taxpayers, is wealth to those who own it. Whatever their concerns for the government's fiscal responsibility, the holders of all those deficit-financing Treasury notes, bills, and bonds feel richer for having them. And the richer they feel, the more they try to spend now and plan to spend in the future.

Since federal deficits add to federal debt, which thus adds to private wealth, they can be expected to increase aggregate demand, or spending. If the economy is booming along at full employment of its resources, further increases in demand raise prices and encourage inflation. But if there is slack in the economy, deficit-induced demand stimulates output and employment.

But for deficits to matter they must be *real* deficits. A real deficit is one which increases the real net debt of the government to the public and hence increases the public's perception of its own real wealth. Thus the vital importance of the inflation correction. For inflation in effect generates an "inflation tax," eating away the value of the public's holdings of those Treasury notes, bills, and bonds, or the cash which they back.

We all know that inflation accelerated sharply in the Watergate Nixon years from 1972 to 1974, and again from 1977 to 1980, during the Carter Administration. In each case, associated

higher interest rates reduced the market value of outstanding
Treasury securities and higher prices further cut their real worth.
The precipitous decline in real market value of the debt the public
held from previous federal borrowing more than offset the increases in public holdings resulting from the new nominal deficits.
In real terms, since the total change in the real market value of
debt held by the public was declining, the federal budget was not
in deficit but in surplus.

In the fall of 1974, utterly misreading the government's real
fiscal and monetary posture, President Ford called the notorious
"WIN" (whip-inflation-now) conference to help plan restrictive
policies just as the economy was moving into a major recession.
And at the end of the Carter years and on into the beginning of
the Reagan era, the false perception of a real deficit fostered the
tight monetary *and* fiscal policies responsible for the even worse
economic drop of 1981–82.

But then, in the latter half of 1982 and in 1983 major tax
reductions became effective. With less inflation and lower interest
rates, the inflation tax was wiped out, or at least suspended. We
now had a real deficit, and a big one, which propelled the 1983–84
recovery. Jack Kemp and the other supply-side tax cutters were
right, for the wrong reasons. Fueled by the deficit, the economy
reacted to classic demand-side stimulus.

This is made clear by a new look at the statistical data, incorporating our inflation-corrected budget measures. Without
correction, even cyclically adjusted or "high-employment" budgets
had appeared in deficit, and increasing deficit, through the sluggish and rising-unemployment decade of the 1970s. That could
be taken to mean that deficits, fiscal policy, and demand did not
matter. The expected stimulus did not take place. Hence the reversion to monetarism and supply siders.

Adjusted for inflation, the "deficits" become surpluses, and
the demand-oriented explanation of stagnation re-emerges. The
less the *inflation-adjusted* surplus or the greater the deficit, the data
confirm, the greater the subsequent growth, or the less the decline, in real gross national product. And the greater that deficit,
the greater the reduction, or the less the increase, in unemployment. With the major swing to a real federal deficit at the end of
1982, unemployment fell, in less than two years, from almost 11
percent to 7 percent.

For those who would attribute all of the gain to a change in monetary policy, we can point to evidence that indicates otherwise. Increases in the monetary base are indeed also associated with growth in GNP and declines in unemployment. But inclusion of monetary variables in our statistical relations does not eliminate the major role of real budget deficits. We offer new confirmation that monetary and fiscal policy *both* matter, and indeed that fiscal policy, as measured by corrected budget deficits, is the more potent.

We present further evidence on the important concern that budget deficits "crowd out" private investment. The argument, of course, is that federal deficits absorb the saving that would otherwise go to finance business capital expenditures. That might indeed occur in a full-employment economy. Over the last thirty years of usually less than full employment though, we find that the stimulus effects of real federal deficits are dominant. They prove positively associated with private investment, and we have "crowding in" rather than crowding out.

Budget deficits have also been blamed for our large recent trade deficits, and while there is more to that story, we do find evidence to support the charge. Real federal deficits are correlated with subsequent increases in imports and decreases in net exports, as economic theory leads us to expect. There is, however, another side to the coin. While our deficits prove a balance-of-trade drag on our economy, they correspondingly stimulate the economies of other nations. The budget deficit of the United States is positively correlated with subsequent growth in output of our major OECD partners.

And deficits in other countries turn out to matter as well. The United Kingdom, with inflation-adjusted budget *surpluses,* has had the slowest economic growth. High-growth Japan, on the other hand, has had the largest real deficits.

Statistical analysis also offers surprises for Wall Street. *Increases* in deficits lead to subsequent *increases* in Dow Jones stock averages. This may be traced to the stimulatory effect of deficits on demand and output and hence on profits. It also relates to the fact that nominal deficits that are not real do not increase the real cost of capital.

Finally, integration of federal deficits and the balance sheet of assets and liabilities permits new insight into the vital issue of our future and our children's future. There has long been concern that federal deficits pass on our burden to future generations. What we really bequeath the future, however, is our physical and human capital. A "deficit" which finances construction of our roads, bridges, harbors, and airports *is* an investment in the future. So are expenditures to preserve and enhance our natural resources or to educate our people and keep them healthy. Federal budgets which are balanced by running down our country's capital are real *national* deficits.

2
Tricks Played by Inflation

INFLATION HAS BEEN CALLED the cruellest tax of all. Whether it is the cruellest is debatable, but in its economic effects, inflation certainly is a tax. We know we have to count it in calculating what the government takes from the public. And therefore we have to count it in reckoning the federal deficit—the difference between the government's outgo and its income.

The significance of a deficit—individual, business, or governmental—is that, unless we dip into capital, we must borrow to finance it. That increases our debt.[1] The federal government, it is true, can finance a deficit by creating money—which economists would call non-interest-bearing debt. That does add some complications but, as we shall see, does not change the essential issue.

What do we do, though, when a dollar isn't a dollar any more? A basic premise in economics—for all schools of economic thought—is that we must avoid "money illusion," the confusion of nominal and real magnitudes. A person earning $60,000 today is obviously no better off than a similar person earning $20,000 twenty years ago, if prices in the marketplace now are three times as high. But similarly, a person with a debt of $60,000 today is no worse off than a person with a debt of $20,000 twenty years

9

ago. *For individuals, businesses, and government, it is the real debt—the debt after adjustment for inflation—that matters.*

If we already owe $100,000 on a mortgage loan on our home and then borrow to spend $5,000 more than our income, our total debt of course rises to $105,000. But suppose, in the meantime, the value of a dollar has fallen by 10 percent because of inflation. That, in effect, cuts the real burden of our existing, mortgage debt to $90,000 just as surely as if, without the inflation, we had somehow paid off $10,000. Adding the $5,000 of new borrowing gives us a new total debt of $95,000. We started with a debt of $100,000. Did our total debt then, in meaningful economic terms, or in dollars of constant purchasing power, rise by $5,000 or fall by $5,000?

But if our real debt declined, does it mean anything to say that we spent more than our income? Or should we rather recognize as part of our income the $10,000 gain in the reduced real value of our debt? If we do, our spending was $5,000 *less* than our income. We did not have a "deficit" of $5,000. *Instead, we had a surplus.*

Inflation is thus not a neutral matter for debtors. They gain. Their creditors lose. American farmers have known this through more than two centuries, from the days of Shays' Rebellion through the Civil War and subsequent struggles over free silver, and on to the present. It certainly became clear to a generation of home buyers, in the 1960s and 1970s, who borrowed to buy homes whose values grew with inflation while the real value of mortgage debt shrank. They flocked to buy, and buy again.

Of course, their lenders in the banks and savings and loans took a beating, as they lent in "good" dollars and were paid back in depreciated ones. And as the inflation continued and people came to expect it to continue, interest rates rose. The latecomers to the game could no longer borrow and buy for a great profit, as the higher interest payments swallowed their inflationary capital gains.

But inflation still quite befouled conventional accounting. Borrowers could report that they were making high, indeed prohibitive interest payments, at rates of 16 percent. As long as inflation was proceeding at 11 percent, however, they were gaining back 11 percent on the depreciation of the dollar, or appreciation of whatever they bought with their loan, so that their *real* rate of interest was only 5 percent.

The situation was quite analogous, if inverse, for lenders. If you put your money in a savings bank or bought a bond as inflation heated up in the late 1960s and 1970s, *you* took a beating, a double beating if you were a bond buyer. As prices rose you found that the money you had turned over to the bank or bond seller was losing value. What you were to get back would be worth less in real terms than what you had lent.

The double beating came along for the bond buyer as interest rates rose in response to expectations of continued inflation. The thirty-year, 8 percent bond sold in 1975 for $1,000 would market or sell for some $585 in 1981. But with prices 55 percent higher in 1981, the value of the $585 in 1981, in terms of the 1975 dollars originally invested, was only $376. That is a $624 loss, which does not come close to being made up by the $480 in interest, in depreciating dollars at that, received over the intervening six years.

Again, as inflation continues, those who buy bonds after interest rates have risen do not lose. They receive enough in higher interest payments to compensate for the loss in the real value of their bonds due to inflation. And, if interest rates stabilize, there is no further drop in the *market* value of bonds. Once more, the only thing that goes wrong is conventional accounting. Bond holders are considered to have income equal to their interest receipts—and pay taxes on that income—without deducting the loss in real value of their bonds due to inflation. The anomaly is all the greater in that the high interest income is paid precisely to compensate for the loss in capital value due to inflation.

Government borrowing reflects the same effects of inflation as private borrowing. And government accounts are similarly bedeviled. The market values of government securities fall when market interest rates rise, and rise when interest rates fall just as do those of the private sector. Holders of government securities take a double beating, when inflation further eats away at real values, just as do holders of private securities. And the real market value of government debt correspondingly declines with rising interest rates and inflation.

For an individual, business, or government, a deficit means a selling off of assets or an increase in debt. A deficit must then increase "net debt," the difference between financial liabilities and financial assets. If there are no changes in market values of financial assets and liabilities, the deficit is thus identically equal to the increase in net debt. Concern over deficits, if it is to make any sense, stems precisely from this fact. *Deficits add to debt.*

But we do not have to be economists to know that what matters is not the numbers written on a bond, or any other piece of paper. What is relevant about the piece of paper is that it has a value, and that value has no meaning unless it is a market value. So it is the market value of debt with which we are properly concerned. And finally, what matters is what that market value is worth in goods or purchasing power, that is, its *real* value.

In the world in which we live, the real market value of debt turns out to reflect much more than the accumulation of past deficits. As we have observed, the market values of existing debt fall as interest rates rise, and their real values fall still further as prices rise. If we want measures of deficits which are equal to increases in the *real, market value of debt,* then we must adjust our measures to incorporate these changes in real market values due to inflation and changing interest rates.

In short, since we are concerned with the impact of federal deficits on the economy, we want measures that reflect changes in the real value of the federal debt held outside of the government. This means measures of the deficit that correspond to changes in the real value of claims of the rest of the economy— the domestic private and state and local sectors—and of foreigners upon the federal government.

Getting those claims straight turns out to be a bit complicated. For one thing, a substantial amount of the federal debt is held by the federal reserve banks, which in turn have liabilities in the form of federal reserve notes—the currency in our wallets and pocketbooks—and the required reserve deposits of private banks and other depository institutions. Social security and other government trust funds own many billions more of federal securities. In addition, we must take into account federally sponsored credit agencies such as the Federal Home Loan Banks, Federal National Mortgage Association and Farm Credit Banks. For all of these we have to convert par values to market values, correct market values for inflation, and subtract financial assets—of loans to private individuals and business as well as U.S. Treasury securities—from liabilities.

In collaboration with Paul Pieper, now at the University of Illinois at Chicago, I have undertaken these compilations, conversions, and corrections for the years from the end of World War II to the present. We have even made projections of the future. Let us go through some of the calculations before noting the results, which are eye-opening.

We begin with the government public debt figures, which reflect the par or face value of government obligations. If the debt were overwhelmingly in very short-term securities or interest rates did not change much over the life of the securities, the difference between par and market values would be small. But in recent years neither of these conditions has been met. A substantial amount of government obligations is medium- and long-term. With varying combinations of tight money and inflation, interest rates rose sharply in the 1970s, and then headed for unprecedented heights. The switch of the Federal Reserve in 1979 to emphasis on curbing the quantity of money and other "monetary aggregates" contributed to that final rise.

Yields on ten-year U.S. Treasury securities thus averaged 2.40 percent in 1954, 7.35 percent in 1970, 9.44 percent in 1979 and 13.91 percent in 1981. The average rate then fell to 13.00 percent in 1982 and 11.10 percent in 1983 before rising to 12.44 percent in 1984. In December 1985, the rate on ten-year securities was sharply down, to 9.34 percent. Other Treasury issues, as well as the broad range of other securities, showed similar fluctuations.

Higher interest rates, as we have pointed out, mean lower prices for outstanding debt securities. A ten-year, 7.5 percent U.S. Treasury bond, issued in 1977 when the market rate was 7.5 percent, could not sell at its principal value of $1,000 in 1981 when the market yield approached 14 percent. Since anyone lending $1,000 when the rate of interest was 14 percent could receive $140 per year, no one was willing to pay $1,000 for a bond paying only $75 per year. Hence, the market price of the $1,000 face-value, 7.5 percent bond had to fall until the $75 per year return on that market price plus the $1,000 return of principal at maturity offered a rate equivalent to the 14 percent on new securities and in the market generally. In 1981, with a market rate of 14 percent, 7.5 percent ten-year bonds issued in 1977 thus had to sell for $725.

As a first step in our corrections, therefore, we construct market-to-par indices for major financial components of government balance sheets.[2] We find that, with par equal to 100, the market-to-par index for the composite of all U.S. government securities was $92.05 at the end of 1969, up to $101.01 for 1976, down to $92.86 for 1980 and up to $101.25 for 1982, then down to $98.23 at the end of 1983 and up again to $99.84 at the end of 1984, as shown in Tables 2.1 and B.14. Fluctuations of this amplitude may not seem large, but when there are $1,800 billion of U.S. government securities outstanding, each one point change in the index implies a change of some $18 billion in market value. Changes in the value of outstanding debt as a consequence of changes in interest rates have been substantial, even in relation to the large deficits of recent years. From 1977 to 1980, with persistent decline in the market-to-par index, holders of the federal debt suffered a $53 billion loss in the market value of their securities. Since rising inflation was the major factor in the increase in interest rates which were responsible, this was essentially an "interest-effect" component of the inflation tax.

In making such calculations we must go beyond the usually cited figures for the gross public debt. For this is a correct measure of neither the total liabilities (interest-bearing and non-interest-bearing) of the federal government (including the associated credit agencies and the Federal Reserve) nor of the critical *net debt*, the difference between total liabilities and total financial assets. We may note, in Table 2.2, illustrative calculations of that net debt.

Total liabilities associated with the U.S. government came, at the end of 1980, to $1,220 billion at par. The par value of financial assets amounted to $592 billion. The par value of net government debt was thus only $628 billion. But with those high interest rates at the end of 1980, Treasury securities were selling at only 94.44 percent of par. The *market* value of total U.S. government liabilities at the end of 1980 was $1,162 billion, $58 billion less than its par value. The market value of U.S. government financial assets was $721 billion, or $129 billion more than par.[3] This mainly reflected a market value of gold that was $141 billion greater than the statutory figure, which is based on the $42 per ounce at which gold is held in Treasury account books. Thus the market value of U.S. government net debt in 1980 was $441 billion, a considerable cry from the original "gross public debt" figure of $930 billion.

The adjustments for 1984 are somewhat different. The par-to-market conversions, in particular, were less. Still, in 1984, we

TABLE 2.1   Market-to-Par Indices
(100 = Par)

(1)	(2)	(3)	(4)
		U.S. GOVERNMENT SECURITIES	
YEAR	*Bills*	*Bonds + Notes*	*Total*
1945	100.0	103.5	102.6
1946	100.0	103.6	102.7
1947	99.9	101.3	101.1
1948	99.8	101.5	101.3
1949	99.9	103.5	102.7
1950	99.8	101.1	101.0
1951	99.7	98.7	99.3
1952	99.7	98.7	99.1
1953	99.8	99.8	99.9
1954	99.9	100.4	100.3
1955	99.7	97.9	98.3
1956	99.6	94.7	90.1
1957	99.6	98.0	98.8
1958	99.5	93.8	96.0
1959	98.8	91.7	94.1
1960	99.4	98.0	98.5
1961	99.3	97.0	97.6
1962	99.3	98.4	98.8
1963	99.1	97.1	97.7
1964	98.9	97.5	97.9
1965	98.6	95.5	96.4
1966	98.6	96.2	97.0
1967	98.5	93.7	95.1
1968	98.1	93.3	94.8
1969	97.7	89.2	92.1
1970	98.6	96.4	97.2
1971	98.9	99.0	99.0
1972	98.6	97.5	97.9
1973	98.0	95.9	96.7
1974	98.1	96.5	97.2
1975	98.5	98.8	98.5
1976	98.7	102.7	101.0
1977	98.1	98.4	98.3
1978	97.2	94.4	95.3
1979	96.6	93.4	94.4
1980	96.0	91.3	92.9
1981	96.5	91.9	93.5
1982	97.5	103.3	101.3
1983	97.1	98.8	98.2
1984	97.5	100.8	99.8

Source: See Appendix C.

TABLE 2.2   The Budget Deficit, Gross Public Debt, and Market Value of Net
Debt, 1980, 1984
(Billions of Dollars)

	1980	1984
A. *Reconciliation of Gross Public Debt and Market Value of Net Debt*		
Gross public debt	930.2	1,663.0
Other liabilities of federal government	120.1	184.1
Liabilities of credit agencies	188.2	285.8
Liabilities of Federal Reserve	173.8	218.4
Less: Debt held by federal government	192.46	289.6
Total U.S. government liabilities at par	1,220.0	2,061.8
Par-to-market conversion	− 58.4	1.5
Total U.S. government liabilities at market	1,161.6	2,063.3
Federal government financial assets	225.3	298.7
Credit agency assets	192.54	298.4
Federal Reserve assets[a]	173.8	218.4
Total U.S. government financial assets at par[a]	591.7	815.5
Par-to-market conversion	129.2	72.0
On gold	141.1	69.9
On other assets	− 11.0	2.1
Total U.S. government financial assets at market	720.9	887.4
Total U.S. government net debt	440.7	1,175.9
B. *Reconciliation of Budget Deficit and Changes in Gross Public Debt*		
Budget deficit on national income accounts	61.2	175.7
Insurance credits to households	8.8	18.1
Change in U.S. financial assets	26.0	27.6
Change in Treasury debt held by U.S. government	7.4	53.3
Less: Change in other U.S. liabilities	11.0	21.1
Less: Mineral rights sales	6.5	7.9
Statistical discrepancy (flow of funds)	− 0.8	6.6
Change in gross public debt	85.1	252.3

Source: Updated from Eisner and Pieper (1984); see Appendix C.

[a] Includes small amount of tangible Federal Reserve assets.

moved from a gross public debt figure of $1,663 billion to a net
debt total of $1,176 billion.

But what is the precise relation between deficits and changes
in debt? In terms of the official gross public debt, it is somewhat
obscure but can be pieced together. In 1984, for example, when
the federal deficit (in the national income accounts) was $176
billion, the gross public debt grew by $252 billion . The differ-
ence, as shown in Section B of Table 2.2, stems from changes in
Treasury debt held within the government, Treasury borrowing
which finances acquisition of other financial assets such as student
and home mortgage loans, insurance credits to households, changes
in U.S. liabilities not included in the public debt, and mineral

rights sales. Year-to-year changes in *net* debt are more closely related to the deficit than changes in gross debt because they are not affected by fluctuations in the mix of federal financial assets and liabilities.

Over all the years from 1946 to 1984, cumulative total deficits were $1,112 billion, not very different from the increase in gross federal debt held by the public over those years, which amounted to $1,077 billion, as shown in Table 2.3. The increase in the market value of net debt, moreover, was about the same as the increase in gross debt held by the public. It rose $1,064 billion, from $229.8 billion at the end of calendar 1945 to $1,175.9 billion at the end of 1984, as shown in Table 2.4 (p. 20).

The market value of net debt varies with changes in interest rates, and a significant factor in such changes is changes in the rate of inflation. As inflation rises it brings on expectations of higher inflation. Lenders demand higher rates of interest because they expect repayment of their loans to be in less valuable dollars. Borrowers are willing to pay higher rates of interest to finance the purchase of houses, automobiles, and business plant, equipment and inventories which they expect to rise in price.

But in addition to the impact of *changes* in expected inflation on the market value of the debt via their effect on market rates of interest, inflation itself erodes the real value of any nominal market value. Unless individuals and businesses are guilty of "money illusion," it is the real value of their assets that should matter. *Hence it is the real value of the federal net debt that should matter.*

By applying the GNP implicit price deflator, a measure of inflation in the overall economy, we have converted our series for both gross public debt and the market value of net debt from current to 1972 dollars. Table 2.4 reveals a near doubling of the market value of net federal debt in *current* dollars from the end of 1945 to the end of 1980. Adjusting for inflation, we show in Table 2.5 that the *real* market value of the net federal debt (in constant 1972 dollars) *declined* over that period by $327 billion, a drop of no less than 58 percent. Even the gross public debt, in real terms, was no larger in 1980 than in 1945. In fact, it declined 27 percent in 1972 dollars, from $682 billion to $496 billion.

The reduction in real net debt reflects large negative "net revaluations." Higher interest rates through 1980, lowering the market value of debt, higher prices of gold increasing the value

TABLE 2.3   Federal Budget Surpluses and Deficits, and Gross Federal Debt, Fiscal Years 1929–84

(1)	(2)	(3)	(4)	(5)	(6)
	SURPLUS OR DEFICIT (−)		GROSS FEDERAL DEBT (END OF PERIOD)		
	On Budget	*Including Off-Budget Outlays*	*Total*	*Held by the Public*	*Held by the Public*
FISCAL YEAR	($ BILLION)		($ BILLION)		(% OF GNP)
1929	0.734	0.734	16.931	NA	NA
1930	0.738	0.738	16.185	NA	NA
1931	−0.462	−0.462	16.801	NA	NA
1932	−2.735	−2.735	19.487	NA	NA
1933	−2.602	−2.602	22.539	NA	NA
1934	−3.630	−3.630	27.734	NA	NA
1935	−2.791	−2.791	32.824	NA	NA
1936	−4.425	−4.425	38.497	NA	NA
1937	−2.777	−2.777	41.089	NA	NA
1938	−1.777	−1.777	42.018	NA	NA
1939	−3.862	−3.862	48.200	41.400	47.260
1940	−3.095	−3.095	50.700	42.800	45.053
1941	−5.013	−5.013	57.500	48.200	44.220
1942	−20.764	−20.764	79.200	67.800	48.777
1943	−54.884	−54.884	142.600	127.800	72.203
1944	−47.004	−47.004	204.100	184.800	91.485
1945	−47.474	−47.474	260.100	235.200	108.387
1946	−15.856	−15.856	271.000	241.900	119.752
1947	3.862	3.862	257.100	224.300	101.356
1948	12.001	12.001	252.000	216.300	88.106
1949	0.603	0.603	252.600	214.300	81.856
1950	−3.112	−3.112	256.900	219.000	82.610
1951	6.100	6.100	255.300	214.300	68.510
1952	−1.517	−1.517	259.100	214.800	63.307
1953	−6.533	−6.533	266.000	218.400	60.448
1954	−1.170	−1.170	270.800	224.500	61.642
1955	−3.041	−3.041	274.400	226.600	59.538
1956	4.087	4.087	272.800	222.200	53.958
1957	3.249	3.249	272.400	219.400	50.565
1958	−2.939	−2.939	279.700	226.400	51.095
1959	−12.855	−12.855	287.800	235.000	49.536
1960	0.269	0.269	290.900	237.200	47.640
1961	−3.406	−3.406	292.900	238.600	46.849
1962	−7.137	−7.137	303.300	248.400	45.312
1963	−4.751	−4.751	310.800	254.500	44.031
1964	−5.922	−5.922	316.800	257.600	41.669
1965	−1.596	−1.596	323.200	261.600	39.666
1966	−3.796	−3.796	329.500	264.700	36.556
1967	−8.702	−8.702	341.300	267.500	34.414
1968	−25.161	−25.161	369.800	290.600	34.957
1969	3.236	3.236	367.100	279.500	30.694

TABLE 2.3   *(continued)*

(1)	(2)	(3)	(4)	(5)	(6)
	SURPLUS OR DEFICIT (−)		GROSS FEDERAL DEBT (END OF PERIOD)		
FISCAL YEAR	On Budget	Including Off-Budget Outlays	Total	Held by the Public	Held by the Public
	($ BILLION)		($ BILLION)		(% OF GNP)
1970	− 2.845	− 2.845	382.600	284.900	29.408
1971	− 23.033	− 23.033	409.500	304.300	29.501
1972	− 23.373	− 23.373	437.300	323.800	28.685
1973	− 14.849	− 14.900	468.400	343.000	27.396
1974	− 4.688	− 6.100	486.200	346.100	25.091
1975	− 45.154	− 53.200	544.100	396.900	26.819
1976	− 66.413	− 73.700	631.900	480.300	29.285
1976TQ[a]	− 12.900	− 14.700	646.400	498.300	28.800
1977	− 44.948	− 53.600	709.100	551.800	29.622
1978	− 48.807	− 59.000	780.400	610.900	29.211
1979	− 27.694	− 40.200	833.800	644.600	27.340
1980	− 59.563	− 73.800	914.300	715.100	27.762
1981	− 57.900	− 78.900	1,003.900	794.400	27.527
1982	− 110.600	− 127.900	1,147.000	929.400	30.512
1983	− 195.400	− 207.800	1,381.900	1,141.800	35.444
1984	− 175.300	− 185.300	1,576.700	1,312.600	36.654
Sum, 1942–45, or change, 1941–45	− 170.126	− 170.126	202.600	187.000	64.167
Sum, 1946–84, or change, 1945–84	− 987.554	− 1,112.438	1,316.600	1,077.400	− 71.734
Sum, 1946–80, or change, 1945–80	− 448.354	− 512.538	654.200	479.900	− 80.625
Sum, 1981–84, or change, 1980–84	− 539.200	− 599.900	662.400	597.500	8.891

Sources: Economic Report of the President February 1985 (Table B-72, p. 318), and data from U.S. Treasury, OMB, and BEA.

[a]Fiscal years until 1976 ran from July 1 of the preceding calendar year to June 30. From 1977 on, the fiscal year began on October 1. TQ denotes the transition quarter, July 1 to September 30, 1976.

of that government asset and, particularly, general inflation, combined to cut the real market value of the net debt to less than half of what it had been at the end of World War II.

The picture changed abruptly in the 1980s. Not only did the nominal deficits grow much larger, but also inflation slowed, gold prices came down, and interest rates fell from their 1981 peaks. The negative net revaluations were thus considerably reduced in

TABLE 2.4   Federal Government Net Debt,
Market Values
(Billions of Dollars)

(1)	(2)	(3)
YEAR	EXCLUDING GOLD	INCLUDING GOLD
1945	249.9	229.8
1950	219.1	196.3
1955	220.9	199.2
1960	224.9	207.1
1965	231.5	217.7
1970	263.5	251.5
1975	396.9	358.2
1980	596.6	440.7
1981	677.6	558.7
1982	895.0	789.6
1983	1,044.3	943.3
1984	1,256.9	1,175.9

Source: See Appendix C.

absolute amount or actually reversed. In the four years of the
first Reagan Administration, the real value of the net debt more
than doubled, rising from $235 billion at the end of 1980 to $517
billion in 1972 dollars at the end of 1984, as shown in Table 2.5.

But most recent history cannot obscure the earlier record.
*With inflation, we can have substantial budget deficits by the official
measure while the real value of the net debt goes down.* The paradox
is that this is true not only for deficits measured in current dollars
but also for so-called constant dollar deficits calculated by the
usual techniques of price deflation. For merely dividing the nominal or current dollar deficit by a price deflator does not take into
account what inflation has done to erode the real value of the
already existing debt.

The juxtaposition, in Table 2.5, of budget surpluses or deficits (for calendar years on national income accounts), and net
revaluations and changes in net debt is striking. It becomes clear
that budget deficits in years of substantial inflation were matched
not by increases in the real value of net debt but by decreases or,
at worst, approximate balance. This was particularly so for the
years 1977 through 1980, when there were very large negative
net revaluations. Thus, in 1977 when the national income account
deficit was $33 billion in 1972 dollars, the net debt rose by only
$2 billion. In 1978, when the reported deficit measured $20 bil-

TABLE 2.5 The Real Value of Federal Debt, 1945–84

(1)	(2)	(3)	(4)	(5)	(6)	(7)	(8)
	GROSS PUBLIC DEBT	NET DEBT	BUDGET SURPLUS OR DEFICIT (−)	NET REVALUATION OF NET DEBT	CHANGE IN NET DEBT	NET DEBT PER CAPITA	CHANGE IN NET DEBT PER CAPITA
YEAR	*($ Billion 1972)*					*($ 1972)*	
1945	681.6	562.0	− 111.0	—	—	4,017	—
1946	545.4	478.5	8.0	− 111.3	− 83.5	3,384	− 632
1947	496.8	405.6	27.0	− 45.4	− 72.9	2,814	− 570
1948	475.7	377.7	15.7	− 11.4	− 27.8	2,576	− 238
1949	491.9	395.0	− 5.0	11.3	17.3	2,648	72
1950	459.1	351.0	17.2	− 32.0	− 44.0	2,305	− 343
1951	450.5	325.3	11.4	− 17.1	− 25.7	2,101	− 205
1952	455.8	327.9	− 6.4	− 6.5	2.5	2,081	− 20
1953	466.0	339.6	− 12.0	0.6	11.8	2,120	39
1954	464.3	344.4	− 10.1	− 5.0	4.7	2,112	− 8
1955	455.4	323.0	7.3	− 16.0	− 21.3	1,947	− 165
1956	431.9	298.3	9.7	− 18.9	− 24.8	1,766	− 181
1957	419.7	297.9	3.5	1.2	− 0.3	1,732	− 34
1958	423.8	300.1	− 15.6	− 15.1	2.2	1,716	− 16
1959	426.3	292.0	− 1.7	− 13.1	− 8.1	1,642	− 74
1960	421.1	300.5	4.4	11.0	8.5	1,663	21
1961	423.5	300.9	− 5.6	− 8.2	0.4	1,638	− 25
1962	426.0	304.9	− 6.0	− 2.7	4.0	1,634	− 3
1963	428.0	298.8	0.4	− 8.4	− 6.1	1,579	− 56
1964	432.7	299.4	− 4.5	− 4.8	0.6	1,560	− 19
1965	426.0	289.0	0.7	− 11.9	− 10.4	1,487	− 73
1966	422.2	285.4	− 2.3	− 8.2	− 3.6	1,452	− 35
1967	427.5	287.2	− 16.7	− 15.4	1.8	1,445	− 7
1968	423.8	281.3	− 7.3	− 14.9	− 5.9	1,402	− 44
1969	412.5	252.9	9.7	− 23.5	− 28.4	1,248	− 154
1970	415.3	268.4	− 13.6	1.9	15.4	1,309	61
1971	432.5	282.6	− 22.9	− 8.8	14.2	1,361	52
1972	439.5	278.6	− 16.8	− 16.3	− 4.0	1,327	− 33
1973	428.6	251.2	− 5.2	− 22.5	− 27.4	1,185	− 142
1974	406.8	219.8	− 10.0	− 24.1	− 31.4	1,028	− 158
1975	445.9	277.0	− 55.2	− 16.0	57.3	1,283	255
1976	481.3	317.1	− 40.1	− 6.3	40.1	1,454	172
1977	498.6	319.5	− 32.8	− 31.4	2.4	1,450	− 4
1978	503.4	295.2	− 19.6	− 39.8	− 24.3	1,326	− 124
1979	496.6	235.9	− 9.8	− 28.3	− 59.2	1,048	− 278
1980	495.9	234.9	− 34.3	− 36.7	− 1.0	1,032	− 17
1981	507.2	275.4	− 32.9	− 22.7	40.5	1,198	166
1982	565.8	373.2	− 71.6	13.7	97.8	1,607	409
1983	643.0	430.0	− 82.8	− 35.3	56.8	1,834	227
1984	730.7	516.7	− 78.6	− 9.5	86.7	2,183	360

Source: See Appendix C.

lion, the net debt actually declined by $24 billion. In 1979, with a budget deficit of $10 billion, the net debt declined by a very large $59 billion. And in 1980, when the deficit again surged to $34 billion, the net debt was virtually unchanged. In sum, *over the four years of the Carter Administration, while the deficits totalled $96 billion in 1972 dollars the net debt thus declined by $82 billion.*

The point is that the major discrepancies between budget deficits and increases in net debt suggest that our conventional measures of the budget deficit are devoid of much of their presumed economic relevance. They are particularly misleading in periods of substantial and varying inflation, and high and fluctuating nominal interest rates. For these contribute to large net revaluations which are a major factor, generally *the* major factor, in the discrepancy between budget deficits and increases in the net debt.

What then is the exact relation between changes in the real value of the net debt, measured in current dollars, and the budget surplus or deficit? Clearly, a surplus itself reduces the debt and a deficit increases it. Higher interest rates, however, lower the market value of debt and hence reduce it. Increases in prices reduce the real value of debt. Off-budget outlays increase debt and increases in the value of Treasury holdings decrease the net debt.

These off-budget items are a bit sticky, conceptually. They are the sum of insurance credits to households, federal mineral sales, credit agency surpluses, net revaluations on foreign exchange and miscellaneous assets, and the "statistical discrepancy" in the Federal Reserve's Flow of Funds Accounts. While they affect the debt, they do not affect directly the net claims on the federal government by the rest of the economy, or the net worth of the rest of the economy. Federal mineral sales, for example, reduce the need to borrow and hence make the debt less than it would otherwise be. They do not, however, make the public any poorer. Thus while the private sector has $7.9 billion less wealth in the form of federal debt it has (at least) $7.9 billion more wealth from its mineral rights acquisitions in 1984.

A similar issue arises with regard to changes in the value of Treasury gold holdings. Higher price tags on Treasury gold will reduce our measure of net debt, which is federal liabilities minus financial assets. But such a reduction in net debt neither reduces the securities held in the private sector nor increases the private

sector's obligations to the government. Hence it too does not affect the wealth of the private sector.

The decrease (increase) in real net debt in current dollars is
actually the sum of the surplus (deficit) in our national income
accounts, interest rate effects (par-to-market adjustment), price
effects (nominal-to-real adjustment), off-budget items, and net
revaluations on Treasury gold. To secure a measure of the impact
of the surplus or deficit on the financial wealth of the individuals
and business of the private sector or, more properly, all sectors
other than the federal government, we should add to the surplus
in national income accounts *only* the interest rate effects and the
price effects. And since this measures changes in the financial
wealth of the economy outside of Washington, it is this "adjusted
surplus" or "adjusted deficit" which, as we shall show, will weigh
heavily on the ebb and flow of the nation's economy.

Calculations of the adjusted surplus or deficit, in current dollars, are presented in Table 2.6. Since in the last four decades
there has almost always been some inflation, which reduced the
real value of the debt, the adjustments have generally moved the
budget toward surplus. Thus, surpluses in the official national
income accounts in the early postwar years were larger by our
adjusted measure. Where there were deficits they were lower (with
exceptions in 1949 and 1953) in the adjusted measure, or they
became surpluses.

Some particularly interesting reversals are recorded. In 1973
and 1974 there were moderate deficits by the official national
income account measure. With inflation accelerating in response
to oil price shocks, our adjusted budget was in substantial surplus.

But the most remarkable differences between official and
adjusted budget measures show up again in the 1977–80 Carter
years. The 1977 deficit of $46 billion is turned into a virtually
balanced budget. The 1978 deficit of $29 billion is converted to
an adjusted surplus of $33 billion. The 1979 deficit of $16 billion
becomes an adjusted surplus of $32 billion. And the deficit of $61
billion which caused so much consternation in 1980 appears now
as an adjusted surplus of $7.6 billion.

Looking at the official deficit figures, Carter Administration
economists and their outside critics agreed that the economy was
suffering from too much fiscal stimulus. Both the deficits and the
stimulus had to be reduced to curb inflation.

Yet there were nagging indications that the economy was

TABLE 2.6   Federal Budget Surplus or Deficit and Change in Real Net Debt
(Billions of Dollars)

(1)	(2)	(3)	(4)	(5)	(6)	(7)	(8)
YEAR	SURPLUS OR DEFICIT (−) ON NATIONAL INCOME ACCOUNTS	INTER-EST RATE EFFECTS	PRICE EFFECTS	ADJUSTED SURPLUS OR DEFI-CIT (−)	OFF-BUDGET ITEMS	REVALUA-TION ON GOLD	DECREASE OR INCREASE (−) IN REAL NET DEBT IN CURRENT $
1946	3.523	0.441	52.459	56.423	−2.100	−3.652	36.660
1947	13.384	3.116	20.388	36.888	−1.075	0.316	36.129
1948	8.316	−0.283	6.368	14.400	−0.550	0.898	14.748
1949	−2.638	−2.157	−3.748	−8.543	−1.086	0.568	−9.061
1950	9.208	2.919	14.951	27.078	−0.201	−3.313	23.564
1951	6.508	3.453	6.393	16.353	−1.081	−0.621	14.651
1952	−3.735	−0.192	3.997	0.071	−1.107	−0.433	−1.470
1953	−7.076	−1.813	1.456	−7.433	0.662	−0.149	−6.920
1954	−6.034	−0.640	3.637	−3.037	0.575	−0.354	−2.816
1955	4.417	3.842	6.042	14.301	−0.746	−0.585	12.969
1956	6.067	3.862	8.242	18.171	−1.770	−0.833	15.569
1957	2.282	−5.609	4.841	1.515	−1.784	0.494	0.225
1958	−10.271	5.917	4.163	−0.190	−0.842	−0.409	−1.441
1959	−1.138	4.160	4.784	7.806	−1.913	−0.438	5.455
1960	3.035	−9.838	2.257	−4.546	−1.075	−0.194	−5.815
1961	−3.886	2.406	3.321	1.841	−1.855	−0.254	−0.268
1962	−4.247	−2.342	4.257	−2.332	−.195	−0.305	−2.832
1963	0.256	2.755	3.298	6.309	−1.711	−0.224	4.374
1964	−3.269	−0.341	3.845	0.235	−0.426	−0.255	−0.447
1965	0.530	3.130	5.864	9.525	1.904	−3.677	7.751
1966	−1.789	−1.734	8.128	4.605	−1.405	−0.472	2.729
1967	−13.180	4.440	7.979	−0.761	−0.211	−0.416	−1.388
1968	−6.049	1.059	11.501	6.511	−3.537	1.856	4.830
1969	8.443	7.528	13.428	29.399	−1.873	−2.905	24.621
1970	−12.435	−13.985	12.217	−14.203	−0.028	0.118	−14.112
1971	−22.025	−3.898	12.498	−13.424	−1.532	1.324	−13.632
1972	−16.819	4.326	12.357	−0.136	−1.269	5.390	3.985
1973	−5.519	3.401	21.264	19.146	−1.488	11.339	28.997
1974	−11.524	−2.006	31.191	17.660	0.040	18.374	36.074
1975	−69.292	−2.519	23.242	−48.559	−5.378	−17.951	−71.888
1976	−53.083	−12.611	21.101	−44.593	−5.077	−3.354	−53.025
1977	−45.879	16.055	29.234	−0.590	−8.568	5.841	−3.318
1978	−29.463	19.125	43.198	32.860	−8.658	12.344	36.546
1979	−16.090	4.605	43.616	32.131	−4.683	69.357	96.805
1980	−61.248	13.725	55.148	7.625	−12.135	6.283	1.773
1981	−64.310	−3.674	49.673	−18.311	−13.103	−47.803	−79.217
1982	−148.165	−62.430	33.351	−177.243	−6.846	−18.174	−202.263
1983	−178.619	42.317	35.096	−101.207	−13.306	−7.869	−122.382
1984	−175.700	−20.583	42.146	−154.137	−16.493	−23.110	−193.740

Source: See Appendix C.

sluggish rather than overheated. I recall asking Carter Economic
Council Chairman Charles Schultze, early in 1980, "What's a nice
guy like you doing trying to bring on a recession?" "Yeah," he
quipped, "but we're not even good at it!" Nevertheless, unemployment, while well below its peak two years later, was approaching 7 percent.

What then was really going on? Mesmerized by those official
deficit figures, most observers insisted that our fiscal policy was
irresponsibly expansionary. That justified Federal Reserve Chairman Paul Volcker's tight money policy as "the only game in town"
to stop inflation.

But the rising interest rates associated with escalating inflation, reinforced by the restrictive monetary posture, had been
driving down the market value of the public's holdings of federal
debt. And the inflation itself was further reducing its real value.
The purchasing power of the public was thus shrinking, not growing.

An inflation-adjusted budget would have told us that we were
actually running a surplus. We were suffering from a tight fiscal
policy *and* tight money. But everyone looked at the official deficit.
The tricks played by inflation were ignored, or never seen.

Murray Weidenbaum, President Reagan's first Economic
Council Chairman, could also be arch. I recall his asking me, with
some prescience, as the 1981 "Economic Recovery Tax Act" was
being passed, "What other Administration had its anti-recession
package in place *before* the recession?" But net tax and expenditure stimulus was not to be realized until late 1982. Initially, the
Reagan Administration acquiesced and persisted in the tight
monetary and fiscal policies it inherited, and it proved considerably "better" at bringing on a severe recession than its hapless
predecessor.

3

Capital Budgeting or Its Lack—and the Nation's Wealth

IF MAJOR AMERICAN CORPORATIONS kept their accounts in the same manner as the federal government, the demand for physical red ink would grow substantially. Many a profitable business would seem to be operating at a loss and, in Washington parlance, would be showing a "deficit." Such a deficit would show that, like the federal government, American businesses have been going more and more into debt.

Can we compare the federal debt with that of private business? Take a look at Table 3.1. The gross debt or liabilities of General Motors grew from $4.3 billion to $27.9 billion from 1970 to 1984. Meanwhile, the debt of a hugely successful company, IBM, grew from $2.6 billion in 1970 to $16.3 billion in 1984. Similar records of increasing debt can be found for almost every successful large business in the United States.

In fact, business debt has been increasing much more rapidly than federal debt. At the end of 1952, gross federal debt held by the public was 62 percent of GNP, while the debt of nonfinancial business came to 32 percent, as shown in Table 3.2. By 1979, the federal debt ratio had *fallen* by more than half, to 26.5 percent, but the business debt figure had risen to nearly double that, or

TABLE 3.1   Assets, Liabilities, and Net Worth, General
Motors and IBM, 1970, 1980, and 1984

	YEARS			
	1970	*1980*	*1984*	*1970 to 1984*
ITEM	($ BILLION)			(% CHANGE)
General Motors				
Assets	14.2	32.2	52.1	+268
Liabilities	4.3	13.0	27.9	+546
Net worth	9.9	19.2	24.2	+146
IBM				
Assets	8.5	24.5	42.8	+401
Liabilities	2.6	9.6	16.3	+530
Net worth	5.9	15.0	26.5	+345

Source: Data for 1984 are from annual reports. "Net worth" figures are what GM
denotes as "net assets" and IBM as "stockholders' equity." IBM figures for 1980
have now been reclassified to conform with the 1984 presentation. They show
1980 assets at $26.8 billion and stockholders' equity at $16.6 billion.

TABLE 3.2   Federal and Other Debt as Percentage of GNP

(1)	(2)	(3)	(4)	(5)	(6)
		STATE AND		NONFINANCIAL	
YEAR	FEDERAL	LOCAL	HOUSEHOLDS	BUSINESS	TOTAL
1952	61.5	8.7	26.0	31.6	127.8
1962	43.6	14.5	44.7	40.5	143.4
1972	27.6	14.7	47.9	50.1	140.3
1973	25.4	14.1	48.7	51.3	139.4
1974	24.5	14.2	49.1	54.3	142.1
1975	27.5	13.7	47.9	52.0	141.1
1976	29.1	13.4	48.9	51.5	142.9
1977	28.8	12.7	50.5	51.5	143.5
1978	27.4	12.0	51.4	50.3	141.0
1979	26.5	11.7	53.9	51.9	144.0
1980	27.1	11.5	53.7	52.0	144.3
1981	27.4	10.7	52.6	52.0	142.6
1982	31.9	11.6	53.8	54.2	151.5
1983	34.3	10.8	55.0	53.0	153.1
1984	36.6	10.8	56.4	55.1	159.0

Sources: Federal Reserve System Board of Governors, Flow of Funds Accounts, "Summary of Credit
Market Debt Outstanding and Credit Market Debt Owed by Nonfinancial Sectors" (Feb. 1985). Years
through 1982 taken from Albert M. Wojnilower, "Discussion," Table 1, p. 105, in Federal Reserve
Bank of Boston (1983).

52 percent. By 1984 the federal debt held by the public had risen to almost 37 percent, but business debt was then 55 percent of GNP.

But investors or others trying to evaluate the fortunes of a corporation hardly look only at gross debt figures. Clearly, they must also concern themselves with assets.

Thus, for example, while General Motors' liabilities grew, so did its assets and net worth. From 1970 to 1984, its assets increased from $14.2 billion to $52.1 billion, and net worth, the difference between assets and liabilities, rose from $9.9 billion to $24.2 billion. In the case of IBM, from 1970 to 1984, assets increased from $8.5 billion to $42.8 billion, while net worth rose from $5.9 billion to $26.5 billion.

So then, with all the talk about government debt, and the deficits which contribute to it, what about looking also at *government* assets and *government* net worth? We are accustomed to thinking of the government taking our money and squandering it. There may of course be some truth in that. But after all, the government does own some roads and some buildings. It has some equipment, nonmilitary as well as military. And it retains title to a great deal of land.

In our earlier work together, Paul Pieper and I constructed and presented, and have now updated, government balance sheets which show the market values (or estimated replacement costs) of all tangible and financial assets as well as liabilities (Eisner and Pieper, 1984, 1985). They indicate that the federal debt has indeed grown, like that of General Motors and IBM, but so have federal assets. The increase in financial assets, as noted earlier, damps the growth in net debt.

It is the growth in value of federal tangible assets, however, which deserves particular attention. In the decade of the 1970s, for example, the value of federally owned structures, as may be noted in Tables 3.3 and B.12, increased from $106 billion to $284 billion. The value of federally owned equipment rose from $95 billion to $229 billion. Inventories went from $59 billion to $136 billion. And the almost certainly underestimates of the value of federal land increased from $45 billion to $175 billion.

Dramatic evidence of the extent of these underestimates may be seen in current Department of the Interior figures on federally owned reserves of oil, gas, and coal.[1] Multiplying the estimated quantities of these reserves by recent market prices, we estimated the *value* of the government oil reserves at $177 billion, gas at

TABLE 3.3   Federal Government Net Debt and Net Worth
(Billions of Dollars)

	1945	1950	1960	1970	1980	1984
Assets						
Tangible	186.2	111.7	205.8	304.6	822.5	1,118.0
Reproducible assets	179.3	102.2	187.4	259.8	648.1	915.2
Residential structures	2.2	2.2	3.2	5.7	20.9	24.5
Nonresidential structures	28.9	39.1	60.8	100.2	262.9	299.6
Equipment	88.3	34.4	65.6	95.3	228.6	395.6
Inventories	59.9	26.5	57.7	58.6	135.7	195.5
Land	6.8	9.5	18.4	44.8	174.4	202.8
Financial	102.8	98.7	124.7	232.8	720.9	887.4
Currency, demand + time deposits	31.3	9.7	12.8	17.6	31.3	40.7
Gold	20.1	22.8	17.8	12.0	155.9	81.0
U.S. government securities	31.5	26.2	35.2	77.5	129.8	172.3
Treasury issues	31.5	26.2	35.1	77.4	120.6	162.7
Agency issues	0.0	0.0	0.0	0.2	9.2	9.6
Mortgages	2.5	2.8	11.2	32.6	132.3	202.6
Other loans	4.7	16.0	25.1	65.2	201.5	288.1
Taxes receivable	9.6	16.5	12.7	5.7	7.1	−16.2
Miscellaneous assets	3.1	3.2	8.4	18.9	47.3	94.9
Total assets	289.0	210.4	330.4	537.4	1,543.4	2,005.4
Liabilities						
Treasury currency + SDR certificates	2.3	2.4	2.7	6.0	13.6	17.5
Demand deposits + currency	31.1	28.2	30.6	52.0	121.5	171.4
Bank reserves + vault cash	19.0	19.9	20.4	31.2	47.3	40.5
Credit market instruments	264.5	224.5	246.7	338.5	841.9	1,613.7
Savings bonds	43.2	49.5	46.5	53.1	68.4	76.1
Other Treasury issues	220.4	173.1	192.5	246.1	625.1	1,296.8
Agency issues	0.9	1.8	7.8	39.3	148.4	240.8
Insurance, retirement reserves	6.5	12.7	20.5	34.9	85.5	139.8
Miscellaneous liabilities	9.2	7.4	10.9	21.8	51.8	80.4
Total liabilities	332.6	295.0	331.8	484.3	1,161.6	2,063.3
Net debt[a]	229.8	196.3	207.1	251.5	440.7	1,175.9
Net worth	−43.7	−84.6	−1.3	53.1	381.8	−57.9

Source: See Appendix C.

[a]Total liabilities minus financial assets.

$169 billion, and coal at $264 billion. That gives a total of $611 billion in federally owned, off-shore and on-shore minerals to be added to our estimates of the value of "land," or separately categorized among assets. There alone is "backing" for more than half of the 1984 net debt. And other estimates set the value of federally owned minerals even higher: $817 billion in 1982 for oil and natural gas rights alone (Boskin, Robinson, O'Reilly, and Kumar, 1985).

Thus, from 1970 to 1980, total liabilities grew what seems an enormous amount, from $484 billion to $1,162 billion, and net debt from $252 billion to $441 billion. But that is only part of the picture. With tangible and financial federal assets each rising by half a trillion dollars in that decade, the growth in total assets considerably exceeded the growth in liabilities.

So, yes, the federal debt did grow as deficit followed deficit. But there was something to show for it. And with all that increase in debt, as with General Motors and IBM, the federal net worth also increased. It rose, according to our conservative estimates, from a modest $53 billion in 1970 to a 1980 figure of $382 billion, and clearly would be shown to have risen much more with proper accounting for federally owned mineral reserves.[2]

Despite this substantial increase in federal net worth in the 1970s (not repeated in the following decade, it must be acknowledged), we kept referring to federal deficits. When private businesses had similar increases in debt, assets, and net worth, we did not think of them as suffering losses or having "deficits." What is the difference?

A significant part of the answer lies in the fact that the federal government, unlike private business and state and local governments, keeps no separate capital budget. When American businesses spend $354 billion on new plant and equipment, as they did in 1984, they do not charge that as a current expense. Profits, or "surplus" are reduced only by depreciation or capital "consumption." But when the federal government makes similar capital expenditures of $77 billion, as it did in (fiscal year) 1984, that goes right into the deficit.

In the great majority of firms where capital expenditures are increasing, whether because of real growth, or inflation, or both, the current depreciation, which is based essentially on previous capital expenditures, is less than current capital spending. For General Motors in 1984, depreciation on old plant and equipment was $2.7 billion while new capital spending was $6.0 billion. For IBM, depreciation was $3.0 billion and capital spending $4.6 billion. Since federal capital expenditures have been increasing too, federal depreciation charges similarly calculated would also be less than federal spending.

If the federal government were to keep separate current and capital accounts, and were also to adjust its depreciation for inflation, the budget picture would look considerably different. In 1984, for example, as shown in Table 3.4, the total national in-

TABLE 3.4   Current and Capital Federal Accounts, 1984

(1)	(2)	(3)	(4)	(5)
	CREDITS	DEBITS	DEFICIT[a]	DEFICIT ÷ GNP
ACCOUNT	($ Billion)			(%)
Current	704.7	860.9[b]	156.2	4.3
Capital	53.6[c]	73.2[d]	19.6	0.5
NIPA	704.7	880.5	175.8	4.8

Source: Bureau of Economic Analysis, updated from Eisner (1984).

[a]Col. 4 is Col. 3 minus Col. 2.

[b]Includes capital consumption allowances of $53.6 billion and current outlays of $807.3 billion.

[c]Capital consumption allowances.

[d]Capital expenditures.

come and product accounts (NIPA) federal sector budget deficit of $176 billion would be decomposed into a capital account deficit of $20 billion and a current account deficit of $156 billion. The difference, though significant, is not overwhelming. But there is more to be said.

First, the $20 billion deficit on capital account in 1984 and the total of $73 billion of federal investment related only to assets acquired by the federal government. But in fiscal 1984, for example, that would omit another $26 billion of federal grants to state and local governments for physical capital investment—for highways, for urban mass transportation and airports, for community and regional development, and for pollution control facilities.

Second, as the Office of Management and Budget points out (*Budget of the United States, Fiscal Year 1986*, p. D-1), a reasonable definition of the category for federal investment is outlays "which yield long-term benefits." The OMB therefore includes among "federal investment-type outlays," along with $34 billion for construction, $67 billion for equipment, and $7 billion for inventory investment, $41 billion for research and development and $22 billion for education and training. Total federal investment (excluding loans and financial investment) thus came to $171 billion in fiscal 1984, almost identical, we might point out, to the fiscal year national income account deficit of $170 billion. The OMB's estimates of nonfinancial federal investment for fiscal 1985 and 1986 are $195 billion and $215 billion, respectively (ibid., Table D-1, p. D-3).

It is thus clear that all of the federal budget deficit, and more, is accounted for by investment. We should, it is true, make some allowance for depreciation or capital consumption. Thus, if we were to put together separate current and capital accounts, with all federal investment-type outlays in the capital account but depreciation as an added current account charge, the current account budget would still not be in balance.

But the figures for the current account deficit would be far less than those to which we have become familiar. When we add the inflation adjustments discussed earlier and relate all this to the growth of population and the economy, we may easily have no deficit left at all.

4

A Variety of Deficits

IF YOU HAVE SEEN A FEW deficits you most certainly haven't seen them all. We have glimpsed how federal budgets and deficits might look if they were presented in accordance with business accounting practice. We have suggested further the implications of capitalizing all investment-type federal expenditures. And we have earlier indicated the major corrections necessary to account properly for inflation, adjusting for changes in the real market value of existing net debt.

But next time someone tells you we must balance the budget, you may want to ask, "Which one?" For there are games to be played with some of the budgets in current use, and new ones keep cropping up.

We might mention first the "unified budget," which is the stuff of presidential recommendations and congressional budget resolutions. It is a consolidated account of the expenditures and receipts of all the federal departments and agencies, and the outlays and receipts of trust funds. These last include the major social security funds, federal employee and railroad retirement funds, the highway trust fund, and a number of others.

The unified budget includes in receipts—or negative expenditures—the proceeds of sales of mineral rights or bonuses on outer continental shelf land leases. It will also henceforth include outlays of currently off-budget federal entities, chiefly for loans to the private sector. We thus have the strange possibility that someone wishing to "balance" the unified budget might do so by selling off the federal loan portfolio, or selling away the nation's natural resources.

Here, I am reminded of the story of my late father-in-law, who unwisely tried to open a law practice in the gloom of 1932. "Had a good day in the office," he quipped as he came home one night. "Sold my desk!"

Inclusion of the social security and other trust funds in the unified budget, though, does make good economic sense. Social security payments are income to their recipients, just as other federal expenditures. And taxes paid for social security reduce disposable personal income just as much as personal income taxes. It hardly makes any difference in what pocket Uncle Sam puts what we give him. Nor does it matter what check book he uses in paying us.

The unified budget has until now included social security expenditures and receipts. It was thus more than a passing oddity when President Reagan in 1984 and 1985 argued repeatedly that cuts in social security benefits would not reduce the deficit. They most certainly would, as he apparently implicitly acknowledged when he approved a Senate Republican plan to reduce benefits by delaying cost of living increases (an approval he subsequently withdrew, to the consternation of some of his legislative supporters).

In fact, the biggest social security fund, that for old age, survivors, and disability insurance, has been projected to show a $6 billion surplus in fiscal 1985 and a $13 billion surplus in 1986. The health insurance trust funds were projected to have surpluses of $4 billion in 1985 and $10 billion in 1986. Perhaps out of concern that social security surpluses would be used to finance deficits in the rest of the budget, Congress has now decreed removal of social security from the unified budget beginning in the 1993 fiscal year. If social security funds are still in surplus as anticipated, their removal from the total will cause what we call "the deficit" suddenly to take a major leap upward.[1]

In any case, many of the oddities and arbitrary shifts associated with the unified budget presented by the Administration and debated by Congress are eliminated in the measure of federal finances in the national income and product accounts. As noted by OMB, "For study of aggregate economic activity, . . . the national income and product accounts (NIPA) provide the most useful measures."

The NIPA federal sector accounts, shown in Table 4.1, differ substantially from the unified budget. They do not include exchanges of assets, as purchases of loans by federally sponsored lending agencies, or sale of mineral rights, which do not enter directly into private income statements. Thus they were not swollen in fiscal 1985 by financial transactions which amounted to no less than $36 billion. And they did not include, as an offset to expenditures, net sales of government land or mineral rights which came to almost $2 billion, and could become much larger if the government proceeded systematically to sell public property to private individuals and business.

With these differences, and others involving the timing of outlays and receipts, NIPA federal expenditures for fiscal 1985 were estimated as $9 billion less than unified budget expenditures, and receipts as $21 billion more.[2] The NIPA budget deficit

TABLE 4.1 Federal Government Receipts, Expenditures, and Surplus or Deficit, National Income Accounts, 1980–84
(Billions of Dollars)

RECEIPTS AND EXPENDITURES	CALENDAR YEAR				
	1980	1981	1982	1983	1984
Total receipts	540.9	624.8	616.7	641.1	704.7
Personal taxes	257.7	298.7	306.2	295.2	315.0
Corporate taxes	70.3	65.7	46.6	59.8	70.8
Indirect business taxes	39.0	56.4	48.4	52.4	55.5
Contributions for social insurance	173.9	204.1	215.5	233.7	263.4
Total expenditures	602.1	689.1	764.9	819.7	880.5
Purchases of goods and services	197.0	228.9	258.9	269.7	295.4
Transfer payments	251.5	286.8	321.6	345.6	353.0
Grants in aid to state and local governments	88.7	87.9	83.9	86.3	93.2
Net interest paid	53.4	73.3	84.4	94.2	116.7
Subsidies less current surplus of government enterprises	11.5	12.3	16.1	23.4	22.3
Less: wage accruals less disbursements	0.0	0.1	−0.0	−0.4	0.1
Surplus or deficit (−)	−61.2	−64.3	−148.2	−178.6	−175.8

Sources: U.S. Department of Commerce (Bureau of Economic Analysis), U.S. Department of the Treasury, and U.S. Office of Management and Budget, as reported in *Economic Indicators*, Nov. 1985, p. 34.

for fiscal 1985 finally turned out, at $194 billion, to be $18 billion less than the unified budget deficit of $212 billion, but $19 billion more than the unified budget deficit of $175 billion when "off-budget" outlays are excluded (*Economic Report of the President February 1985*, p. 32).

Some experts suggest that discussions of federal debt and deficits are generally wide of the mark by ignoring vast amounts which are not included in official measures. In particular, we are told, the government has vast unfunded obligations for social security, federal employee and military retirement programs, and other contingency obligations such as loan and credit guarantees. These dwarf the so-called public debt.

In fact, as of the end of the 1982 fiscal year, the Treasury listed "liabilities" accountable to the public of $1,085 billion and, in addition, payments due on "undelivered orders" of $475 billion, and net "contingency" obligations of $5,658 billion, the latter for loan and credit guarantees, insurance commitments, and retirement and annuity programs, including social security. Adding all these apples and oranges together (which the Treasury does not do), we would come to a total of $7,218 billion, as shown in Table 4.2.

The retirement and annuity programs, in particular, involve calculating the present value of anticipated receipts or assets as

TABLE 4.2   Federal Liabilities and Contingency Obligations[a]
(Billions of Dollars)

	FISCAL YEARS		
ITEM	1982	1983	1984
Liabilities to public	1,085.5	1,316.1	1,493.5
Undelivered orders	474.7	405.4	485.5
Net contingency obligations	5,657.8	4,208.0	4,756.4
Loan and credit guarantees	346.7	553.3	627.7
Insurance commitments	2,079.6	2,338.7	2,636.8
Annuity programs	3,150.1	1,245.6	1,414.7
Retirement pay	834.5	814.8	857.1
Social security	2,219.2	336.8	464.4
Hospital insurance	577.9	485.1	501.8
Old age and survivors insurance	2,297.6	−95.9	−49.7
Disability insurance	−656.3	−52.4	12.3
Other annuity programs	96.4	94.0	93.2
Other contingency obligations	81.5	70.6	77.1
Total	7,218.0	5,929.6	6,735.4

Sources: U.S. Department of the Treasury, Financial Reports Branch, and *Treasury Bulletin.*
[a]Net assets (−)

well as obligations. Results are sensitive to assumed discount rates, which are not the same for different programs, as well as uncertain and varying projected outgo and income.

The Treasury thus estimated a net deficiency of $2.3 trillion on social security's old age and survivors insurance as of the end of fiscal 1982. This figure was turned, by 1982 legislation, into a surplus of $96 billion at the end of fiscal 1983. Total "debt" of the Treasury, including net contingency obligations, then came to $5,930 billion.

Consistent with the principle that the deficit should equal the increase in debt over the corresponding period, we could, ignoring corrections for changing real market values of obligations due to inflation and changing interest rates, calculate that fiscal 1983 actually showed a *surplus* of $1,288 billion, the amount that the present value of total Treasury obligations was reduced! But since total obligations rose to $6,735 billion over the next year, we would swing to a deficit of $806 billion in fiscal 1984. Can we really take these measures of surplus and deficits seriously?

The financing, or lack of financing, of the vast government programs and obligations underlying such calculations may have substantial impacts on the economy. They are clearly, however, in varying ways different in character and implications from the formal, current debt. If only because of the great volatility in their measures, we should be prudent—as some have not been—in our evaluation of their effects on the economy.

A considerable amount of recent work, for example, has tried to detect the effects on consumption and saving when changes occur in implicit social security debt. But measures of the magnitude of that debt vary widely with assumptions as to future government policy. They also differ with assumptions as to public perceptions and expectations (Leimer and Lesnoy, 1982). I myself have found (Eisner, 1983a) substantially greater and clearer effects of direct government debt than of measures of "net social security wealth." As pointed out by the U.S. Treasury,

> Clearly there is a vast difference between items . . . where the liability is certain or relatively precise . . . and . . . where the possible future liability is highly speculative and may never arise . . . The [latter] amounts, if they can be projected at all, are stated . . . without regard to probability of occurrence . . . and without deduction for existing and contingent assets which would be available. . . . (*Statement of Liabilities and Other Financial Commitments*, p. 2).

It is clear that construction of measures of government commitments that go beyond net current liabilities would take us into uncharted and unfathomable waters. The task would face huge uncertainty regarding the anticipated tax receipts to meet the commitments. One not implausible assumption, particularly after the recent changes in the social security law, is that we can expect taxes generally to be adjusted so that the net actuarial value of government obligations and the taxes to pay for them will approximate zero. *They would then contribute nothing to an enlarged measure of the deficit, or to the public's perception of its net wealth.*

To examine the economic implications and impact of budget deficits, a number of other measures are useful, if not indispensable. In particular, it is crucially important to distinguish between structural and cyclical deficits. The structural deficit is the deficit that would occur aside from cyclical variations in the economy. Hence it is defined for some given level of economic activity or employment. In the United States, it has usually been measured at a "high employment level," ranging until recently from 4 percent to 5.1 percent. The cyclical deficit is then the additional deficit which actually occurs or would occur as employment or economic activity varies from the levels used in defining the structural deficit. The structural deficit is also dubbed the "cyclically adjusted" deficit.

These distinctions are important in judging the significance and policy implications of the deficit. The cyclical deficit or cyclical component of the total deficit reflects the impact of the economy on the deficit, rather than the impact of the deficit on the economy. When the economy slows and unemployment rises, tax receipts from income and corporate profits decline. With fewer people working, contributions for social security and unemployment insurance also decline. With production and purchases down, revenues from excise taxes and import duties fall. Yet government expenditures do not decline in the face of a recession. Even without introduction of additional government programs, expenditures rise automatically as payments for unemployment benefits increase with the greater unemployment. Thus, the lower the level of economic activity and the greater the rate of unemployment, the less will be tax revenues and the greater will be expenditures and, hence, the greater will be the budget deficit.

The economy has a long history of fluctuations not necessarily stemming from changes in government expenditures or taxes.

Low points in the path of the economy are likely to be associated with *resultant* deficits. A simple statistical analysis would hence generally show a positive correlation between the relative size of the budget deficit and the rate of unemployment. The relation between taxes and expenditures, and income and employment, however, should make clear that any inference that deficits *cause* unemployment would be erroneous.

The structural, cyclically adjusted, standardized-employment, high-employment, or full-employment budget surpluses or deficits, via their effects on aggregate demand, offer at least first-order measures of the impact of fiscal policy on the economy. Changes in the structural deficit, by definition, exclude purely cyclical changes in federal outlays or in tax receipts. Changes in tax *rates* or government expenditures which are not automatic consequences of cyclical fluctuations do affect the structural deficit. An increase in tax rates can generally be expected to lower the structural deficit, while an increase in government expenditures can be expected to raise it.

Factors other than changes in legislated government expenditures and tax rates may also affect the structural deficit. Higher prices, for example, particularly as reflected in higher incomes, have generally reduced the deficit. With our progressive structure of income tax rates, and depreciation deductions tied to the original cost of capital assets, higher prices have swollen tax revenues more than they have increased government expenditures. With the introduction of indexing of individual income tax rates, however, higher prices and incomes would no longer result in a higher proportion of personal income being taxed. And if President Reagan's May 1985 proposal of inflation adjustments to "capital cost recovery" were adopted, higher prices would no longer increase revenues from business income taxes.

At the same time, a restrictive monetary policy which raises interest rates would not only foster a cyclical deficit by slowing down the economy. It would also increase the structural deficit by increasing the already substantial interest payments on the existing federal debt.

This suggests still another useful measure of the deficit, one which excludes interest payments. A "primary" budget, which is balanced aside from interest payments on the debt, has particular analytical significance. If there is an existing debt, a balanced primary budget would imply a total budget in deficit. The debt would then grow each year by the amount of the interest payments and the deficit would remain in a constant ratio to the debt, equal to the rate of interest. On the not unreasonable assumption that the real interest rate equals the real rate of growth of output, the debt and deficit would remain indefinitely a constant proportion of gross national product.

As compared to the national income and product federal deficit of $175.8 billion in 1984, the primary deficit was $59.1 billion. For the first quarter of 1985, the primary deficit was down to an annual rate of $32.6 billion, less than 1 percent of GNP.

There are indeed still other adjustments to the measure of the deficit which may prove relevant. One would involve the portion of the deficit which can be financed, without contributing to inflation, by the direct or indirect creation of money. This would correspond to the rate, in a growing economy, at which the public would like to increase its holding of real cash balances, that is, money adjusted for inflation.

And of course, not to be forgotten are those adjustments necessary to secure measures of deficits corrected for inflation, which we presented in Chapter 2. These will play a major role in the story we have yet to unfold.[3]

5

Deficit, Deficit, Who's Got the Surplus?

ONE BASIC FINANCIAL FACT escapes most public discussion of debt and deficits: for every debtor there must be a creditor. People, businesses, and state and local governments—and foreigners—own the Treasury bills, notes, and bonds that constitute the federal debt.

Individuals and businesses are apt to think of their own debts as a burden, since they are obligations to others. If the government debt is owed to foreign governments or their nationals, the analogy to private debt is clear. Others are the creditors. But if the government debt is owed to its own citizens and businesses, what then? The debt of the government must constitute financial assets for those who hold it. While debt may be a burden, are not financial assets a blessing?

At the end of 1980, just before the Reagan Administration took office, of the total gross public debt of $930 billion, by official measure, $314 billion were held by U.S. government agencies and trust funds and the Federal Reserve Banks, as may be seen in Table 5.1. State and local government held another $88 billion of that debt. American banks, businesses, individuals, and "other miscellaneous investors" held $399 billion. Foreign and interna-

TABLE 5.1   Gross Public Debt of U.S. Treasury by Holder

(1)	(2)	(3)	(4)	(5)
	1980	1984	1980	1984
HOLDER	($ Billion)		(% of Total)	
U.S. government agencies and trust funds	192.5	289.6	20.7	17.4
Federal Reserve Banks	121.3	160.9	13.0	9.7
State and local governments	87.9	181.6[a]	9.4	10.9[a]
Commercial banks	112.1	183.4	12.1	11.0
Money market funds	3.5	25.9	0.3	1.6
Insurance companies	24.0	82.3	2.6	4.9
Other companies	19.3	51.1	2.1	3.4
Individuals	117.1	143.8	12.6	8.6
Foreign and international	129.7	192.8	13.9	11.6
Other miscellaneous	122.8	351.6[a]	13.2	21.1[a]
Total	930.2	1,663.0	100.0	100.0

Source: Treasury Bulletin as reported in Federal Reserve Bulletin, August 1985, p. A30.

[a]Projected from second quarter, 1984, proportions of state and local and other miscellaneous holdings.

tional holders accounted for only $130 billion, or less than 14 percent of the total gross public debt. And while foreign ownership was up to $193 billion by the end of 1984, that accounted then for a smaller proportion, less than 12 percent of the total.

Since the American government debt has been and still is overwhelmingly held by Americans, does its magnitude affect anything other than the distribution as opposed to the amount of our national income, product, and wealth? One measure of the burden of the debt is the taxes to be levied to pay interest and, to be less realistic, to pay off the principal of the debt. But if the taxes are paid by Americans and the interest and principal payments are received by Americans, costs to taxpayers are matched by the benefits received by debt holders. If taxpayers receive interest and principal payments in the same proportion in which they pay taxes, not even the distribution of income or wealth is affected.

It is the relatively rich, it may be argued, who own most of our securities of all kinds, and the relatively rich who pay a large share of taxes. It would thus appear that a large public debt does not particularly affect the distribution of income as between rich and poor. Of course, some rich may own the Treasury bills, notes, and bonds and other rich may pay more in taxes. We are then left with some possibilities of the debt affecting distribution. But if this is the whole story, it is indeed a small story for the panic criers among us to tell.

In sum, again, if for every debtor there must be a creditor, for every borrower there must be a lender. Just as someone out there must be owning the federal debt, when the government borrows to finance a deficit, someone else must have a surplus to do the lending. And if the federal government is spending more than it is taking in in taxes, others must be getting from the federal government more than they are giving to it. Those "others" are private households (and nonprofit institutions), business, state and local governments, or foreigners.

Any that doubt this fundamental identity between federal deficits and everybody else's surpluses can check the historical data of the last four decades. Except for our inability to get all the numbers right, the "statistical discrepancy," federal deficits are always exactly matched by other surpluses—state and local, private or foreign. Our rare federal surpluses are in turn matched by others' deficits.

Just look at some of the numbers shown in Table 5.2. In 1945 there was a huge federal, war deficit of $42 billion. The private sector—individuals, business, and nonprofit institutions—was in surplus by $34 billion, state and local governments by another $3 billion and foreigners by $1 billion, with the statistical discrepancy accounting for the remainder.

In 1975, when the reported federal deficit reached a record $69 billion, the private *surplus* attained a record $77 billion. In 1983, our new record federal deficit of $179 billion was matched by a private surplus of $100 billion, state and local surpluses of $44 billion, and now a substantial surplus of foreigners—our increasing debt to the rest of the world—of $34 billion.

In 1984, with a federal deficit of $176 billion, the private sector surplus was only $37 billion. The balance was made up by state and local surpluses of $53 billion, a particularly large foreign surplus of $93 billion, and a statistical discrepancy of − $7 billion. For the first time, the major portion of a large deficit was vis à vis the rest of the world rather than Americans.[1]

In most of the years since 1945, however, the foreign sector was in deficit to the United States. In the relatively few, mainly recent years that we were in deficit to the rest of the world, their surplus, as shown in Table 5.3, never amounted to as much as one percent of our gross national product until 1983. It then attained 2.6 percent in 1984, as against a federal deficit of 4.8 percent. But mostly, the federal deficit has been matched by surpluses in the other *domestic* sectors.

TABLE 5.2   Surplus and Deficit (−) by Sector, 1945–84 (Billions of Dollars)

(1)	(2)	(3)	(4)	(5)	(6)
	GOVERNMENT				
YEAR	Federal	State and Local	PRIVATE	FOREIGN	STATISTICAL DISCREPANCY
1945	−42.1	2.6	34.1	1.3	4.1
1946	3.5	1.9	−1.1	−4.9	0.5
1947	13.4	1.0	−6.7	−9.3	1.5
1948	8.3	0.1	−4.5	−2.4	−1.6
1949	−2.6	−0.7	3.7	−0.9	0.6
1950	9.2	−1.2	−11.1	1.8	1.3
1951	6.5	−0.4	−8.4	−0.9	3.2
1952	−3.7	0.0	2.7	−0.6	1.7
1953	−7.1	0.1	3.4	1.3	2.3
1954	−6.0	−1.1	5.4	−0.2	2.0
1955	4.4	−1.3	−4.0	−0.4	1.3
1956	6.1	−0.9	−0.3	−2.8	−2.1
1957	2.3	−1.4	5.1	−4.8	−1.2
1958	−10.3	−2.4	13.4	−0.9	0.2
1959	−1.1	−0.4	1.8	1.2	−1.3
1960	3.0	0.1	2.1	−2.8	−2.4
1961	−3.9	−0.4	8.2	−3.8	−0.1
1962	−4.2	0.5	5.1	−3.4	2.1
1963	0.3	0.5	2.0	−4.4	1.7
1964	−3.3	1.0	8.9	−6.8	0.1
1965	0.5	0.0	6.2	−5.4	−1.2
1966	−1.8	0.5	2.9	−3.0	1.4
1967	−13.2	−1.1	17.1	−2.6	−0.3
1968	−6.0	0.1	8.7	−0.6	−2.1
1969	8.4	1.5	−5.7	−0.4	−3.9
1970	−11.5	1.9	14.4	−3.2	−1.5
1971	−21.3	2.6	13.9	0.7	4.1
1972	−16.1	13.5	−5.8	5.1	3.3
1973	−5.6	13.4	−2.1	−6.5	0.8
1974	−13.5	6.8	5.8	−2.9	3.7
1975	−69.3	5.5	76.6	−18.3	5.5
1976	−53.1	16.6	36.5	−5.1	5.1
1977	−45.9	28.0	2.8	13.6	1.4
1978	−29.5	30.3	−12.6	14.3	−2.6
1979	−15.0	30.4	−15.7	1.8	−1.5
1980	−60.0	30.6	33.5	−6.3	2.3
1981	−63.2	37.6	25.7	−5.8	5.6
1982	−148.2	32.9	109.1	6.6	−0.5
1983	−178.6	44.1	100.1	33.9	0.5
1984	−175.8	52.9	36.9	93.4	−7.4

Source: *Economic Report of the President February 1985,* Table B-25, p. 262, and, for 1984, *Survey of Current Business,* Table 5.1, p. 14.

TABLE 5.3   Surplus and Deficit (−) by Sector, 1945–84 (Percent of GNP)

(1)	(2)	(3)	(4)	(5)	(6)
	GOVERNMENT				
YEAR	*Federal*	*State and Local*	PRIVATE	FOREIGN	STATISTICAL DISCREPANCY
1945	− 19.8	1.2	16.1	0.6	1.9
1946	1.7	0.9	− 0.5	− 2.3	0.2
1947	5.7	0.4	− 2.9	− 4.0	0.6
1948	3.2	0.0	− 1.7	− 0.9	− 0.6
1949	− 1.0	− 0.3	1.4	− 0.3	0.2
1950	3.2	− 0.4	− 3.9	0.6	0.5
1951	2.0	− 0.1	− 2.5	− 0.3	1.0
1952	− 1.1	0.0	0.8	− 0.2	0.5
1953	− 1.9	0.0	0.9	0.4	0.6
1954	− 1.6	− 0.3	1.5	− 0.1	0.5
1955	1.1	− 0.3	− 1.0	− 0.1	0.3
1956	1.4	− 0.2	− 0.1	− 0.7	− 0.5
1957	0.5	− 0.3	1.1	− 1.1	− 0.3
1958	− 2.3	− 0.5	3.0.	− 0.2	0.0
1959	− 0.2	− 0.1	0.4	0.2	− 0.3
1960	0.6	0.0	0.4	− 0.6	− 0.5
1961	− 0.7	− 0.1	1.6	− 0.7	0.0
1962	− 0.7	0.1	0.9	− 0.6	0.4
1963	0.1	0.1	0.3	− 0.7	0.3
1964	− 0.5	0.2	1.4	− 1.1	0.0
1965	0.1	0.0	0.9	− 0.8	− 0.2
1966	− 0.2	0.1	0.4	− 0.4	0.2
1967	− 1.7	− 0.1	2.1	− 0.3	0.0
1968	− 0.7	0.0	1.0	− 0.1	− 0.2
1969	0.9	0.2	− 0.6	0.0	− 0.4
1970	− 1.2	0.2	1.5	− 0.3	− 0.2
1971	− 2.0	0.2	1.3	0.1	0.4
1972	− 1.4	1.1	− 0.5	0.4	0.3
1973	− 0.4	1.0	− 0.2	− 0.5	0.1
1974	− 0.9	0.5	0.4	− 0.2	0.3
1975	− 4.5	0.4	4.9	− 1.2	0.4
1976	− 3.1	1.0	2.1	− 0.3	0.3
1977	− 2.4	1.5	0.1	0.7	0.1
1978	− 1.4	1.4	− 0.6	0.7	− 0.1
1979	− 0.6	1.3	− 0.6	0.1	− 0.1
1980	− 2.3	1.2	1.3	− 0.2	0.1
1981	− 2.1	1.3	0.9	− 0.2	0.2
1982	− 4.8	1.1	3.6	0.2	0.0
1983	− 5.4	1.3	3.0	1.0	0.0
1984	− 4.8	1.4	1.0	2.6	− 0.2

Source: Table 5.2.

Public deficits, then, create private surpluses. We cannot eliminate one without wiping out the other. Achieving public surpluses—paying off the debt—must mean private deficits.

All this may seem like trick accounting. In fact, it has a great deal of economic significance. On the one hand, a federal budget deficit, by adding to the financial assets of the private sector, makes it richer. On the other hand, the added wealth of the private sector is the federal debt itself.

That, though, is only the beginning. With greater wealth, those of us in the private sector, and state and local governments as well, will be inclined to spend more. And the federal deficit itself will imply greater private income and hence greater private spending.

But before we go further in this important story, we should essay a fuller view of the effects of government deficits. To do so will demand a little courage, as we take the plunge into some relevant economic theory.

6

Deficits and the Economy: The Theory, Part I

FEDERAL DEBT AND DEFICITS do matter, and can matter very much. To see how, we have to ignore most of the rhetoric and fit both debt and deficits into a meaningful theory of how the economy operates. We shall risk offense to currently ascendant popular fashion as we pose four questions about some key analytical relationships.

1. How do the debt and deficits affect the bottom line, the total production of goods and services and the national income earned from this production?
2. How do the debt and deficits affect employment and unemployment?
3. How do the debt and deficits affect the composition of total production, particularly as between current consumption and investment for the future?
4. How do the debt and deficits affect prices and the rate of inflation?

Supply and Demand

We begin with classical notions of supply and demand. What becomes tricky, however, is that for our purposes we must be primarily concerned not with the supply and demand for peanuts, or automobiles, or electrical machinery, or any one commodity or group of commodities. We must focus rather on the *aggregate* supply and demand, for all of the goods and services produced in the economy.

Aggregate supply is then taken to be the total amount of goods and services that the residents of the nation are ready to offer. This depends clearly on the quantity and quality of the population wishing to work and how many hours and how hard they wish to work. It depends also upon the land and other natural resources. It depends further upon the capital of buildings, roads, equipment, and inventories—public and private—used in production. And it depends finally upon the system which puts all these together.

But it takes more than supply to sustain production. In our economy, business takes orders from neither commissar nor pope. Firms produce to make profits, and they cannot make profits if they cannot sell their output. For supply to result in production firms must also see demand. For the economy as a whole that means there must be an aggregate demand to match the total of what can be supplied.

In the old pre-Keynesian or classical economics of half a century ago, aggregate demand presented no problem. According to "Say's Law," named after the early nineteenth-century French economist, Jean-Baptiste Say, it was proclaimed that "supply created its own demand." The reasoning was that whenever anyone supplied productive resources it was in order to enjoy that output or to trade it for some other output. Since for each individual act of supplying resources of land, labor, or capital, there was then an equivalent demand, the sum of all demand would equal the sum of all supply, or the aggregate output to be produced.

As an argument against those who insist that progress dooms us to glut and that new people coming to work—women, youth, minorities, and immigrants—must take jobs away from those already employed, the argument had some usefulness. As a dogma denying the possibility that a free market can leave us with unused capacity of men and machines, it left its adherents open to ridicule.

For the reality is that in much of the world, and certainly in the private enterprise or capitalist world, unemployment is an enduring, if variable, fact of life. In the United States, whether we face the 10.7 percent official rate of December 1982, the worst point in our recent recession, or the 7.1 percent of the fall of 1985, unemployment remains the critical if not the most important parameter of economic policy. Whatever other impact they may have, economic measures and activities must be evaluated in terms of their effect upon employment.

This is not merely a matter of concern for jobless individuals or for their families who depend upon them. Since fewer people working means less total production, unemployment affects the welfare of the nation. It entails not only the lost product of workers but also that of machines left idle with their masters. Unless we are to "liquidate" those directly touched by unemployment, a loss in total production is in fact shared by much of the population. Whether it is borne in higher taxes for unemployment benefits and welfare payments, lower dividends and declines in the stock market, or in a greater cost–price squeeze for farmers, the loss in output is real and widely if unevenly suffered.

The complaint of John Maynard Keynes, in setting forth the foundation of the modern revolution in macroeconomic theory, was that the "classical" economists, ignoring the possibility of insufficient aggregate demand, *assumed* that the economy was in a perpetual state of full employment. These theorists then based all of their economic reasoning on that assumption. Unemployment could only occur, by their logic, because workers or their unions foolishly insisted on wages higher than their productivity, or government interfered with the free workings of the economic system. Faced with the fact of involuntary and persistent unemployment, "the classical theorists," according to Keynes, "resemble Euclidean geometers in a non-Euclidean world who, discovering that in experience straight lines apparently parallel often meet, rebuked the lines for not keeping straight—as the only remedy for the unfortunate collisions which are occurring" (Keynes, 1936, p. 16).

The Supply Side

Whether the economy is or can be assumed to be at full employment makes all the difference for the implications of government debt and deficits. Conclusions that apply to the world of full employment are negated if not reversed in a world of unemployment. This in turn relates to the issue raised by Say's Law, where aggregate demand can always be relied upon to equal aggregate supply. If it can, then the only limit to total production is aggregate supply. Hence the way to increase employment and output is exclusively to work on increasing supply—the two-century-old foundation of the extremes of current "supply-side economics."

Of course the supply side is important. It may be said that God gave economists two eyes, one to watch demand and the other to watch supply. So no self-respecting economist would suggest that supply can be ignored. And the government debt and the choice between deficits and taxes do in principle affect supply. Let us consider how.

For one thing, virtually all taxes affect economic behavior.[1] Cigarette taxes discourage smoking by making it more expensive. Similarly, tariffs discourage imports. It is widely argued that income taxes discourage both employment and saving, thus reducing the supply of labor and capital, respectively. They are presumed to discourage employment because, given the choice between leisure and work, the tax on payment for work makes work relatively less desirable and leads some of us to forgo a job, or reduce our hours of work or intensity of effort.

And to the extent that we save in order to secure a return, interest or dividends on our savings, the fact that the return is taxed is deemed to make the saving less worthwhile. Saving is refraining from consuming and therefore frees, for the production of capital goods, the resources which would otherwise be used to produce consumption goods. Less saving hence means a lower supply of capital.

If income taxes decrease the supply of labor and capital, should we look to other taxes or to substituting "deficit financing" of government expenditures? A deficit financed by borrowing will tend to raise interest rates as the government competes for loanable funds. By classical theory, the higher interest rates might be expected to draw forth more saving. But with a government deficit, savers would be buying government bonds instead of corporate bonds. The public dis-saving would more than offset the increased private saving. This would reduce the supply of capital for private capital formation—private investment would be "crowded out." If the deficit is financed by "printing" money, the classical view is that this would surely raise prices, including wages, but it is hard to see why that would reduce supply.

We might infer that the deficit in itself may be better for supply than income taxes, or any variant of them such as payroll or corporate profit taxes, which would particularly discourage employment and corporate activity respectively. Perhaps that is why supply siders, such as Congressman Jack Kemp, so adamantly oppose tax increases to reduce the deficit.

We recall, however, that deficits add to debt, in the form of money or interest-bearing securities. And the government debt constitutes a portion of the financial assets of the private sector of the economy. Hence the greater the federal debt, and the greater the interest payments on Treasury securities, the greater the wealth and income enjoyed by the nation's citizens or, more narrowly, residents who hold the federal obligations.

If the owners of the securities think themselves richer as a consequence of this government debt, they will have less need for work. They will use some of their wealth to "buy" leisure, reducing their supply of labor. Further, if people think themselves wealthy they will, according to classical theory, feel less need to accumulate more wealth. They will save less and reduce the supply of capital as well as the supply of labor. The government debt would thus seem to reduce supply, and deficits increase the debt.

This line of reasoning has to elicit some counterarguments. These include the suggestion, just offered, that deficits are better for supply than income taxes because income taxes discourage work and saving. The notion that taxes reduce the supply of labor and capital depends, in the jargon of economic theory, on the "substitution effect." A lesser after-tax return to work leads people to substitute leisure for labor. A lesser after-tax return to saving leads people to consume currently rather than accumulate capital.

Simply enough, someone contemplating a job paying, let's say, six dollars per hour, has to reckon whether the wage is worth it. If taxes will take away a third, so that the take-home pay will be only four dollars, the prospective worker may decide to cultivate his—or her—garden instead.

Similarly, a couple contemplating a $5,000 ocean cruise may weigh the merit of saving the money, and going next year, or in thirty years, after retirement. If they can invest $5,000 and secure a six percent per year return, they can put the cruise off one year and have $300 to spare. Or they can put it off to retirement and have $23,717 to spare. But if they face a one-third tax on the earnings from their investment, the gain from putting off the trip one year is reduced to $200. And the gain from saving until retirement is reduced by more than half, to $11,217. The couple might just decide to enjoy ocean breezes now.

But this ignores the income and wealth effects. All taxes in themselves make us poorer. If we are poorer we need to work harder in order to enjoy the standard of living to which we aspire. Again in terms of economic theory, since we are able to have less, what we have is more precious and the marginal utility or benefit of having more is greater. Hence we are driven to work harder by taxes, essentially to make up for the after-tax income that we lose. We might contemplate working 20 hours a week on that six dollars an hour job, to earn $120, if we had no taxes to pay. If we were anxious to get $120, for whatever purpose, application of a one-third tax, reducing our take-home pay to four dollars per hour, might induce us to increase our hours to thirty.

And similarly, a tax on saving forces us to save more to accumulate a desired amount of wealth, for retirement or any other purpose, since we cannot rely on as much wealth being accumulated from the return on saving. We might just have decided that we wanted to be able to enjoy $28,717 in our retirement: the $5,000 from the foregone ocean voyage and all the accumulated earnings that we could have from them if we did not have to pay taxes. With a one-third tax rate reducing the annual return to 4 percent instead of 6 percent, however, we would have to put aside $8,854 now to accumulate to a total of $28,717 in thirty years. If we are determined to have that retirement nest egg, the tax would thus induce us to save $3,854 more than we would have saved otherwise.

There are, of course, other taxes besides those on income. In particular, there are excise taxes, import duties, and inheritance taxes at the federal level, and sales and property taxes on state and local levels. In general, taxes on goods and services are likely to distort the allocation of resources from what they would be in a tax-free system. The higher prices including the taxes would not only discourage the purchase of taxed commodities. Since prices are higher, real incomes are lower and what we can buy with our wages is less. Therefore, we may again be tempted to substitute leisure for work. But once more, because of the income or wealth effect, people feeling poorer may decide to work harder to make ends meet.

Inheritance taxes, like income taxes, are presumably ambiguous in effect. We may be discouraged from working and saving to leave an estate, to the extent that we feel the government will tax so much of it away that we might as well not bother. But if we are really determined to leave a substantial estate, we will work all the harder and save all the more to compensate for the taxes we anticipate the government will collect. Of course, if inheritance tax rates become prohibitively high, saving to leave to our heirs will dry up unless the tax can be avoided. If the tax rate is 100 percent, the game is over.

In the way of proposed taxes, value-added taxes or consumption taxes, excluding the portion of income saved from taxation, would not have the negative effects on saving that some see in the income tax. We already have all kinds of "tax incentives," though, for saving and investment. These include accelerated depreciation, capital gains exclusions, the investment tax credit, and interest deductibility for business borrowing, all rationalized as necessary to make up for the anti-saving effects of the income tax. To switch now from an income tax to a consumption tax without dropping these special provisions would bias our choices in the direction of more saving than we would undertake in a tax-free economy. But it is not clear that that is desirable. Government *may* know better how much we should deprive ourselves of current consumption in order to invest in our futures, but this case has not been made.

If all of this leaves us with a somewhat fuzzy notion as to the ultimate impact of alternative courses regarding taxes, deficits, and debt, that is the nature of the problem. There is really little to report *on the supply side* that is clear, unambiguous, and important. The confident assertions of the supply-side panaceas are not readily sustainable.

An Extreme Example of Supply-Side Effects on Labor

In principle, debt does have effects on labor supply, but for them to become important the debt has to be many times its present magnitude. It has indeed to be so large that real interest income on the debt becomes a dominant supplement and potential substitute to real income from working. Those who do not find this obvious, or who wish an instructive example, can walk with us through Table 6.1.

On the first line we set forth what is not far from the current situation, although in the interest of simplicity numbers are rounded liberally. We thus put the debt at $2,000 billion, but for convenience ignore the fact that a fair part of that is not held by the public. We assume interest payments at 10 percent, somewhat higher than the actual current rate. This means that with federal expenditures exclusive of interest payments at some $800 billion, total federal government outlays are $1,000 billion.

Now, assuming earned income (or national income) is $3,000 billion, taxable income including the federal interest payments equals $3,200 billion. It then takes an average tax rate of 25 percent to collect the $800 billion in taxes necessary to keep the deficit from exceeding $200 billion. That means that income after taxes comes to $2,400 billion. If nobody bothered to work and there were hence no *earned income,* total income, restricted to receipts of federal interest payments, would be only $150 billion.

If the debt were $18,000 billion, fully nine times the amount assumed to correspond to the current situation, the average tax rate necessary to keep the deficit to $200 billion, as indicated on the second line of Table 6.1, would be 50 percent. With a debt of $66,000, an average tax rate of 75 percent would be necessary to keep the deficit down to $200 billion. It may be noted that in this last case, while total income after taxes would still be $2,400 billion, income after taxes, from just the federal interest payments, would amount to a substantial $1,650 billion.

What does that imply for the individual household? Let us assume that an average household, earning some $30,000 per year, shares proportionally not only in earned income but in holdings of federal debt and hence in interest payments on that debt, and also shares equally in taxes. Then, in the current situation, that household would be receiving $2,000 in interest payments from its holdings of federal debt and have a total taxable income of $32,000. It would pay 25 percent of that in taxes and have $24,000 left after taxes. If the income earners in that household decided to loaf and earn nothing, their interest receipts would leave them with an after-tax income of only $1,500. This alternative would hardly seem desirable. We can therefore expect in

TABLE 6.1 Burden of the Debt: Earnings

(1)	(2)	(3)	(4)	(5)	(6)	(7)	(8)
						INCOME AFTER TAXES	
						Total	Without Earned Income
DEBT HELD BY PUBLIC	FEDERAL EXPENDITURES EXCLUSIVE OF INTEREST PAYMENTS	FEDERAL INTEREST PAYMENTS AT 10% [0.1 × (1)]	EARNED INCOME	TAXABLE INCOME [(3) + (4)]	TAX RATE (%)	[(5) − (6) × (5)]	[(3) − (6) × (3)]
Economy: Billions of Dollars							
2,000	800	200	3,000	3,200	25	2,400	150
18,000	800	1,800	3,000	4,800	50	2,400	900
66,000	800	6,600	3,000	9,600	75	2,400	1,650
Individual Household: Dollars							
20,000	—	2,000	30,000	32,000	25	24,000	1,500
180,000	—	18,000	30,000	48,000	50	24,000	9,000
660,000	—	66,000	30,000	96,000	75	24,000	16,500

the current situation that members of the typical household may groan about their taxes but continue working.

But if the debt were nine times as great, this typical household would own $180,000 of government securities and receive interest payments of $18,000. It would have a taxable income of $48,000 but have to pay 50 percent in taxes so that it would still have only $24,000 left after taxes. Household members would now realize that if they decided to quit their jobs and forgo earned income, their substantial interest receipts would leave them $9,000 per year after taxes. This, though, may still seem insufficient to give up work.

Suppose finally we get to the point, where along with a national income of $3,000 billion, we enjoy interest receipts of $6,600 billion on a federal debt of $66,000 billion. With the 75 percent average tax rate necessary to keep the deficit at $200 billion, we might then have some very serious consequences for the supply of labor.

For the "typical" American family, holding a proportionate amount of the national debt, would now have a total gross income of $96,000, composed of $30,000 in salary and wages and $66,000 in interest income on its Treasury securities. With the average tax rate of 75 percent necessary to finance interest payments, the family would again find that, if its members continue working, it would have a net income after taxes of $24,000. But by giving up all work and its accompanying salary or wage, members of the family could still enjoy $16,500 of after-tax income from their interest receipts. It may be argued that a significant number of people would opt for the $16,500 and a life of complete leisure rather than the hard work necessary to raise the $16,500 to $24,000.

Before we get too concerned about this fateful possibility, we should recognize of course that it is very remote. Even calculated on the basis of a nominal interest rate of 10 percent, it would require a debt of $66 trillion, no less than thirty-three times as large as our current gross public debt. And if, as we shall suggest later, the appropriate measure of real income on the debt requires application of a *real* rate of interest, say 4 percent, the debt would have to be in the order of $165 trillion![2] Accustomed as we may be to astronomical numbers in dealing with the debt, these figures take us quite out of our galaxy and any reasonable economic relevance.

Effects of the Debt on Saving

There are some further effects that a debt may have on the supply
of capital, on the assumption that income is given. We can illus-
trate these in Table 6.2, where we assume a national income of
$3,000 billion, real wealth of $13,000 billion[3] and, initially, a federal debt again of $2,000 billion.

The critical relations here are those associating consumption
and saving with wealth. As we have suggested earlier, the greater
we consider our existing wealth the less need, presumably, we
have to accumulate more wealth to consume in the future. Hence,
the more we are likely to consume now. In a rough conformity
with statistical evidence (see, for example, Ando and Modigliani,
1963), we assume that each additional dollar of wealth, other
things equal, will cause us to consume ten cents more. But saving
equals income minus consumption. Thus, if income remains fixed,
each additional dollar of wealth must also mean ten cents less of
saving.

Since the federal debt is wealth to its holders, we find consumption and saving varying with the amount of that debt. On
the first line, roughly describing the current situation, we then
have consumption of $2,700 billion and saving of $300 billion. If
the debt is $200 billion more (perhaps one year from now as a
result of a deficit this year of $200 billion), *with income unchanged*,
consumption would be $2,720 billion, leaving only $280 billion

TABLE 6.2 Burden of the Debt: Saving
(Billions of Dollars)

Consumption = 0.7 Income + 0.1 Wealth − 900
Saving   = Income − Consumption
Saving   = 0.3 Income − 0.1 Wealth + 900
Wealth   = Real Wealth + Federal Debt

(1)	(2)	(3)	(4)	(5)	(6)
		WEALTH			
INCOME	Real	Federal Debt	Total	CONSUMPTION	SAVING
3,000	13,000	2,000	15,000	2,700	300
3,000	13,000	2,200	15,200	2,720	280
3,000	13,000	2,400	15,400	2,740	260
3,000	13,000	3,000	16,000	2,800	200
3,000	13,000	4,000	17,000	2,900	100
3,000	13,000	5,000	18,000	3,000	0

for saving. Raising the debt by 50 percent, to $3,000 billion, would reduce saving to $200 billion. A debt of $4,000 billion would cut saving to $100 billion. And a debt of $5,000 billion, two and a half times our current debt, would cut saving to zero, given our assumptions.

But how good are our assumptions? What turns out to be crucial is the one that income remains the same, regardless of consumption. If households are trying to buy more automobiles, television sets, and trips to Palm Springs and Las Vegas, would not the product of these goods and services, and hence the national income, be increased? The way to rule out that likelihood is to assume that the economy is operating at full employment with no excess capacity. Then more cannot be produced. Hence if consumers succeed in inducing more production of consumption goods this can only be at the expense of investment goods, and saving and investment must be reduced. In this instance, we do have a real crowding out of investment as a consequence of a budget deficit which increases the debt. Martin Feldstein, Pete Peterson, and Felix Rohatyn would in this case appear to be right.

But even here, with the full employment assumption that total production cannot be increased, there is a question. How will business react if it understands this same theory of the wealth effect on consumption? According to the principle of "rational expectations," business will see consumers buying more now and know that they also plan to buy more in the future out of their greater perceived wealth. Will not business then try to invest more so as to have the additional plant and equipment necessary to produce additional goods to meet the greater consumer demand? If so, there will be increases in both consumption demand and investment demand. The result, since these demands cannot be met, would be an increase in prices. Prices would in fact rise until the *real* value of the debt is reduced sufficiently for there no longer to be excess demand to drive prices up further.

The only complication relates to a possible shortage of money, given the need to finance higher-price transactions. That shortage would drive up interest rates and this would reduce certain types of investment: business spending for plant and equipment and construction of new housing would be curbed. But if that is the problem it could and should be solved simply by increasing the quantity of money. There would then be no change in real interest rates and no real effects of an increase in debt. Indeed, because of the inflation, we would end up with no *real* increase in the debt!

The purported crowding out of investment is thus traced to the failure of monetary policy to allow the supply of money to grow with the demand. Even under the assumption most favorable to the argument—that total production is fixed—investment is not necessarily reduced by the deficit-created debt.

7

Deficits and the Economy: The Theory, Part II

WE HAVE SO FAR CONCENTRATED on a world in which full employment is assured—or assumed. This is a world where all who want to work are working, and are working as much as they want. It is a world where all that we can produce is produced. There is no problem of being able to sell our output. The way to increase production—and income—is therefore to increase our *ability* to produce, that is, to increase supply. And we have explored potential effects of deficits on supply—finding them somewhat more enigmatic than many chose to believe.

But every businessman knows that getting the goods is only half the problem, if that much. What is critical is being able to sell what you can produce. For any single firm that is a problem of the demand for *its* products. For the economy as a whole it is a problem of total, or *aggregate* demand.

It is here that we will find major effects of federal budget deficits and federal debt. They *can* have a significant impact on aggregate demand. This impact can be good or bad, depending on the situation of our changing, dynamic economy, and depending on just how large the deficits and debt really are. The latter issue brings to the fore some of the critical questions of measurement we have been discussing. But the first essential question is, however large the deficit or debt, what difference does it make? Why should the deficit—the difference between government expenditures and government tax revenues—matter?

To answer this, we must build upon a body of theory and analysis well known to most economists, and indeed to a generation or two of survivors of freshman economics courses. We also have to be familiar with some of the recent reservations and objections to this theory and analysis. If we are convinced beforehand that the reservations and objections have been sufficient to negate the analysis, we have in effect decided that deficits do not matter. Those so convinced have perhaps read too far already, and might well pursue a more promising pastime. Those still concerned may want to plunge on with us into the theory.

Deficits, Debt, and Aggregate Demand

The first thing to understand then is that when the government buys goods and services it contributes to aggregate demand. Whether the expenditures are worthwhile, useless, or counterproductive is beside the point. Government purchases constitute demand. To any business, sales of goods to the government are just as lucrative as sales to a private purchaser (and given the notorious government buying habits, frequently more lucrative).

The first objection to this argument is that government demand must replace private demand. One can indeed imagine certain scenarios in which this would occur. For example, government expenditure to build roads may reduce private demand for railroad cars. But this very example also suggests the frailty of the argument. Government road construction may stimulate private demand for automobiles, buses, and trucks and gasoline, filling stations and motels. While government expenditures may prove a substitute for private expenditures, they may just as well stimulate additional private expenditures.

Government expenditures which do not entail the purchase of goods and services contribute to demand indirectly. Such expenditures include interest payments on the debt and the general category of transfer payments—social security and unemployment benefits, payments to veterans of the armed forces, and government employee retirement benefits. The more individuals receive in the way of these payments, the bigger is their personal income and the greater their consumption demand—spending for food and clothing, television sets, travel, and cars.

While both government expenditures for goods and services and transfer payments and interest payments contribute to aggregate demand, the bang for the buck is generally surer and greater in the case of the direct government purchases. For each dollar of government purchases of goods and services is a dollar of demand. The other dollars, received in transfer payments and interest, must be *spent* by individuals (or business) before they become effective demand. Since people tend to save some portion of additional income—the marginal propensity to consume of economic theory is considered to be less than one—each dollar of transfer payments or interest incomes is expected to add less than a dollar to purchases of goods and services. But all government spending contributes to demand.

Taxes, on the other hand, reduce demand. What we pay to the government in taxes we cannot spend. As with transfer and interest payments, however, the impact of taxes on demand is not likely to be dollar for dollar. Imposing a tax on a particular commodity, such as cigarettes, raises its price and is thus expected to reduce the quantity purchased. Total spending for the taxed commodity may even go down by considerably more than tax payments increase, as buyers shift to other, untaxed commodities that are now relatively less expensive. (Tax payments may even decline if the quantity of the taxed good purchased decreases by a greater percentage than the tax rate increases.)

But taxes in the aggregate may be expected to reduce spending by less than their amount. We generally save some of our income, and if our income goes up we tend to save more. That means, however, that if taxes are raised, thus reducing our after-tax or "take-home" income, we tend to consume less but also save less. For every dollar that after-tax income is lowered, consumption may be lowered, for example, by only eighty cents, as saving is then reduced by twenty cents. (Note, of course, that consumption equals income minus taxes minus saving.)

The issue is even more sharply drawn when we recognize that, while taxes are always grouped with death as inevitable, we know death will come eventually but taxes may rise and fall throughout our lifetime. Since any change in taxes may therefore prove less than permanent, it makes sense to change our current consumption by less than the change in after-tax income due to a change in taxes. For example, if taxes on our income are cut by $1,000 this year but we think they may be back up again next year, we are not likely to increase our consumption by $1,000 of riotous living now only to have to cut back fully later. We may rather use part of our current $1,000 gain to increase current consumption, and save a good part of it to keep up a higher level of consumption in the future.

An increase in government expenditures for goods and services, as we have noted, implies an equal direct increase in aggregate demand. Since the corresponding increase in taxes, to preserve a balanced budget, will reduce aggregate demand by less, we have the proposition that, even with a balanced budget, equal increases in taxes and government spending for goods and services will increase aggregate demand. Indeed under certain simplifying assumptions, it can be shown that the ultimate in-crease in demand, when taxes rise by as much as the government expenditures, will be exactly equal to the amount of increase in government spending (Salant, 1957).

But that applies to balanced-budget spending. What about a deficit, which occurs when government spending is *not* matched by taxes. Since taxes do bring about some—undoubtedly substan-tial—reduction in private expenditures or demand, government spending contributes more to demand if it is deficit-financed than if it comes with a balanced budget.

This then is the Keynesian or "income-expenditure" view of the role of deficits. Government spending on goods and services adds to demand even if fully covered by taxes. If it is deficit-financed it adds more, probably much more. And while govern-ment transfer payments fully supported by tax revenues do not add to demand, if they are deficit-financed they do. So, budget deficits increase aggregate demand, and hence stimulate the econ-omy. The widely expressed view that excessive deficits will bring on a recession has no place in this analysis. Since deficits *increase* demand, they can hardly be charged with creating a situation in which firms must cut output and employment because they can-not find buyers for their products.

Classical economists are quick to remind us that we cannot properly explain or predict economic behavior on the basis of the short run alone. Despite the reminder by Keynes, "in the long

run we are all dead," all economists recognize that current economic behavior is affected by our desire to optimize over a ho-
rizon that extends beyond today's sunset. In this context, today's
deficit becomes tonight's debt. Our analysis cannot be complete,
therefore, without integrating the implications of a current deficit
with those of the debt to which it contributes.

Economists find this best elucidated in terms of 1985 Nobel
prize winner Franco Modigliani's life cycle theory (Modigliani and
Brumberg, 1954; Ando and Modigliani, 1963), which, along with
the permanent income theory of the consumption function of
earlier Nobel Laureate Milton Friedman (Friedman, 1957), has
contributed significantly to the Keynesian theory of aggregate
demand. According to the life cycle theory, households decide
current consumption and plan future consumption on the basis
not merely of current income but also of their wealth and expected future income. Reasonable assumptions about individual
preferences or the utility to be derived from consumption imply
that an increase in current wealth will cause households to allocate
some of that wealth to increase current consumption. They will
also set aside a major portion of it, however, to increase consumption in the future.

The critical long-term role of the deficit now becomes clear.
The federal deficit adds to the federal debt and the debt is wealth
to its holders. Whatever their concerns for the government's finances, the greater are public holdings of that debt, the wealthier
the public see themselves, regarding their own portfolios, and,
hence, the more ready they are to spend. They will be willing to
spend more on current consumption, and will plan to spend more
on consumption in the future as well.

All this is illustrated in Table 7.1 which, for those not fright-
ened by numbers, will repay careful study. It is indeed built around
that standard elementary analysis which has been taught to almost
two generations of college freshmen. The important additional
twist, though, is that private consumption spending, in good neoclassical fashion—and consistent with the formulations of Modigliani and Friedman—is made to depend not only on officially
measured income but upon private wealth or net worth.

The standard analysis indicates that equilibrium GNP, and
hence the real income earned, which we can for our purposes
consider identical, will tend to an "equilibrium" value at which
there is no excess demand: namely, a point at which the aggregate
demand equals total output. If there is excess demand, business

TABLE 7.1   The Debt and Aggregate Demand
(Billions of Dollars)

$AD = C + ID + G + NE$		
$C = 0.8(Y - T) + 0.1\,NW - 1{,}500$		
$ID = 0.15Y + 80$		
$NW = RW + D$		
$T = 0.2Y$		
$G = 860$		
$NE = 380 - 0.12Y$		
$RW = 13{,}000$		
$C = 0.64Y - 200 + 0.1D$		
$X = AD - Y$		
$X \gtreqless 0 \rightarrow \Delta Y \gtreqless 0$		

AD = aggregate demand
C = consumption
ID = investment demand
Y = income = GNP
T = taxes net of transfers
NW = net worth of private sector
RW = real wealth of private sector
D = federal debt
NE = net exports
G = government expenditures for goods and services
X = excess demand

(1)	(2)	(3)	(4)	(5)	(6)	(7)	(8)
Y	C	ID	G	NE	AD	X	EQUILIBRIUM
A. Debt = $2,000 billion							
4,100	2,624	695	860	−112	4,067	−33	↓
4,000	2,560	680	860	−100	4,000	0	=
3,900	2,496	665	860	−88	3,933	+33	↑
B. Debt = $2,330 billion							
4,100	2,657	695	860	−112	4,100	0	=
4,000	2,593	680	860	−100	4,033	+33	↑
3,900	2,529	665	860	−88	3,966	+66	↑

will try to produce more to meet it. If excess demand is negative, that is, aggregate demand is less than what is being produced, business will cut production rather than be stuck with goods and services that people do not want and will not buy.

In example A, with a debt of $2,000 billion, total wealth, including real wealth of the private sector, will be $15,000 billion and the equilibrium output will be $4,000 billion. For at any greater output, aggregate demand would be less than output, and at any lesser output, aggregate demand would be greater than output. Thus, at an output of $4,100 billion, aggregate demand, the sum of consumption plus investment demand plus government purchases of goods and services plus net exports, would be only $4,067 billion, leaving a shortage of demand of $33 billion. When business consequently reduces production it finds consumption declining, as people's incomes, out of which they consume, decline, and investment demand declines as well. Only when output and income are down to $4,000 billion, is aggregate demand no longer less than output. Similarly, if output and income were below their

equilibrium level, say $3,900 billion, there would be excess de-
mand driving output up to the $4,000 billion equilibrium.

What can change that equilibrium is a change in any of the
components of aggregate demand—a change in the table's col-
umns for consumption, investment demand, government expenditures, or net exports. As we commonly explain in our economics principles classes, equilibrium output would be raised if
business were persuaded to buy more new plant and equipment,
thus raising the investment demand column, if government itself
bought more goods and services, thus raising the "G" column, or
if foreigners could be persuaded to buy more of our goods and
services, thus raising the net export column. (In this last case,
since net exports have been shown negative, reflecting our current unfavorable balance of trade, initially it would mean making
the figures less negative.)

But how can we bring about any of these outcomes? To the
extent that we can control our government, one apparent solution
is to have the government itself spend more. That solution is
perhaps too readily rejected, except with regard to military expenditures, by those whose prime concern appears to be to reduce
the role of government.

If the government spending route is rejected, what about net
exports? The problem here is that foreigners are not that readily
subject to our control and we may not be able to induce them to
buy more of our goods and services. We could conceivably raise
net exports by reducing our imports, but the objections to the
protectionist measures that might accomplish this are formidable.

They would in fact be likely to boomerang. A high dollar and
cheap foreign currencies caused United States imports to surge.
But a reduction of imports by the United States would mean a
reduced supply of dollars to foreigners. Less supply, making the
dollar scarcer, would cause the dollar to appreciate, that is, again
raise its exchange value in foreign currency. This would make
foreign goods still cheaper, and thus raise imports again and hurt
our exports, even without likely foreign retaliation. On the other
hand, a monetary policy that might reduce the value of the dollar
would tend to help net exports. But we will consider that later,
along with the potential effects of easier monetary policy in raising investment demand.

Our focus here is on the debt and, however paradoxically to
some, a *larger* debt can help! We will assume that the debt is

perceived by the public as part of its net worth. Then, as illustrated in equations at the top of Table 7.1, the higher that perceived net worth or wealth, the greater will be consumption. (In fact we have evidence, to be shown later, that greater holdings by the public of federal debt apparently directly or indirectly tend also to increase business investment demand.)

Thus, in example B of Table 7.1 we show that, for a higher debt, $2,330 billion, the consumption column is higher. At an income of $4,000 billion, consumption is not $2,560 billion but $2,593 billion. Similarly, at an income of $4,100 billion, consumption is not $2,624 billion but $2,657 billion. One may note that, as a consequence of this increase of $33 billion for any given increase in income, there is an increase in the *equilibrium income* of $100 billion. The fact that $33 billion will, in this illustration, get us an increase of $100 billion, evidences the "multiplier," also well known to the last two generations of students of modern economics.

We should acknowledge that the numbers are illustrative, although taken roughly from current statistical data and hardly to be viewed as unreasonable. But whether they are accurate is not critical. The direction of movement as a consequence of an increase in debt is clear and unambiguous, at least under the assumptions we have made.

There are some other implications, frequently missed, which can be drawn from this analysis. If a larger debt implies greater aggregate demand, then an *increasing* debt implies *increasing* aggregate demand. And the faster the debt is increasing, the faster is aggregate demand increasing. As long as there is the capacity or potential supply, the increases in demand bring about corresponding increases in output. But the greater the federal deficit, the greater the increase in the debt. Thus, we can expect a positive correlation, other things equal, between deficits, which *increase* the debt, and *increases* in GNP. The federal deficit, appropriately adjusted, should be related not merely to GNP, but to the *change* or *growth* in GNP.

It is also significant to note that this analysis applies not only to the explicit debt of the government. It applies to any government commitments which add to households' perception of their wealth or expected future income. This led Martin Feldstein, the distinguished Harvard economist, President of the National Bureau of Economic Research and former Chairman of President

Reagan's Council of Economic Advisers, to a provocative conclusion. Implicitly assuming that aggregate demand could not affect employment and output, he claimed that our social security system, by bringing about increased consumption, has so depressed saving that it has reduced our private capital stock by more than a third.[1] Feldstein argued that current generations perceive their wealth in the form of expected social security income as greater than the taxes that they expect to pay for social security. Hence, as with any government debt constituting private assets, private consumption is increased and, since output and income cannot rise, saving decreases. Feldstein purported to show that, in fact, increases in net social security wealth were associated with such movements in consumption and saving.

Feldstein's argument has indeed been challenged on both empirical and theoretical grounds by a number of economists (Barro, 1974, 1978; Barro and MacDonald, 1979; Leimer and Lesnoy, 1982; Eisner, 1983a). The data, after correction of computational errors in Feldstein's original work, do not generally support his argument with regard to social security wealth. But the most far reaching, if not yet widely recognized objections, are theoretical. They relate to the fact that greater wealth should lead households to increase current consumption *and* plan more consumption for the future.

For, picking up some of the important kernels of truth in the concepts of rational expectations, we should assume that businesses understand the economy as well as we do. If they see current consumption increased by added wealth, they will also anticipate that future consumption will be increased. They would then want to acquire additional capital to be used in additional production to satisfy the increased future consumption demand. Hence increased wealth, in the form of social security or explicit federal debt held by the public, will generate *both more current consumption demand and more current investment demand* for the capital to satisfy future consumption demand. There is no reason, a priori, to conclude that the current demand for private capital must decline. Indeed, if employment and output can be increased, both social security and debt could generate more consumption *and* more investment.[2] Business will be able to produce more to meet our demand for more bread today, and build a new bakery now, as well, to meet our demand for more bread tomorrow.

An Argument That Debt and Deficits Do Not Matter

There is an alternative view which challenges the validity of this entire approach. Robert Barro (1974) argued that the private sector of the economy should not in theory and does not in practice regard government debt as net wealth. For while holders of government bonds would clearly feel wealthier, all other things equal, than if they did not have them, other things are not equal. In particular, corresponding to the wealth perceived in bonds, there must be an expectation of taxes to pay the interest on the bonds and/or eventually to pay off the principal. If people are rational, they recognize then that their assets in the form of their holdings of government debt are fully balanced by corresponding liabilities in the form of future taxes.

There would seem to be one obvious answer to that. The holders of government debt are alive today to enjoy their wealth but taxes to pay off the debt will be borne in part by future generations. Hence those currently alive and making economic decisions that affect aggregate demand *are*, on balance, wealthier.

Barro has an answer to this, however. We can be expected to take into account not only our own well-being but that of our children and grandchildren.

Thus, assume that the government runs a deficit which adds to our holdings of government debt. Before we decide to consume more we think of the higher future taxes to service this debt which will be borne by our children and grandchildren. If we do not correct for this new situation, they will have to consume less. Since there is nothing about the deficit that changes our preferences for our own consumption against those of our heirs, we set aside for them an additional estate equal to the excess of the value of our new holdings of government bonds over the additional taxes that we ourselves have to pay. Thus, we are not made to feel wealthier by the deficit and our contribution to aggregate demand is unaffected.

If the Barro argument is accepted, government debt and deficits hardly matter. There is an equivalence between government expenditures financed by taxes and government expenditures financed by borrowing. In the first instance, taxes are paid currently to finance the expenditures. In the second instance, taxes are paid in the future. The argument has been labeled the

"Ricardian Equivalence Theorem" (Buchanan, 1976) after the famed classical economist David Ricardo, who suggested it early in the nineteenth century (Ricardo, 1871). In fact, having raised the argument, Ricardo dismissed it as implausible. Why? Because the public would just not evaluate uncertain future taxes of uncertain incidence as the equivalent of the certain taxes currently foregone. Ricardo indicated that potential victims of future taxes might even emigrate to avoid them. We might better refer to a "Ricardian Non-Equivalence Theorem" (Buiter and Tobin, 1979).

After stressing supply-side concepts, Barro has in fact argued against aiming for a balanced budget and has suggested that, instead, the deficit should vary directly with government expenditures. The reasoning here is that, to keep the budget balanced in the face of fluctuating government expenditures, we would have to vary tax rates. But taxes, particularly marginal tax rates, affect the supply of labor and capital. If we were to vary tax rates with government expenditures, we would then be introducing inefficient variations over time in the supply of the factors of production (Barro, 1979, 1986).

The equivalence theorem has hardly carried the day in current economic thought, however, and that is as it should be. Some of its frailties are obvious. For one thing, some of us have no children and anticipate no grandchildren. If we leave an estate, it is the inadvertent consequence of not being able to anticipate correctly our final needs and the date of our death. Taxes to be paid by future generations are none of our concern and if the government makes us wealthier by giving us bonds instead of receipts for current taxes, we do feel wealthier and spend more.

Others of us do have children but are convinced that they and our grandchildren will be sufficiently wealthy that they need nothing from us, or are sufficiently ungrateful that they deserve nothing from us or, in any event, should be left to shift for themselves. For us too, the burden of taxes on the next generation is of no concern.

Still another consideration, in the real world, is the possibility, which must occur to us, that taxes will not be raised in the future as a result of today's borrowing. Perhaps the government will simply borrow again, or even just print money, to meet future interest and principal obligations.

We can indeed turn the argument around if we rule out the classical, market-clearing assumption that aggregate demand will always be equal to aggregate supply and that we will always have full employment. Deficits may then, as we have seen, contribute to higher employment and a greater gross national product. If this is what we anticipate, continued deficit financing, as opposed to a continued balanced budget, may lead us to anticipate a greater gross national product for our children as well as for ourselves. It will therefore lead us to consume all the more ourselves, leaving less for our children, in the confident expectation that they will be better off anyway.

And there are further formidable objections to the equivalence theorem. Even if we had children, were fully as concerned about them as we are about ourselves, and felt that we should compensate them for the higher taxes that we expect them to have to pay as a result of current deficits, we would still not be likely to view the expected future taxes as a burden fully equivalent to our current wealth and holdings of government debt. For in economics, "time is money." We cannot compare future burdens with current benefits without appropriate adjustment.

The adjustment is in terms of the rate of interest or discount which we use to convert future amounts to "present values." Thus, if the rate of interest is 10 percent, $110 a year from now has a present value of $110/(1 + 0.1) or $100. Similarly, $121 to be received or paid two years from now, with the interest rate still 10 percent per year, has a present value of $121/(1 + 0.1)^2, again $100.

The lower the rate of interest or rate of discount, however, the greater the present value of any future amount. Thus, for example, if the rate of interest were only 4 percent, $110 a year from now would be worth $110/(1 + 0.04) or approximately $106, instead of $100. And the $121 two years from now at an interest rate of 4 percent per year would mean a present value of $121/(1 + 0.04)^2, or about $112, instead of $100. The differences become striking for amounts further in the future. At 10 percent, $1,000 to be received in 20 years is worth $148.68 now. At 4 percent it is worth $456.39, more than three times as much.

The present value—or market value—of government debt held by the public is derived by applying the rate of interest on government securities to discount their future interest and principal payments. But even if private individuals and businesses can expect with certainty to pay taxes equal to the amount of these government interest and principal payments, the rate of discount

can make a difference. It is only logical that those of us antici-
pating such obligations discount at the rate of interest appropriate
for private borrowing and lending, clearly much higher than that
on government securities. The present value of future tax liabilities is thus less, and considerably less than the present or market
value of the government debt, and government debt still represents, on balance, net worth to the private sector of the economy.

This is illustrated in Table 7.2, which shows what the present
value of expected future taxes would be if households expected
to have to pay taxes equal to the interest payments on a permanent debt of $2,000 billion. It is assumed that the Treasury has
to pay a 10 percent rate on both existing securities and any new
refinancing as current securities mature. If the household interest
rate were also 10 percent and, of course, if households were fully
convinced that they would have to pay taxes to finance these interest payments, they would then find the present value of their
expected taxes equal to the value of the debt and its net value to
the public would be zero.

If, to fit the facts, we assume the interest rate available to
households is higher, they are clearly better off to have the wealth
in government debt now, even if they have to pay taxes over
future years to meet the interest cost of that debt. At a household
interest rate of 12.5 percent, for example, the present value of
taxes to pay forever the interest on a 10 percent, $2,000 Treasury
bond, would be only $1,600, thus leaving a net value of debt to
the public of $400. Thus, even if households felt responsible for
future taxes to finance the current debt, their holdings of that

TABLE 7.2   Burden of the Debt: Future Taxes

(1)	(2)	(3)	(4)	(5)
		HOUSEHOLD INTEREST RATE TO BE USED TO CALCULATE PRESENT VALUE	PRESENT VALUE OF TAXES EQUAL TO INTEREST PAYMENTS	NET VALUE OF DEBT TO PUBLIC
DEBT	INTEREST PAYMENTS ON DEBT AT 10%		[(2) ÷ (3)]	[(1) − (4)]
($ Billion)		(%)	($ Billion)	
2,000	200	10	2,000	0
2,000	200	12.5	1,600	400
2,000	200	16	1,250	750
2,000	200	18	1,111	889
2,000	200	20	1,000	1,000

debt would make them feel richer. And, as shown in Table 7.2, the higher the household interest rate, the less the present value of taxes and the greater the net value of debt to the public.

We can thus safely return to the mainstream of our argument. Deficits do matter because they add to the debt held by the public and hence contribute to aggregate demand. But recall again that two directions of analysis are open. We may make the classical assumption that we always have full employment, or what was more recently defined by Milton Friedman (1968), "the natural rate of employment." Aggregate demand then cannot affect the rate of unemployment, except at most temporarily, and hence cannot affect output or the gross national product, except temporarily. What then is the result of any increase in aggregate demand stemming from an increase in debt held by the public as a consequence of a budget deficit?

The answer must be that the increase in aggregate demand implies that some or all of us try to buy more. Since we are at full employment, and implicitly full capacity, our efforts to buy more cannot bring about more production. The consequence then is simple. More spending for the same amount of goods must mean that prices rise. The consequence of a budget deficit for an economy at full employment would appear to be inflation.

This argument, however, must be qualified in a number of important ways. First, we must remember that the economy is not stationary. With the population and the labor force growing and productivity per worker tending to increase, the maintenance of full employment implies that gross national product or the output of goods and services of the nation is increasing. Hence to maintain full employment, aggregate demand must be increasing. We can well therefore envisage a balanced growth in aggregate demand, balanced in the sense that all components of that demand will grow in proportion.

Suppose, for example, the rate of growth of real gross national product is the substantial but not impossible 4 percent per year of some Reagan Administration forecasts. That would mean that aggregate demand could and should grow at 4 percent per year so that full employment output could be purchased with no increase in prices. Balanced growth of all of the factors in aggregate demand would then require a 4 percent per year growth in the amount of public debt. If we take that at roughly $2 trillion, this implies an $80 billion increase in the debt over the next year or, of course, a deficit of $80 billion. Under conditions of economic growth, then, a significant deficit and increase in the debt is compatible with full employment and price stability. A balanced budget, under these circumstances, would constitute a drag on the economy, requiring other factors in aggregate demand to make up for the failure of public holdings of government debt to keep pace with economic growth.

What this means is that a deficit per se, within the classical analysis, should not be expected to contribute to inflation. Only a deficit which is too large would prove inflationary. *And this means a deficit which makes the debt grow more rapidly than the real value of output.*

Suppose now, with the economy at full employment (or the "natural" rate of unemployment) and growing in real terms at 4 percent per year, the government runs a budget deficit so large that the federal debt is growing at 10 percent per year. What then should happen? If the money supply were also allowed to grow at 10 percent per year, we could expect GNP in current dollars to grow at a 10 percent rate. Prices would then be increasing at some 6 percent per year, so that real aggregate demand and the real value of the debt would be growing at the assumed 4 percent rate of real economic growth. If the money supply grew at less than the 10 percent per annum increase in the federal debt, we should expect some relative shortage of money and higher interest rates, with a somewhat lesser rate of increase in prices.

This would indeed have real consequences for the economy, presumably reducing the rate of investment or capital accumulation, and thus raising current consumption at some expense to our future well-being. These consequences, though, follow not from the deficit and increase in debt but from the failure to provide a neutral monetary policy. For presume that monetary policy remains neutral, in the sense that the quantity of money is allowed to grow at the same rate as the debt and the money value of all other variables in the economy. The old quantity theory of money, expanded to account for debt, will then hold sway. Prices will increase by the difference between the identical rates of growth of the quantities of money and debt and the rate of increase of real output. Increasing the deficit—and hence the rate of increase in the debt—will then only affect the rate of inflation. It will have no effect, or virtually no effect, on real output.

The qualification is necessary here because of the "Tobin–Mundell Effect" (see, for example, Tobin, 1965, and Mundell, 1963). This suggests that since inflation implies continued loss in the real value of money, individuals and businesses faced by inflation brought on by deficits (or by any other factor) will try to hold less of their wealth in the form of money. They will then turn to the real alternatives of capital and land, whose values keep up with inflation. As these preferences for real assets are met, real interest rates will fall, and investment and the quantity of real capital in the economy will rise. With the assumption of full employment, greater investment must mean a reduction in current consumption. But the deficits and inflation would thus have led to the accumulation of more capital, which would increase future output.

I would not want to make much of this argument. At best, it ignores the loss in real services of money balances. Having less money on hand does, after all, force us to borrow more often and buy and sell more frequently as we reduce the size of our transactions. If money thus contributes to output, or to our convenience, whether its contributions are measured in gross national product or not, the forced shift to a greater proportion of physical capital relative to money may actually reduce the value of goods and services available to the nation.

We may safely conclude that, under the classical assumption of full employment, the size of the debt and amount of deficits need affect only the level of prices and rate of inflation, and not aggregate real output of the economy.[3]

Deficits When There May Be Unemployment

It is another matter when we admit the possibility of insufficient aggregate demand and involuntary unemployment. Again deficit-financed government spending contributes more to aggregate demand than does fully tax-financed or balanced-budget spending. And the larger publicly held debt created by the deficit may be expected to increase both current and future demand.

Unlike the full-employment situation, however, since additional workers can be hired, more output can be produced when aggregate demand is greater. To the extent that the economy is near full employment, higher aggregate demand may bring higher prices. There is every reason to believe, though, that some of the greater demand will bring greater output. Both economic theory and data indicate that when the economy is operating significantly below full employment, changes in demand in fact have much more effect upon output than upon prices (see, for example, Gordon, 1981, 1982).

Thus, provocative as this may seem to some of the public or body politic, when we have substantial unemployment, a deficit, indeed a large deficit, is helpful. Action to reduce a deficit in the face of unemployment is likely to make the unemployment worse.

It is easy to secure agreement that a budget deficit should not be reduced by increasing taxes when there is significant unemployment. The fate of Walter Mondale and his pledge to raise taxes during the 1984 presidential campaign helped close that argument, at least for a while.

What is somehow not so widely recognized is that the essential argument against reducing the deficit by raising taxes applies as well to reducing the deficit by cutting government spending. As we noted earlier, government spending contributes to demand and cutting government spending reduces demand by as much as does raising taxes. If the cut in government spending is a cut in government purchases of goods and services, rather than merely a cut in transfer payments, reduced government spending will reduce demand dollar for dollar by more than would an equal increase in taxes. And a decrease in demand will reduce business output and therefore reduce employment.

We are thus left with the conclusion that deficits and debt do matter. Under conditions of full employment, a deficit that raises the debt at a more rapid rate than real economic growth will raise prices. Under conditions of unemployment, a deficit that raises the debt by more than the growth in output will tend to increase output, and reduce unemployment below what it would otherwise have been.

Deficits then can be too big or too little. It all depends. If the problem is inflation brought on by excess demand, reductions in the deficit are in order. If, rather, the problem is unemployment due to a shortage in demand, a deficit or bigger deficits are in order. All this indeed had become the conventional wisdom of economic thinking over the decades prior to the anti-Keynesian counterrevolution of the 1970s. That counterrevolution took its justification at least in part from the apparent failure of the economy to react to deficits and debt in the manner we have here indicated. Unemployment *and* inflation increased in the face of apparently increasing budget deficits. What went wrong?

The answer is that appearances are deceiving, if our measures of debt and deficits are wrong. This should become clear as we proceed now to bring together our theory and corrected measures of the facts.

8

Deficits and the
Economy: The Facts

To THE CHARGE THAT NOTHING is inevitable except death and taxes we might well add deficits and debt. A look at Table 8.1, or back at Table 2.3 (p. 18), would appear to confirm such a view. The federal budget was in deficit in all but eight of the fifty-five years from 1931 through 1985. In fact, in the twenty-five years since 1960 only one, 1969, had no deficit. The last sixteen years have presented an unbroken picture of deficits.

World War II saw what were then huge deficits, totaling $170 billion for the years 1942 through 1945. The total gross federal debt over that period rose by $203 billion.

From 1946 through 1984, budget deficits, net of surpluses, totaled $988 billion and, including off-budget outlays, totaled $1,112 billion. And over that period, the gross federal public debt increased by $1,317 billion. This is a history, which in at least general terms, is well etched in the public consciousness. It has been the stuff of many sober pronouncements and warnings, and has frequently agitated political debate. A number of additional items of information, however, complicate the picture, and also put it in better perspective.

First, when numbers are changing rapidly over time, partic-

TABLE 8.1 Federal Receipts and Outlays, and Surplus or Deficit as Percentage of Outlays and GNP, Fiscal Years 1929–84

(1)	(2)	(3)	(4)	(5)	(6)	(7)
		OUTLAYS, INCLUDING OFF-BUDGET OUTLAYS		SURPLUS OR DEFICIT (−)		
					As % of	
FISCAL YEAR	RECEIPTS ($ Billion)	($ Billion)	(As % of GNP)	($ Billion)	OUTLAYS	GNP
1929	3.86	3.13	3.03	0.73	23.47	0.71
1930	4.06	3.32	3.43	0.74	22.23	0.76
1931	3.12	3.58	4.30	−0.46	−12.92	−0.56
1932	1.92	4.66	6.96	−2.74	−58.70	−4.09
1933	2.00	4.60	8.10	−2.60	−56.59	−4.58
1934	3.02	6.65	11.00	−3.63	−54.63	−6.01
1935	3.71	6.50	9.46	−2.79	−42.96	−4.06
1936	4.00	8.42	10.88	−4.43	−52.54	−5.72
1937	4.96	7.73	8.94	−2.78	−35.91	−3.21
1938	5.59	6.77	7.72	−1.78	−26.27	−2.03
1939	4.98	8.84	10.09	−3.86	−43.68	−4.41
1940	6.36	9.46	9.95	−3.10	−32.73	−3.26
1941	8.62	13.63	12.51	−5.01	−36.77	−4.60
1942	14.35	35.11	25.26	−20.76	−59.13	−14.94
1943	23.65	78.53	44.37	−54.88	−69.89	−31.01
1944	44.28	91.28	45.19	−47.00	−51.49	−23.27
1945	45.22	92.69	42.71	−47.47	−51.22	−21.88
1946	39.33	55.18	27.32	−15.86	−28.73	−7.85
1947	38.39	34.53	15.60	3.86	11.18	1.75
1948	41.77	29.77	12.13	12.00	40.31	4.89
1949	39.44	38.83	14.83	0.60	1.55	0.23
1950	39.49	42.60	16.07	−3.11	−7.31	−1.17
1951	51.65	45.55	14.56	6.10	13.39	1.95
1952	66.20	67.72	19.96	−1.52	−2.24	−0.45
1953	69.57	76.11	21.06	−6.53	−8.58	−1.81
1954	69.72	70.89	19.46	−1.17	−1.65	−0.32
1955	65.47	68.51	18.00	−3.04	−4.44	−0.80
1956	74.55	70.46	17.11	4.09	5.80	0.99
1957	79.99	76.74	17.69	3.25	4.23	0.75
1958	79.64	82.58	18.64	−2.94	−3.56	−0.66
1959	79.25	92.10	19.41	−12.86	−13.96	−2.71
1960	92.49	92.22	18.52	0.27	0.29	0.05
1961	94.39	97.70	19.18	−3.41	−3.49	−0.67
1962	99.68	106.80	19.48	−7.14	−6.68	−1.30
1963	106.56	111.30	19.26	−4.75	−4.27	−0.82
1964	112.60	118.50	19.17	−5.92	−5.00	−0.96
1965	116.80	118.20	17.92	−1.60	−1.35	−0.24
1966	130.80	134.50	18.57	−3.80	−2.82	−0.52
1967	148.80	157.50	20.26	−8.70	−5.53	−1.12
1968	153.00	178.10	21.42	−25.16	−14.13	−3.03
1969	186.90	183.60	20.16	3.24	1.76	0.36
1970	192.80	195.60	20.19	−2.85	−1.45	−0.29
1971	187.10	210.20	20.38	−23.03	−10.96	−2.23
1972	207.30	230.70	20.44	−23.37	−10.13	−2.07
1973	230.80	245.70	19.62	−14.90	−6.06	−1.19
1974	263.20	269.40	19.53	−6.10	−2.26	−0.44

TABLE 8.1   (continued)

(1)	(2)	(3)	(4)	(5)	(6)	(7)
		OUTLAYS, INCLUDING OFF-BUDGET OUTLAYS		SURPLUS OR DEFICIT ($-$)		
					As % of	
FISCAL YEAR	RECEIPTS ($ Billion)	($ Billion)	(As % of GNP)	($ Billion)	OUTLAYS	GNP
1975	279.10	332.30	22.45	-53.20	-16.01	-3.59
1976	298.10	371.80	22.67	-73.70	-19.82	-4.49
1976TQ[a]	81.20	96.00	22.21	-14.70	-15.31	-3.40
1977	355.60	409.20	21.97	-53.60	-13.10	-2.88
1978	399.70	458.70	21.93	-59.00	-12.86	-2.82
1979	463.30	503.50	21.36	-40.20	-7.98	-1.71
1980	517.10	590.90	22.94	-73.80	-12.49	-2.87
1981	599.30	678.20	23.50	-78.90	-11.63	-2.73
1982	617.80	745.70	24.48	-127.90	-17.15	-4.20
1983	600.60	808.30	25.09	-207.80	-25.71	-6.45
1984	666.50	851.80	23.79	-185.30	-21.75	-5.17

Sources: Economic Report of the President February 1985, Table B-72, p. 318, and data from U.S. Department of the Treasury, Office of Management and Budget, and Bureau of Economic Analysis.

[a]Fiscal years until 1976 ran from July 1 of the preceding calendar year to June 30. From 1977 on, the fiscal years began on October 1. TQ denotes the transition quarter, July 1 to September 30, 1976.

ularly with economic growth and inflation, it is important to put the figures in some kind of relative terms. The gross federal debt held by the public, for example, grew from $235 billion at the end of the 1945 fiscal year to $1,313 billion by the end of the 1984 fiscal year. But our national income and gross national product grew relatively more over those years. Thus, as may have been noted in Table 2.3, while the gross federal debt held by the public was 108.4 percent of gross national product at the end of fiscal 1945, despite the very large dollar growth in that debt over the following years, it had fallen, as a percentage of gross national product, to 27.8 percent by the end of the 1980 fiscal year. With all the subsequent red ink and increase in the debt, at the end of the 1984 fiscal year the debt as a ratio of GNP had risen to only 36.7 percent, still well below the 108.4 percent figure of 1945 (and the 119.8 percent figure of 1946).

There are some analogous observations to make with regard to our annual budget deficits. They surged during the years of World War II, but then were generally modest until they rose toward the end of the Vietnam War, and surged again after 1981. Over all these years federal outlays and receipts have been fluctuating—generally growing—and gross national product has increased enormously. How can we get an appropriate view of the *relative* size of the deficit?

One way of securing a broader perspective is to note what has happened to the deficit as a percentage of outlays. In Table 8.1 we can see that while the proportion of federal outlays which is deficit-financed stood at a substantial 21.8 percent in fiscal 1984, this was far from a record. During the depression fiscal year of 1932 (from July 1, 1931 through June 30, 1932), although the deficit was "only" $2.7 billion, 58.7 percent of federal outlays were deficit-financed. And during the war years, that proportion soared, rising to 70 percent in 1943. In the presumably fiscally responsible administration of Dwight Eisenhower, in fiscal 1959, the ratio rose to 13.96 percent. During the peak-deficit, Vietnam fiscal year of 1968, the ratio was slightly higher, some 14.13 percent.

The size of the deficit relative to the economy as a whole may be reasonably captured by the ratio of the deficit to gross national product. That ratio was also relatively high in depression and war years but fairly small over the rest of the period until the years from 1982 on.

But how can we measure the effects of deficits on the economy? Do they cause inflation or recession? Do they reduce unemployment or crowd out investment? Do they stifle economic growth or stimulate it? Do they increase our foreign debt and wreck our balance of trade, or do they contribute to world prosperity?

A simple, naive approach would be to relate the federal deficit to some of the broad aggregates in which we are interested. We might check the correlations among deficits and gross national product, business investment, or the rates of unemployment or inflation. The difficulty, a common one in economics, is especially serious here: we cannot distinguish between cause and effect.

The problem is that the economy affects the deficit, perhaps as much as or more than the deficit can be expected to affect the economy. When economic conditions are good, incomes, profits, and employment are high. Treasury receipts, tied as they are to individual and business income taxes and payroll taxes on employment, are hence high. Further, government expenditures for unemployment benefits and welfare payments will be less when the economy is prosperous.

The combination of higher tax receipts and lower expenditures means a lower deficit. But it is clearly the high GNP, income, profits, and employment that have caused the low deficit, and not the reverse. Since high rates of saving and investment generally accompany high GNP, income, and profits, they too would be associated with smaller deficits. The inference that the smaller deficits brought on the higher saving and investment would be similarly unwarranted.

The inverse relation between deficits and inflation is somewhat more complex. At first blush it might appear that inflation would be neutral in its effects on the deficit. While higher prices would mean larger nominal incomes and hence greater tax payments to the Treasury, the government would also have to pay more for what it buys. If federal salaries and social security benefits are indexed to the cost of living, we might conclude that expenditures and receipts would both be increased by inflation and the deficit therefore not changed.

There are, however, a number of complications. First, income taxes have historically risen more than in proportion to the increases in income brought on by inflation. This has happened because of the notorious "bracket creep"—inflation has pushed more of income into taxable brackets and into higher brackets with higher tax rates.

While indexing of exemptions and tax brackets to the price level has now essentially ended that contribution of inflation to a more than proportional enhancing of individual income tax payments, the effect of inflation in bringing more than proportional increases in business tax payments remains. This stems from the failure of original cost depreciation deductions to rise with inflation, as well as swollen inventory profits of firms which use FIFO ("first-in, first-out") accounting. For revenues reflect current higher prices, while accounting costs of materials and fixed capital are based on the lower prices of bygone days.

Inflation also brings about more than proportionate increases on the expenditure side. These stem from the higher interest rates and hence greater Treasury interest payments as inflation expectations take hold.

In the past, bracket-creep effects of higher prices were such that inflation tended on balance to reduce deficits. But such an association of higher inflation with lower deficits can *not* then warrant the inference of the inverse relation—that *deficits* reduce *inflation*.

Actual budget deficits are therefore not a good measure of fiscal policy. The Administration and the Congress might be following a tight fiscal policy, keeping discretionary expenditures down and tax rates up, and yet a recession would create a substantial deficit. Indeed the tight fiscal policy, by depressing aggregate demand, might bring on such a recession.

To ascertain what deficits do to the economy, we need a measure that is uncontaminated by what the economy does to deficits. Economists have been able to develop a measure that removes some of the contamination, that brought on by cyclical fluctuations in income and employment. As mentioned in Chapter 4, it has been variously called the full-employment, high-employment, and standardized-employment budget, the cyclically adjusted budget, and the structural budget.

Whatever its name, the important thing about this budget is that it presents estimates of what expenditures and receipts, and hence the deficit, *would be* if the economy were at a level of activity independent of cyclical variations in employment, output, and income. Since the cyclical variations in output and income are closely associated with those of employment and unemployment, the budget has usually been defined for a constant rate of unemployment.

The Bureau of Economic Analysis of the U.S. Department of Commerce has in fact constructed a series of high-employment budget surpluses and deficits beginning in 1955. "High" employment was initially taken to mean 4 percent unemployment, but that figure was raised in several steps in later years, apparently on the assumption that structural or demographic change in the economy was increasing the amount of unemployment—unfortunately frequently called the "natural" rate of unemployment—which should be accepted as consistent with high employment. It was argued, particularly, that the population contained increasing proportions of youths and urban blacks, with high rates of even noncyclical unemployment, and these increasing proportions were forcing up the national average of unemployment which was attainable.

The comparison of actual and high-employment budgets is intriguing. From 1955 through 1965, as shown in Table 8.2, the actual budget was in deficit five times and in surplus six. The high-employment budget was never in deficit. When the actual budget was in surplus the high-employment budget was more so.

TABLE 8.2   Actual and High-Employment Federal Budget Surpluses and
Deficits on National Income Account, 1955–84

(1)	(2)	(3)	(4)	(5)
	ACTUAL	HIGH-EMPLOYMENT	ACTUAL	HIGH-EMPLOYMENT
YEAR	($ Billion)		(% of GNP)	
1955	4.4	5.2	1.10	1.30
1956	6.1	7.9	1.44	1.87
1957	2.3	6.1	0.51	1.37
1958	−10.3	0.0	−2.28	0.00
1959	−1.1	5.4	−0.23	1.11
1960	3.0	12.1	0.60	2.39
1961	−3.9	7.1	−0.74	1.35
1962	−4.2	3.0	−0.75	0.53
1963	0.3	7.4	0.04	1.24
1964	−3.3	1.1	−0.51	0.17
1965	0.5	0.9	0.08	0.13
1966	−1.8	−5.6	−0.24	−0.74
1967	−13.2	−15.1	−1.65	−1.89
1968	−6.0	−11.0	−0.69	−1.26
1969	8.4	4.9	0.89	0.52
1970	−12.4	−4.6	−1.25	−0.46
1971	−22.0	−11.3	−2.04	−1.05
1972	−16.8	−12.1	−1.42	−1.02
1973	−5.5	−9.5	−0.42	−0.72
1974	−11.5	−0.3	−0.80	−0.02
1975	−69.3	−29.1	−4.47	−1.88
1976	−53.1	−17.4	−3.09	−1.01
1977	−45.9	−20.4	−2.39	−1.06
1978	−29.5	−15.9	−1.36	−0.73
1979	−16.1	−2.0	−0.67	−0.08
1980	−61.2	−17.1	−2.33	−0.65
1981	−64.3	−3.2	−2.17	−0.11
1982	−148.2	−32.6	−4.83	−1.06
1983	−178.6	−59.7	−5.40	−1.81
1984	−175.8	−108.6	−4.80	−2.96

Source: See Appendix C.

All this reflected the fact that actual unemployment was more
than the high-employment rate over this period. Hence actual tax
revenues were less while government expenditures were more.

From 1966 to 1969, with the boom aggregate demand produced by the Vietnam War, actual unemployment was less than
the 4 percent high-employment rate. (That is an interesting com-
mentary on our view of "high" employment even then. We have
now settled for still more unemployment!) The low unemployment of those years caused the three actual deficits to be *less* than
the high-employment deficit, and the 1969 surplus to be greater.

The 1970s ushered in the era of unrelenting federal deficits.

For none of the last sixteen years has the budget been balanced, let alone in surplus. Those who saw deficits as evidence of unbridled government spending contributing to inflation seemed to have some support for their views. Inflation rose through most of the decade of the 1970s, peaking in 1981. But then, as deficits soared to unprecedented heights in 1982, inflation rates dropped precipitously.

The deficits were widely interpreted, nevertheless, as evidence of expansionist fiscal policy. Richard Nixon had said in 1972, "We are all Keynesians now." If the Keynesian analysis which had presumably come to dominate policy making were correct, should not unemployment have been low and the economy sizzling? In fact, unemployment was inching up and the economy was sluggish. What was wrong?

One try at an answer was that it was the actual budget that showed the repeated and generally growing deficits. As we have observed, these deficits may have been essentially the product of poor economic conditions, rather than their cause. We may point, for example, to the then record deficit of $69 billion in 1975. Clearly that was largely the result of the sharp 1974–75 recession. Unemployment after all averaged 8.5 percent in 1975. If we had looked at the high-employment budget might we have had a different picture?

But now comes the shocker. The high-employment budget deficit was less than the actual deficit throughout the 1970s and into the 1980s, but it too was never quite balanced, coming close only in 1974. Indeed, in 1975 the high-employment budget also showed a record deficit. And high-employment deficits seemed generally to be getting larger, not smaller.

It might be said that with growth in the economy and inflation everything was getting larger. The deficit figures would be more comparable over time if they were adjusted for this growth. A simple way to do this is to present the deficit figures as percentages of GNP. As we can also see in Table 8.2, however, this does not change the basic picture. Actual deficits as a percentage of GNP set post–World War II records. But high-employment budgets also showed an unmistakable trend to deficit.

Indeed, the high-employment budget was never in deficit and was usually substantially in surplus until the Vietnam War. By 1966, however, the high-employment budget moved to deficit and remained in deficit thereafter, with the solitary exception of the tax-surcharge year of 1969. It would thus appear that the original charge that fiscal policy had been overly expansive is supported—or at least not contradicted—by the history of the high-employment budget deficit.

We come now to our critical departure. Recall that, in terms of our theory and the usual assumptions by all schools of economic thought that people and business are not guilty of "money illusion," we should adjust deficits for inflation. We have indicated earlier that the real, actual surplus or deficit may be viewed as essentially the sum of three components: 1) the nominal surplus or deficit as currently measured; 2) an adjustment for changes in the market value of government financial assets and liabilities due to changes in interest rates; and 3) an adjustment for changes in real value due to changing general price levels incident to inflation. An identical or analogous set of adjustments is appropriate for the high-employment budget surplus or deficit.

We can then calculate the adjusted high-employment budgets which, by correcting for these inflation effects, come closer to measuring real surpluses or deficits and the consequent thrust of fiscal policy on aggregate demand. Applying our calculations of net revaluations on net debt, Paul Pieper and I originally adjusted the official high-employment budget surplus series for the years 1955 through 1981. Maintaining the 5.1 percent unemployment benchmark for high employment in effect in the official series since 1975, we have now extended our calculations to 1984.

The results, shown in Table 8.3, are dramatic. Inflation and rates of interest were low and relatively steady in the early 1960s, prior to escalation of our military involvement in Vietnam. Corrections to the official high-employment budget surplus are hence generally small in those early years.

But in later, more inflationary years, when the official high-employment budget as well as the actual budget moved substantially into deficit, the corrections are striking. *In the 1970s, the entire perceived trend in the direction of fiscal ease or expansion is eliminated or reversed.* The high-employment budget surplus, fully adjusted for price and interest effects, was higher as a percent of GNP for every year from 1977 through 1981 than the surplus of all but two of the years from 1966 through 1976. The only exceptions were the tax-surcharge year of 1969 and the oil-price-shock year of 1974. With similar exceptions, the surplus adjusted only for

TABLE 8.3   High-Employment Surplus as Percentage of GNP, 1955–84

(1)	(2)	(3)	(4)	(5)	(6)
	SURPLUS OR DEFICIT ($-$) ON NATIONAL INCOME ACCOUNTS				
YEAR	Official	Adjusted for Price Effects	Adjusted for Interest Effects	Adjusted for Price and Interest Effects	% CHANGE IN GNP
1955	1.30	2.81	2.26	3.77	6.72
1956	1.87	3.83	2.79	4.74	2.14
1957	1.37	2.46	0.11	1.20	1.82
1958	0.00	0.93	1.32	2.24	-0.42
1959	1.11	2.09	1.96	2.94	5.99
1960	2.39	2.83	0.45	0.89	2.15
1961	1.35	1.99	1.81	2.45	2.63
1962	0.53	1.28	0.12	0.87	5.78
1963	1.24	1.79	1.70	2.25	4.02
1964	0.17	0.78	0.12	0.72	5.27
1965	0.13	0.98	0.58	1.43	6.04
1966	-0.74	0.33	-0.97	0.11	5.97
1967	-1.89	-0.89	-1.33	-0.34	2.70
1968	-1.26	0.06	-1.14	0.18	4.62
1969	0.52	1.94	1.32	2.74	2.79
1970	-0.46	0.77	-1.87	-0.64	-0.18
1971	-1.05	0.11	-1.41	-0.25	3.39
1972	-1.02	0.02	-0.66	0.39	5.66
1973	-0.72	0.89	-0.46	1.14	5.77
1974	-0.02	2.15	-0.16	2.01	-0.64
1975	-1.88	-0.38	-2.04	-0.54	-1.18
1976	-1.01	0.22	-1.75	-0.52	5.41
1977	-1.06	0.46	-0.23	1.30	5.51
1978	-0.73	1.26	0.15	2.15	5.03
1979	-0.08	1.72	0.11	1.91	2.84
1980	-0.65	1.45	-0.13	1.97	-0.30
1981	-0.11	1.57	-0.23	1.45	2.52
1982	-1.06	0.02	-3.10	-2.01	-2.13
1983	-1.81	-0.75	-0.53	0.54	3.70
1984	-2.96	-1.81	-3.53	-2.37	6.78

Source: See Appendix C.

price (and not including interest) effects was higher in every year from 1978 to 1981 than in any other year back to 1963.[1]

So some significant rewriting of recent economic history is perhaps in order. Inflation could hardly be ascribed to excess demand associated with increasing fiscal ease and stimulus if, at least by the appropriately corrected high-employment budget measure, there was no such movement to fiscal ease. Some explanation of sluggishness in the economy, climaxed by the severe 1981–82 recession, might then be found in a relatively tight fiscal policy, as measured by the adjusted high-employment budget surplus, as well as in the widely blamed (or credited) role of monetary policy.

The record of deficits from 1982 on is another matter. We shall come to that later. For now we want to present a systematic analysis of the statistical relations of budget deficits to the economy. And we will find that prevailing views reflect the distortions of improper measures, the most important of which, again, are those tricks played by the effects of inflation.

A few illustrations can begin to set the record straight, and tell a dramatic new story. First, Figure 8.1 shows the widening gap between official and price-adjusted high-employment budget surpluses or deficits as inflation began to heat up in the late 1960s. The two measures moved up and down in broadly similar fashion. But by the mid-1970s the price-adjusted budgets were some 1.5 to 2 percentage points more in surplus or less in deficit than the unadjusted, official high-employment budgets.

What about the relation between budget deficits and the economy? In Table 8.4 we relate annual changes in real gross national product for the years 1967 to 1984 to previous high-employment surpluses or deficits. GNP change is tabulated as greater or less than the median growth of 3 percent over this period.

In the upper left-hand panel we see again that the official high-employment budget was in deficit in seventeen years, in nine of which GNP growth was more than 3 percent and in eight of which it was less. For the one year of surplus (1969), subsequent growth was less than 3 percent (in fact, virtually zero), but one year does not offer very much evidence. In the lower left-hand panel, however, we observe that the *adjusted* budget was in surplus in twelve of the years. *For the years that it was in surplus, subsequent GNP growth was more than 3 percent only three times, and less than 3 percent nine times. For all of the six years that it was in deficit, subsequent GNP growth was more than 3 percent.*

The official high-employment budget surplus or deficit is in fact also closely related to subsequent growth in GNP. This relation becomes clear when we recognize that inflation makes a true surplus appear as a deficit in the official accounts, and recategorize our official budgets accordingly. Thus, in the upper right-hand panel of Table 8.4, we divide the period into years when the previous official high-employment deficit was less than

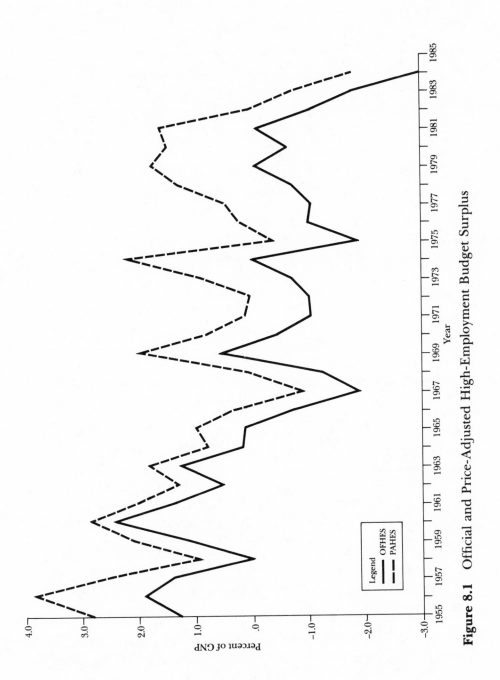

Figure 8.1 Official and Price-Adjusted High-Employment Budget Surplus

89

TABLE 8.4   High-Employment Surpluses and Deficits, and Growth in GNP, 1967–84

1. *Official Budget*

PREVIOUS HIGH-EMPLOYMENT BUDGET	ΔGNP ≳ 3%			PREVIOUS HIGH-EMPLOYMENT BUDGET	ΔGNP ≳ 3%		
	Greater	*Less*	*Total*		*Greater*	*Less*	*Total*
Surplus	0	1	1	Deficit < 1%	1	8	9
Deficit	9	8	17	Deficit > 1%	8	1	9
Total	9	9	18	Total	9	9	18

2. *Price- and Interest-Adjusted Budget*

PREVIOUS HIGH-EMPLOYMENT BUDGET	ΔGNP ≳ 3%			PREVIOUS HIGH-EMPLOYMENT BUDGET	ΔGNP ≳ 3%		
	Greater	*Less*	*Total*		*Greater*	*Less*	*Total*
Surplus	3	9	12	Surplus > 1%	1	7	8
Deficit	6	0	6	Surplus < 1% or deficit	8	2	10
Total	9	9	18	Total	9	9	18

1 percent of GNP and years when it was more than 1 percent. We find that for the nine years when the deficit was less than 1 percent, subsequent GNP growth was greater than 3 percent in only one case. For the nine years when the deficit was more than 1 percent, subsequent GNP growth was more than 3 percent in eight cases.

Recategorization of the price- and interest-adjusted high-employment budget as in *surplus* by more or less than 1 percent (or in deficit) shows similar results. For the eight years in which the surplus was more than 1 percent, subsequent GNP growth was greater than 3 percent in only one. For the ten years when the adjusted budget was in surplus by less than 1 percent or was in deficit, subsequent GNP growth was greater than 3 percent eight times.

But a single picture may be worth a thousand words, or as many statistics. I update from the Eisner and Pieper *American Economic Review* article of March 1984 a striking one. Figure 8.2 juxtaposes the percentage change in real gross national product and the previous year's price-adjusted high-employment deficit as a percent of real gross national product.

The two curves, it must be conceded, show a remarkable fit.

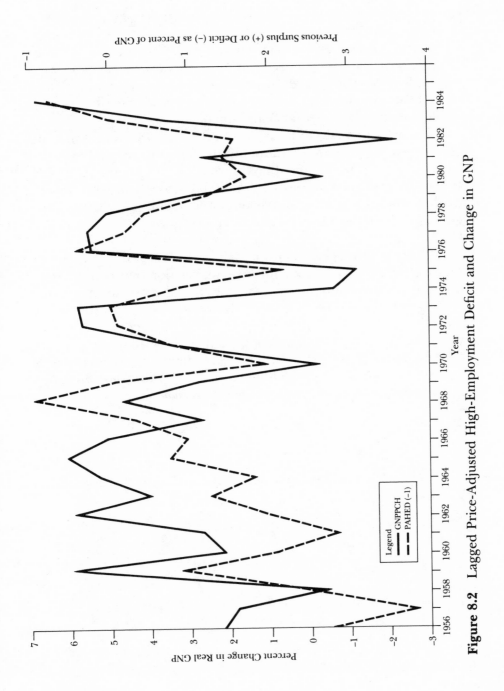

Figure 8.2 Lagged Price-Adjusted High-Employment Deficit and Change in GNP

91

The greater the deficit, the greater the next year's increase in GNP. The less the deficit, the less the increase or the greater the decline in the next year's GNP. And Figure 8.2A shows the same relation in a two-variable scatter diagram. The simple two-by-two distributions of Table 8.4 are confirmed and amplified.

Changes in real GNP, as is well known, are closely but inversely related to changes in unemployment. Production requires labor and the more people that are working the greater is output. When unemployment goes up, real GNP growth slackens or actually becomes negative. When unemployment goes down, GNP goes up. And the faster unemployment goes down, the faster GNP rises.

In view of the relation between the deficit and GNP, we should thus expect a similar close, but inverse, relation between the deficit and changes in unemployment. Figure 8.3 confirms this. Converting the inverse relation with the deficit into a direct one, it plots the percentage point change in unemployment and the previous year's ratio of the price-adjusted high-employment *surplus* (the negative of the deficit). The close fit of the two curves is again outstanding. *Higher surpluses—or lesser deficits—are associated with greater increases or lesser decreases in unemployment.*

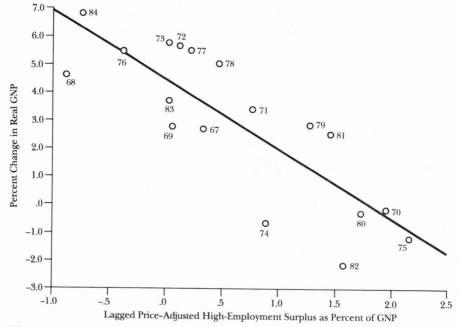

Figure 8.2A   Lagged Price-Adjusted High-Employment Surplus and Change in GNP, 1967–84, Scatter

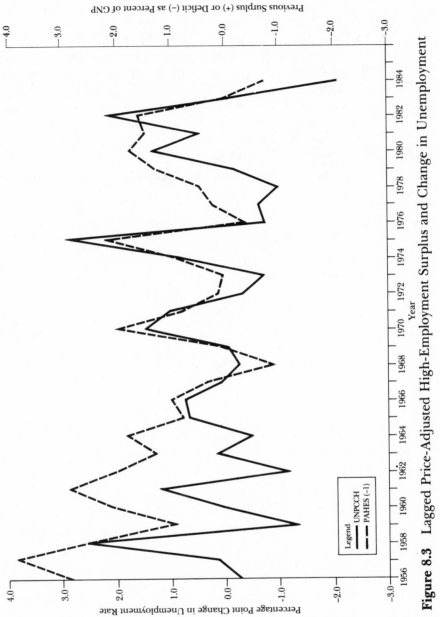

Figure 8.3 Lagged Price-Adjusted High-Employment Surplus and Change in Unemployment

93

These findings are sustained in more rigorous, statistical analysis. In a number of least squares regressions we relate our various measures of high-employment surpluses and deficits to growth in GNP and changes in unemployment. We also examine effects of changes in the monetary base to ascertain the role of monetary policy and its possible interaction with the budget variables. And we further explore effects on the various components of GNP, thus casting some light on the investment "crowding out" argument as well as the explosive issue of trade deficits. A full presentation of this statistical analysis is offered in the next chapter.

9

More Facts:
A Statistical Analysis

WHAT FOLLOWS IS NOT FOR everybody. It is a more rigorous statistical analysis of annual time series data for the United States economy. Those who find the going tough may want to tread lightly through the tables and their exposition and move on to the summary at the end of the chapter.

What we have done is to take our observations from 1956 to 1984 and carry out a number of least squares regressions. They provide estimates of the quantitative relations between key variables in the economy and budget deficits, both as officially reported and as we have corrected them. We thus offer evidence, for example, on how much the rate of growth of GNP and the rate of change of unemployment were affected, on the average, by each percentage point change in the ratio of budget deficits to GNP. We also learn what happened to important components of GNP, such as private investment and net exports. And we note the comparative roles of deficits and monetary variables.

Recognizing 1967 as something of a watershed in inaugurating accelerating inflation and subsequently slower rates of growth and higher unemployment, we initially divided our observations into two groups: 1956 to 1966 and 1967 to 1984. Looking first at the official high-employment budget *surplus* (OFHES), we note in equations (9.1) and (9.3) of Table 9.1 that it was clearly negatively related to subsequent growth in real GNP and positively related to subsequent changes in unemployment in both periods. For 1956 to 1966, each percentage point of greater surplus (lesser deficit) was associated with approximately 1.8 percent lesser growth in real GNP. For the 1967–84 period, each percentage point of surplus, again expressed as a ratio of GNP, was associated with 3.3 percentage points less of growth in real output.

A balanced official high-employment budget in the earlier period would have "predicted" a 5.7 percent growth in real GNP. For the later, 1967–84 period, however, a balanced official high-employment budget would have predicted a rate of growth of GNP of only 0.1 percent. A balanced official high-employment budget would have been associated with a *de*crease of 0.9 percentage points in subsequent unemployment during the 1956–66 period, but an *in*crease of 1.5 percent in unemployment in the 1967–84 period.

The official high-employment budget was thus in both periods significantly related to subsequent movements in the economy. But why is a balanced official high-employment budget during the later years, 1967 to 1984, associated with an economy of virtually no growth and of increasing unemployment? *Because a balanced official high-employment budget, with high inflation, is a budget really in substantial surplus.* Confirmation of this is found in the relations involving the inflation-adjusted high-employment budget.

We note first, from the values of the constant term, b_{02}, that a balanced, *price-adjusted* high-employment budget, from 1967 on, predicts a 4.4 percent growth in real GNP and a 0.5 percent decline in unemployment. But recall from Table 8.3 that in 1981, when there was an official high-employment deficit equal to 0.11 percent of GNP, the high-employment budget adjusted for price effects was in surplus by 1.57 percent of GNP. The 1.57 percentage point swing to deficit necessary to eliminate the price-adjusted budget surplus would then have created an official deficit equal to 1.68 percent of GNP. Our equation involving the official high-employment budget suggests that if it had been in deficit by that much, GNP would have risen by 5.7 percent and unemployment would have declined by 1.1 percentage points.[1]

Evidence of the distorting effects of inflation may be found

TABLE 9.1 High-Employment Budgets and Changes in Real GNP and Unemployment

$Y_t = b_{01} + b_{11}HES_{t-1}$ for $t = 1956, \ldots, 1966$
$Y_t = b_{02} + b_{12}HES_{t-1}$ for $t = 1967, \ldots, 1984$

(1)	(2)	(3)	(4)	(5)	(6)	(7)	(8)	(9)
EQUATION AND MEASURE OF *HES*	DEPENDENT VARIABLE (*Y*)	REGRESSION COEFFICIENTS[a]				SIGNIFICANCE LEVEL OF DIFFERENCE IN REGRESSIONS	$\hat{R}^2$	D–W
		1956–66		1967–84				
		b_{01}	b_{12}	b_{02}	b_{12}			
(9.1) OF	ΔGNP	5.678 (0.923)	−1.837 (0.727)	0.137 (0.677)	−3.312 (0.644)	0.0001	.529	1.71
(9.2) PA	ΔGNP	7.187 (1.125)	−1.731 (0.516)	4.421 (0.447)	−2.491 (0.416)	0.0001	.622	2.10
(9.3) OF	ΔUN	−0.880 (0.426)	0.792 (0.336)	1.452 (0.313)	1.490 (0.297)	0.0002	.503	2.18
(9.4) PA	ΔUN	−1.175 (0.585)	0.566 (0.269)	−0.455 (0.233)	1.087 (0.216)	0.002	.494	2.27

[a]Ordinary least squares; standard errors are shown in parentheses.

Y = dependent variable: ΔGNP or ΔUN
HES = high-employment budget surplus as percent of GNP
OF = official
PA = price-adjusted
ΔGNP = percent change in gross national product
ΔUN = percentage point change in unemployment
R^2 = adjusted coefficient of determination
D–W = Durbin–Watson ratio

in the contrasting differences between the implications of balanced budgets for 1956–66 and 1967–84 in the official and the price-adjusted HES equations. These indicated that a balanced official high-employment budget implied a rate of growth of real GNP some 5.5 percentage points less in the later period (5.678 − 0.137), while a balanced price-adjusted high-employment budget predicted a rate of growth of GNP only 2.8 percentage points less (7.187 − 4.421).[2]

What is more, the adjusted budget measures generally did at least as well in capturing the impact of fiscal thrust, and in most cases better, as measured by the fit of the relation or values of $\hat{R}^2$, than did the official high-employment budget. This would indeed be consistent with the hypothesis, in econometric terms, that there was an errors-in-variable problem in the official budget equations. The true relation, we may suggest, involves an *adjusted* high-employment budget. In the earlier period, when the rate of inflation was low, the relations were fairly similar. In the later period with high inflation, there were differences which could not be ignored.

The relations involving one-year lagged, adjusted high-employment budget surpluses became poorer, however, when interest effects, or par-to-market adjustments of the value of the debt, were incorporated. The difficulty here may stem from the high variability of interest rates and the consequent par-to-market corrections. These would cause private creditors to view day-to-day interest effects as largely transitory. They may not react to changes in bond prices until the new prices are seen to persist. A par-to-market correction based on market values of securities on December 31 may hence not be promptly or fully reflected in the aggregate demand of the subsequent year.

We therefore estimated relations in which changes in GNP and employment were functions of distributed two-year lags of the high-employment surplus. Results shown in Table 9.2 indicate that with two-year lags interest effects did matter, and the price- and interest-adjusted surplus (PIAHES) also outperformed the official surplus.

Thus, the less the high-employment budget surplus, or the greater the deficit, the more GNP and unemployment turned for the better. Further, satisfactory growth in output and constant or declining unemployment would have been associated with a balanced official high-employment budget in the non-inflationary

TABLE 9.2 High-Employment Budgets and Changes in Real GNP and Unemployment, Distributed Lags

$Y_t = b_{01} + b_{11}HES_{t-1} + b_{21}HES_{t-2}$ for $t = 1957, \ldots, 1966$
$Y_t = b_{02} + b_{12}HES_{t-1} + b_{22}HES_{t-2}$ for $t = 1967, \ldots, 1984$

(1)	(2)	(3)	(4)	(5)	(6)	(7)	(8)	(9)	(10)	(11)
EQUATION AND MEASURE OF HES	DEPENDENT VARIABLE (Y)	REGRESSION COEFFICIENTS[a]						SIGNIFICANCE LEVEL OF DIFFERENCE IN REGRESSIONS	$\hat{R}^2$	$D\text{–}W$
			1957–66			1967–84				
		b_{01}	b_{11} $(t-1)$	b_{21} $(t-2)$	b_{02}	b_{12} $(t-1)$	b_{22} $(t-2)$			
(9.5) OF	ΔGNP	5.634 (1.275)	−1.798 (0.786)	0.104 (0.851)	0.166 (0.866)	−3.315 (0.680)	0.040 (0.690)	0.005	0.491	1.73
(9.6) PIA	ΔGNP	7.757 (1.357)	−0.261 (0.453)	−1.502 (0.488)	4.392 (0.494)	−1.237 (0.324)	−0.999 (0.321)	0.001	0.576	2.15
(9.7) OF	ΔUN	−0.900 (0.581)	0.805 (0.358)	0.041 (0.388)	1.650 (0.395)	1.484 (0.310)	0.279 (0.315)	0.003	0.479	2.25
(9.8) PIA	ΔUN	−1.228 (0.631)	−0.242 (0.211)	0.757 (0.194)	−0.420 (0.230)	0.403 (0.151)	0.531 (0.149)	0.002	0.548	2.28

[a]Ordinary least squares; standard errors are shown in parentheses.

Y = dependent variable: ΔGNP or ΔUN
HES = high-employment budget surplus as percent of GNP
OF = official
PIA = price- and interest-adjusted
ΔGNP = percent change in gross national product
ΔUN = percentage point change in unemployment

years from 1956 to 1966, but would apparently have required a substantial official deficit in the more inflationary years from 1967 to 1984. And finally, we found that budget deficits calculated after adjustment for inflation and changes in interest rates fit the data better than the official, unadjusted budgets and reduced the differences between the two periods.

These results, however, are certainly open to challenge. After all, the economy is complex and many variables are correlated with each other. Why pick out the high-employment budget surplus as critical? Perhaps some other variable or variables, themselves correlated with the high-employment budget deficit, were the really causal factors. The relations involving the high-employment budget surplus or deficit may thus be spurious. This means that if we were to alter the high-employment budget—by changing tax rates or government expenditures, for example— we would not get the results we have implied unless we changed the other factors as well. And conversely, if we changed the other factors, changing the high-employment budget surplus or deficit would not matter.

The Role of Monetary Policy

Among the many factors thus far ignored, the roles of money and monetary policy cry out for attention. This is so in part because strict monetarists insist that it is the quantity of money *alone* that matters for aggregate economic activity. They argue that if budget deficits do seem to stimulate the economy, it is because the deficits are associated with increases in the quantity of money. But Keynesians and supply siders also believe that money matters, even if they see other important forces as well.

As long as the Federal Reserve tries to stabilize interest rates or "maintain orderly conditions" in securities markets, changes in the quantity of money may well be associated with budget surpluses and deficits. For the bigger is the budget deficit, the greater will be Treasury borrowing and the greater, hence, the upward pressure on interest rates if the Federal Reserve does not relieve that pressure by some compensatory buying of Treasury securities. When the Fed buys Treasury securities, though, it increases the monetary base and bank reserves, thus setting off a multiple expansion of the money supply, especially of demand deposits against which there are substantial reserve requirements.[3]

In fact, changes in the money supply have been positively associated with federal budget deficits. Hence it is possible that the negative relation we have found between changes in GNP and the high-employment surplus merely reflects a positive relation with changes in the monetary base. For the less the surplus, that is, the more the deficit, the more the Federal Reserve increases the monetary base by buying Treasury securities. We should, then, examine the role of changes in the monetary base. We might point out that, although similar relations might be expected (and are found) involving other monetary aggregates such as M1 and M2, use of the monetary base is conceptually cleaner. For the monetary base is under the more direct control of the Federal Reserve and may less reflect the reverse relation, in which it is the GNP and the economy which affect money.

Since the Federal Reserve offers a consistent monetary base series which starts in 1959, we were able to begin our series of *changes* in the monetary base with 1960. We could thus begin with 1961 GNP in estimating relations involving *lagged* values of the high-employment surplus and real changes in the monetary base.

We may first regard results of re-estimating, for the years 1961 to 1984, the relation between changes in GNP and the high-employment surplus. Since we had only six relatively noninflationary years, from 1961 to 1966, while estimating a separate constant term for those years, we did not assume separate regression coefficients for earlier and later periods. The results for the high-employment surplus, shown in equations (9.9) and (9.10) of Table 9.3, are, nevertheless, fairly similar to and consistent with the results for the somewhat larger number of observations, from 1955 to 1984, shown in Table 9.1. Again, both the official and price-adjusted high-employment surpluses are significantly negatively related to subsequent changes in GNP. Each percentage point more of deficit was associated, on the average for all of the years from 1961 to 1984, with from 2.3 to 2.6 percentage points more in growth (or less in decline) of GNP. And the fit for the equation with the price-adjusted surplus was again considerably better than that for the official surplus.

But the results of equation (9.11) show, as anticipated, that changes in the monetary base are strongly related to changes in GNP. The coefficient in this case is, as predicted, positive and

TABLE 9.3   High-Employment Budgets, Changes in Monetary Base, and Changes in GNP

$\Delta GNP_t = b_{01}X_1 + b_{02}X_2 + b_1 HES_{t-1} + b_2 \, \Delta MB_{t-1}$
$\qquad X_1 = 1, X_2 = 0 \quad \text{for } t = 1961, \ldots, 1966$
$\qquad X_1 = 0, X_2 = 1 \quad \text{for } t = 1967, \ldots, 1984$

(1)	(2)	(3)	(4)	(5)	(6)	(7)	(8)
			REGRESSION COEFFICIENTS[a]				
	Constant		High-Employment Surplus		Change in Monetary Base		
EQUATION	1961–66 (b_{01})	1967–84 (b_{02})	OFFICIAL (b_1)	PRICE-ADJUSTED (b_1)	(b_2)	$\hat{R}^2$	D–W
(9.9)	7.442 (0.867)	0.759 (0.595)	−2.567 (0.519)	—	—	.556	1.70
(9.10)	8.633 (0.846)	4.298 (0.417)	—	−2.288 (0.363)	—	.669	1.88
(9.11)	3.228 (0.722)	2.023 (0.409)	—	—	12.898 (2.282)	.618	1.99
(9.12)	5.181 (0.973)	1.113 (0.497)	−1.433 (0.540)	—	8.678 (2.561)	.704	1.58
(9.13)	6.432 (1.250)	3.348 (0.569)	—	−1.463 (0.496)	6.528 (2.909)	.721	1.70

[a]Ordinary least squares; standard errors are shown in parentheses.

ΔGNP = percent change in GNP
HES = high-employment surplus as percent of GNP
ΔMB = real change in monetary base as percent of GNP

highly significant. The high-employment budget deficits "predict" changes in GNP, but so do changes in the monetary base.

This leads us directly to the critical test of relating changes in GNP to both the high-employment surplus and changes in the monetary base. Results for the official and price-adjusted surpluses in equations (9.12) and (9.13), respectively, show *both* the budget surplus or deficit and changes in the monetary base to be statistically significant. Further, the adjusted values of $\hat{R}^2$ are higher when both variables are included.[4]

In addition, coefficients of the budget variables are considerably less in absolute magnitude with addition of the monetary base variable, and the coefficient of the monetary base variable is sharply reduced when either budget variable, but particularly the adjusted budget variable, is included. These equations confirm the consensus judgment among economists that fiscal policy, measured by the high-employment surplus, and monetary policy, measured by the change in the monetary base, both matter.

We have earlier alluded to the possible difference in lag

structure for the consequences of interest effects and other components of the adjusted high-employment budget surplus. Fluctuations in market values of securities may well be viewed as in considerable part transitory. Changes in the real value of public holdings of federal debt that are due to official deficits and changes due to price inflation may both tend to be serially correlated, that is, show some stability, while changes in market values due to changes in interest rates, as we pointed out, bounce around. The interest effects may thus have to persist before they are taken fully into account.

This judgment gained support from the relatively poor fit of equations involving the price- and interest-adjusted budget with only one lagged value and the improvement with the two-year-lagged equation. By combining both adjustments—price and interest—and the official surplus in one variable, however, we are constraining the lag structure to be the same for all of the components. We might expect a still better fit and better parameter estimates, that is, a sharper and more accurate view of the relation, if we separate the interest effects—the changes in market values of securities due to changing interest rates—from the other components of the budget surplus. We hence estimated equations with the separate interest effects in two lagged variables, along with official and price-adjusted surpluses with one lag.

We may observe first, in Table 9.4, that the interest effect is significantly negative and its inclusion in this manner improves the fit, substantially reducing the unexplained variance of changes in GNP. In equations without the money variable, addition of the interest effect raises $\hat{R}^2$ to .692 and .728 in equations (9.14) and (9.15) from its values of .556 and .669 in Table 9.3's equations (9.9) and (9.10). The interest effects in equations (9.16) and (9.17), with the monetary base variable, raise $\hat{R}^2$ to .780 and .765, respectively.

The significance and magnitudes of the negative coefficients of the interest effect are robust against introduction of the monetary base variable. And the interest effect on the deficit, with appropriate lags, seems to have affected growth in GNP with about the same force as the other components of the adjusted deficit. Equation (9.17) in Table 9.4 indicates that each percentage point of deficit is associated on the average with 1.246 percentage points more of growth of GNP over the next year. Interest effects which reduced the real deficit by one percentage point of GNP

TABLE 9.4 High-Employment Budgets, Interest Effects, and Changes in Monetary Base and GNP

$$\Delta GNP_t = b_{01}X_1 + b_{02}X_2 + b_1 HES_{t-1} + b_2 IE_{t-1} + b_3 IE_{t-2} + b_4 \Delta MB_{t-1}$$
$$X_1 = 1, X_2 = 0 \quad \text{for } t = 1961, \ldots, 1966$$
$$X_1 = 0, X_2 = 1 \quad \text{for } t = 1967, \ldots, 1984$$

(1)	(2)	(3)	(4)	(5)	(6)	(7)	(8)	(9)	(10)	(11)
		Constants			REGRESSION COEFFICIENTS[a]					
EQUATION	MEASURE OF HES	1961–66 (b_{01})	1967–84 (b_{02})	HES_{t-1} (b_1)	IE_{t-1} (b_2)	IE_{t-2} (b_3)	ΣIE ($b_2 + b_3$)	ΔMB (b_4)	$\hat{R}^2$	$D–W$
(9.14)	OF	6.814 (0.749)	1.091 (0.514)	−2.173 (0.465)	−0.566 (0.393)	−1.386 (0.416)	−1.945 (0.656)	—	.692	1.75
(9.15)	PA	7.854 (0.825)	4.051 (0.389)	−1.893 (0.363)	−0.184 (0.367)	−1.048 (0.412)	−1.232 (0.644)	—	.728	1.81
(9.16)	OF	5.195 (0.837)	1.269 (0.438)	−1.406 (0.471)	−0.547 (0.331)	−1.063 (0.368)	−1.611 (0.565)	6.824 (2.316)	.780	1.59
(9.17)	PA	6.067 (1.174)	3.292 (0.526)	−1.246 (0.466)	−0.285 (0.344)	−0.931 (0.387)	−1.217 (0.598)	5.547 (2.760)	.765	1.66

[a]Ordinary least squares; standard errors are shown in parentheses.

ΔGNP = percent change in GNP
HES = high-employment surplus as percent of GNP
IE = interest effect as percent of GNP
ΔMB = real change in monetary base as percent of GNP
OF = official
PA = price-adjusted

tended to be associated with reductions in GNP within two years of almost the identical amount, 1.217 percent (0.285 percent plus 0.931 percent).

Alternate formulations without the first lagged interest effect variable, for which the coefficient showed only a low level of significance, are shown in Table 9.5. The fit is very slightly poorer in the official budget equation and almost identical in the price-adjusted surplus equation. When a separate price effect variable is added in equation (9.20), its coefficient is not statistically significantly different from zero but is negative and of the same order of magnitude as the coefficients of the high-employment surplus and the interest effect. *The three components of our fully adjusted budget surplus—the official surplus, the price effect, and the interest effect—all affect the rate of growth of GNP in the predicted manner.*

As we have noted, the variables that drive GNP up generally drive unemployment down. Similar relations with the percentage point change in unemployment as the dependent variable are seen in Tables 9.6 and 9.7 (p. 108). Once more, the high-employment surplus and the separate price and interest effects all have the predicted signs, in this case positive. A greater real surplus or a lesser real deficit are associated with less favorable movements of the unemployment rate. The separate price effect is, however, again not statistically significant and the coefficients of the first lagged interest effect variable, also not statistically significant, in this case have the "wrong" sign. The coefficients of the monetary base variable in the unemployment equations have the predicted negative sign but they do not all pass the 0.05 level significance test.

We conclude that the high-employment budget surplus, official and/or price-adjusted, the separate interest effects on the market value of debt, and changes in the monetary base are all factors significantly related to the growth of output and are correspondingly related to changes in the rate of unemployment. With interest effects and the monetary base in the equation, the price-adjusted budget deficit itself does not contribute any more to explaining changes in GNP than does the official budget deficit, but the official budget equation is "helped" by the larger difference between constant terms for the brief, early, less inflationary period and the later more inflationary one. The price-adjusted

TABLE 9.5 High-Employment Budgets, Price Effects, Delayed Interest Effects, and Changes in Monetary Base and GNP

$$\Delta GNP_t = b_{01}X_1 + b_{02}X_2 + b_1 HES_{t-1} + b_2 PE_{t-1} + b_3 IE_{t-2} + b_4 \Delta MB_{t-1}$$

$X_1 = 1, X_2 = 0$ for $t = 1961, \ldots, 1966$
$X_1 = 0, X_2 = 1$ for $t = 1967, \ldots, 1984$

(1)	(2)	(3)	(4)	(5)	(6)	(7)	(8)	(9)	(10)
		Constants		REGRESSION COEFFICIENTS[a]					
EQUATION	MEASURE OF HES	1961–66 (b_{01})	1967–84 (b_{02})	HES_{t-1} (b_1)	PE_{t-1} (b_2)	IE_{t-2} (b_3)	ΔMB_{t-1} (b_4)	$\hat{R}^2$	D–W
(9.18)	OF	5.209 (0.874)	1.326 (0.456)	−1.312 (0.488)	—	−0.878 (0.366)	6.899 (2.418)	.761	1.66
(9.19)	PA	6.268 (1.139)	3.333 (0.518)	−1.306 (0.456)	—	−0.825 (0.362)	5.211 (2.708)	.769	1.70
(9.20)	OF	6.055 (1.283)	2.727 (1.614)	−1.371 (0.495)	−0.938 (1.036)	−0.834 (0.371)	5.513 (2.872)	.758	1.67

[a]Ordinary least squares; standard errors are shown in parentheses.

ΔGNP = percent change in GNP
HES = high-employment surplus as percent of GNP
PE = price effect as percent of GNP
IE = interest effect as percent of GNP
ΔMB = real change in monetary base as percent of GNP
OF = official
PA = price-adjusted

TABLE 9.6 High-Employment Budgets, Interest Effects, and Changes in Monetary Base and Unemployment

$\Delta UN_t = b_{01}X_1 + b_{02}X_2 + b_1 HES_{t-1} + b_2 IE_{t-1} + b_3 IE_{t-2} + b_4 \Delta MB_{t-1}$
$\quad X_1 = 1, X_2 = 0 \quad$ for $t = 1961, \ldots, 1966$
$\quad X_1 = 0, X_2 = 1 \quad$ for $t = 1967, \ldots, 1984$

(1)	(2)	(3)	(4)	(5)	(6)	(7)	(8)	(9)	(10)	(11)
		Constants		REGRESSION COEFFICIENTS[a]						
EQUATION	MEASURE OF HES	1961–66 (b_{01})	1967–84 (b_{02})	HES_{t-1} (b_1)	IE_{t-1} (b_2)	IE_{t-2} (b_3)	ΣIE ($b_2 + b_3$)	ΔMB_{t-1} (b_4)	$\hat{R}^2$	D–W
(9.21)	OF	−0.618 (0.394)	0.935 (0.206)	0.682 (0.221)	−0.067 (0.156)	0.470 (0.173)	0.403 (0.266)	−2.200 (1.089)	.736	1.97
(9.22)	PA	−1.200 (0.522)	−0.106 (0.234)	0.677 (0.207)	−0.202 (0.153)	0.394 (0.172)	0.192 (0.266)	−1.284 (1.229)	.747	1.80
(9.23)	OF	−1.140 (0.320)	0.992 (0.220)	0.929 (0.199)	−0.061 (0.168)	0.574 (0.178)	0.513 (0.281)	—	.693	1.90
(9.24)	PA	−1.613 (0.342)	−0.284 (0.162)	0.826 (0.150)	−0.226 (0.152)	0.421 (0.171)	0.196 (0.267)	—	.746	1.78

[a]Ordinary least squares; standard errors are shown in parentheses.

ΔUN = percent change in unemployment
HES = high-employment surplus as percent of GNP
IE = interest effect as percent of GNP
ΔMB = real change in monetary base as percent of GNP
OF = official
PA = price-adjusted

107

TABLE 9.7 High-Employment Budgets, Price Effects, Delayed Interest Effects, and Changes in Monetary Base and Unemployment

$$\Delta UN_t = b_{01}X_1 + b_{02}X_2 + b_1 HES_{t-1} + b_2 PE_{t-1} + b_3 IE_{t-2} + b_4 \Delta MB_{t-1}$$
$$X_1 = 1, X_2 = 0 \quad \text{for } t = 1961, \ldots, 1966$$
$$X_1 = 0, X_2 = 1 \quad \text{for } t = 1967, \ldots, 1984$$

(1)	(2)	(3)	(4)	(5)	(6)	(7)	(8)	(9)	(10)
		REGRESSION COEFFICIENTS[a]							
		Constants							
EQUATION	MEASURE OF HES	1961–66 (b_{01})	1967–84 (b_{02})	HES_{t-1} (b_1)	PE_{t-1} (b_2)	IE_{t-2} (b_3)	ΔMB_{t-1} (b_4)	$\hat{R}^2$	D–W
(9.25)	OF	−0.616 (0.385)	0.942 (0.201)	0.693 (0.215)	—	0.493 (0.161)	−2.191 (1.065)	.747	1.93
(9.26)	PA	−1.058 (0.521)	−0.070 (0.237)	0.635 (0.209)	—	0.470 (0.165)	−1.522 (1.239)	.737	1.72
(9.27)	OF	−0.820 (0.574)	0.605 (0.722)	0.707 (0.221)	0.225 (0.464)	0.482 (0.166)	−1.858 (1.285)	.737	1.85

[a]Ordinary least squares; standard errors are shown in parentheses.

ΔUN = percent point change in unemployment rate
HES = high-employment surplus as percent of GNP
IE = interest effect as percent of GNP
ΔMB = real change in monetary base as percent of GNP
OF = official
PA = price-adjusted

budget variable would seem a safer predictor over periods where inflation varied substantially.

But now, what about the composition of gross national product? What is the evidence on crowding out of investment and on exports and imports, recognizing that the effects of the budget deficit and changes in the monetary base on GNP are the sum of their effects, direct or indirect, on the various components of GNP.[5] From regressions of these components, shown in Tables 9.8 and 9.9, we note first, in equations (9.28) and (9.29) that *the price-adjusted high-employment surplus is significantly and negatively related to both consumption and investment. Deficits appeared to "crowd in," not "crowd out" investment.*

And most interestingly, the surplus coefficient is significantly *positive* in the net exports equation. This indicates that the greater the adjusted budget deficit, the greater are subsequent imports and/or the less are subsequent exports. The positive effect of the deficit on imports (negative effect of the surplus) is confirmed in equation (9.41) of Table 9.9.

We may presume that greater adjusted high-employment deficits, by bringing about a greater gross national product and national income, bring about greater expenditures on foreign goods. To the extent that the deficit induces an inflow of foreign capital it may also contribute to raising the international value of the dollar. This, too, encourages imports and may, as well, discourage U.S. exports.

There are two important consequences, one domestic and one foreign, of this negative effect of our budget deficits on net exports. On the domestic side, we have a "leakage" of income and demand outside of our economy. We see in equation (9.33) of Table 9.8 that each percentage point of price-adjusted high-employment deficit was associated with an increase in "domestic demand" equal to 2.1 percent of GNP. It was also associated, however, with a reduction in net exports equal to 0.4 percent of output; the estimated impact of one percentage point of deficit on subsequent GNP is only 1.6 percent. We find then that the deficit leads Americans to spend more and that stimulates more production, but some of it involves Japanese Toyotas and Sonys, French wines, and English sweaters.

But if this "leakage" reduces the favorable impact of budget deficits on our own output, it correspondingly contributes to the

TABLE 9.8 High-Employment Budgets, Changes in Monetary Base, and Changes in Components of GNP

$\Delta COM_t = b_{01}X_1 + b_{02}X_2 + b_1 PAHES_{t-1} + b_2 \Delta MB_{t-1}$
$X_1 = 1, X_2 = 0$ for $t = 1962, \ldots, 1966$
$X_1 = 0, X_2 = 1$ for $t = 1967, \ldots, 1984$

(1)	(2)	(3)	(4)	(5)	(6)	(7)	(8)	(9)
		Constants		REGRESSION COEFFICIENTS[a]				
EQUATION	COMPONENT (COM)	1962–66 (b_{01})	1967–84 (b_{02})	$PAHES_{t-1}$ (b_1)	ΔMB_{t-1} (b_2)	$\hat{R}^2$	D–W	$\hat{\rho}$
(9.28)	Consumption	3.401 (0.675)	2.339 (0.303)	−0.642 (0.263)	2.393 (1.592)	.580	1.91	.092
(9.29)	Investment	2.613 (1.176)	1.135 (0.541)	−1.383 (0.414)	3.587 (2.411)	.570	1.99	.282
(9.30)	Government	1.195 (0.558)	0.483 (0.270)	−0.113 (0.172)	−0.660 (0.981)	.354	1.52	.473
(9.31)	Net exports	−1.615 (1.273)	−0.766 (1.012)	0.399 (0.137)	1.625 (0.811)	.512	1.45	.836
(9.32)	GNP	6.208 (1.296)	3.371 (0.585)	−1.568 (0.479)	7.172 (2.830)	.735	2.03	.174
(9.33)	Domestic demand	7.405 (1.506)	3.934 (0.675)	−2.141 (0.560)	5.149 (3.295)	.767	1.93	.155

[a]Least squares with Cochrane–Orcutt, first-order autoregressive corrections; standard errors are shown in parentheses.

ΔCOM = change in component as percent of GNP
$PAHES$ = price-adjusted high-employment surplus as percent of GNP
ΔMB = real change in monetary base as percent of GNP

TABLE 9.9 High-Employment Budgets, Changes in Monetary Base, and Changes in Five Components of GNP

$\Delta COM_t = b_{01}X_1 + b_{02}X_2 + b_1 PAHES_{t-1} + b_2 \Delta MB_{t-1}$
$X_1 = 1, X_2 = 0$ for $t = 1962, \ldots, 1966$
$X_1 = 0, X_2 = 1$ for $t = 1967, \ldots, 1984$

		REGRESSION COEFFICIENTS[a]						
		Constants						
(1)	(2)	(3)	(4)	(5)	(6)	(7)	(8)	(9)
EQUATION	COMPONENT (COM)	1962–66 (b_{01})	1967–84 (b_{02})	$PAHES_{t-1}$ (b_1)	ΔMB_{t-1} (b_2)	$\hat{R}^2$	D–W	$\hat{\rho}$
(9.34)	Consumer durables	1.039 (0.363)	0.601 (0.163)	−0.382 (0.139)	1.049 (0.806)	.549	1.79	.186
(9.35)	Nondurables and services	2.340 (0.400)	1.725 (0.179)	−0.252 (0.153)	1.444 (0.944)	.508	1.96	.089
(9.36)	Fixed investment	1.610 (0.690)	0.821 (0.328)	−0.802 (0.211)	2.727 (1.257)	.669	1.93	.446
(9.37)	Change in inventories	0.824 (0.587)	0.246 (0.261)	−0.464 (0.235)	0.737 (1.406)	.352	1.94	−.124
(9.38)	Federal	0.607 (0.528)	0.177 (0.254)	−0.098 (0.166)	−0.892 (0.940)	.220	1.59	.463
(9.39)	State and local	0.542 (0.252)	0.308 (0.128)	−0.012 (0.062)	0.182 (0.362)	.515	1.98	.611
(9.40)	Exports	0.008 (0.513)	0.278 (0.239)	0.005 (0.186)	1.736 (0.973)	.204	1.86	.401
(9.41)	Imports	0.991 (0.371)	0.751 (0.170)	−0.457 (0.143)	0.170 (0.835)	.456	1.64	.096

[a]Least squares with Cochrane–Orcutt, first-order autoregressive corrections; standard errors are shown in parentheses.

ΔCOM = change in component as percent of GNP
$PAHES$ = price-adjusted high-employment surplus as percent of GNP
ΔMB = real change in monetary base as percent of GNP

111

demand for foreign products. With our gross national product in the neighborhood of $4,000 billion, each percentage point of deficit, according to equation (9.41), contributes to an increase in demand for foreign goods and services of $18 billion (0.457 percent of $4,000 billion). We should then anticipate a role for the U.S. budget deficit in the economies of other nations. The lesser increase in domestic output will have a counterpart in greater growth of output elsewhere, as we shall shortly confirm with some striking new evidence.

Summary of Findings

1. The high-employment budget deficit is a substantial predictor of subsequent changes in output and employment. Greater deficits have been associated with more favorable outcomes in gross national product and unemployment.
2. The price- or inflation-adjusted high-employment budget deficit has been a better predictor of changes in output and unemployment than the unadjusted official budget deficit. It explains, particularly, a good deal of the difference between the results of deficits in less inflationary and more inflationary periods.
3. Change in the monetary base, an indicator of monetary policy, also proves a good predictor of growth in output. It is, by itself, a somewhat better predictor than the official high-employment surplus but a somewhat poorer predictor than the price-adjusted surplus.
4. In multivariate relations, both the high-employment surplus and changes in the monetary base are highly significant. The role of the high-employment surplus is not merely that of a proxy for associated changes in the money supply. If anything, the high-employment surplus variables add more to the equation including the monetary base than the monetary base adds to the equations including the high-employment surplus. The role and significance of the monetary base variable is reduced with introduction of interest effects on the market value of debt.
5. The interest effects on the market value of federal debt appear to require two years rather than one for most of their consequences. With two-year distributed lags, equa-

tions with the price- and interest-adjusted high-employment surplus show a good fit; those with one-year lags do not. The "best" equations are those which allow the interest effect to be estimated separately over two years while the budget surplus and changes in the monetary base have their separate effects over one year.

6. The stimulatory effects of budget deficits show up significantly in both consumption and investment. Rather than "crowd out" investment, budget deficits have tended to crowd it in. Their stimuli to aggregate demand and total output have apparently outweighed deficits' absorption of private saving or the possible negative effects of interest rate movements.

7. There is evidence that budget deficits increase our trade deficit. They have been significant, in particular, in increasing imports. This indicates a "leakage" of income and demand to foreign economies, contributing to their growth but lessening the favorable impact of budget deficits on our own.

8. Our results are thus consistent with the theory that real budget deficits, taking into account changes in the real value of outstanding debt brought on by inflation and changes in interest rates, stimulate demand and raise output and employment, when capacity and the supply of labor permit.

10

Deficits and the Rest of the World

BUDGET DEFICITS HAVE been blamed for much in the United States. Our deficits have also been charged with creating havoc in other economies. In particular, they have been viewed as draining capital from the rest of the world. To the extent that they have contributed to rising interest rates in the United States, it is felt that they have forced other nations to follow their own tight money policies to reduce the loss of investment funds. This has been presumed to have had the consequence of curbing other nations' growth and contributing to their unemployment.

What can we say about the role of budget deficits in other nations? Have they had impacts similar to those of budget deficits in the United States? Will correction of budget measures for inflation cast new light on the role of fiscal policy elsewhere?

In another statistical analysis with Paul Pieper, prepared for a European conference and publication,[1] I have undertaken such corrections. We have examined in particular the relation of United States deficits to economic growth elsewhere. Our results, we shall note, are in sharp conflict with conventional wisdom.

By way of anticipation, larger inflation-adjusted budget deficits have been associated with *greater* rather than lesser rates of growth within OECD countries, although the apparent effect has been small. But inflation adjustments alter sharply the relative deficits among countries. The United Kingdom, for example, with very slow growth, turns out to have had substantial budget surpluses after inflation adjustment. And *Japan, with the fastest growth, has had the greatest deficits.* Finally, and most significantly, larger, inflation-adjusted budget deficits in the United States have been associated with distinctly, and considerably, *higher* subsequent growth in gross domestic product in the other nations.

Pieper and I undertook inflation adjustments in preliminary fashion to structural or high-employment budgets in Canada, France, West Germany, Italy, Japan, and the United Kingdom. We did not, however, include interest rate effects on the market value of government financial assets and liabilities. The underlying structural deficits and debt figures may lack the full relevance and consistency over time, let alone across nations, that we have associated with the high-employment budget deficit and the adjustments that we have made to it in the United States. Nevertheless, the results of our parallel analysis with data for the years 1970 through 1982 for these six advanced industrial nations are striking.

First, the ratios of net debt to gross domestic product in 1970 and their movements from 1970 to 1982 varied widely among nations, as may be seen in Table 10.1. Canada and France had relatively low ratios of net debt to GDP in 1970, while West Ger-

TABLE 10.1   General Government Net Financial Assets ($+$) or Debt ($-$), 1970, 1982
(Percentage of GDP)

(1)	(2)	(3)	(4)
COUNTRY	1970	1982	CHANGE 1970–82
Canada	−11.6	−17.9	−6.3
France	−10.2	−11.0	−0.8
W. Germany	+5.8	−20.7	−26.5
Italy	−35.0	−63.4	−28.4
Japan	+6.6	−23.8	−30.4
U.K.	−66.4	−36.7	+29.4
U.S.[a]	−26.7	−25.8	+0.9

Sources: See Appendix C.

[a]Includes Federal Reserve Banks and federal credit agencies.

many and Japan actually had surplus positions. The debt ratios for Italy and, particularly, the United Kingdom were large compared to that for the United States. From 1970 to 1982 the ratio of net debt to GDP rose modestly in Canada, was relatively unchanged in France and the United States, rose substantially in West Germany, Italy, and Japan, and *fell* dramatically in the United Kingdom.

Looking then at the price or inflation effects on government financial assets and liabilities, inflation *reduced* the net *creditor* positions of West Germany and Japan for a number of years, as shown in Table 10.2. But this is akin to increasing net debt, that is, increasing the budget deficit, or reducing the surplus. The inflation effects served to reduce net debt in Canada and France and, in the later years, in West Germany and Japan, but were modest in these cases, thus contributing moderately to reducing the adjusted deficit. They were very large, however, in Italy and in the United Kingdom, reaching highs of, respectively, 12.2 and 10.3 percent of GDP, and sharply reducing adjusted deficits in those countries.

Building on series of data developed by Alex Cukierman and Jorgen Mortensen (1983) for the European Economic Community, we put together measures of the general government surplus

TABLE 10.2   Price Effects on Government Financial Assets
or Debt ($-$), 1970–82[a]
(Percentage of GDP)

(1)	(2)	(3)	(4)	(5)	(6)	(7)	(8)
YEAR	CANADA	FRANCE	W. GERMANY	ITALY	JAPAN	U.K.	U.S.
1970	0.2	0.7	−0.1	1.9	−0.6	5.0	1.2
1971	0.5	0.7	−0.2	1.8	−0.3	4.9	1.2
1972	0.5	0.7	−0.1	3.1	−0.4	4.1	1.0
1973	0.7	0.8	−0.1	5.3	−1.1	5.0	1.6
1974	0.6	1.3	0.0	10.1	−1.2	9.3	2.2
1975	0.7	1.0	0.2	5.1	−0.2	10.3	1.5
1976	0.5	1.1	0.3	10.6	0.2	6.3	1.2
1977	1.0	1.0	0.3	6.6	0.3	5.4	1.5
1978	1.0	1.1	0.3	6.6	0.4	4.1	2.0
1979	1.2	1.4	0.7	10.9	0.9	7.1	1.8
1980	1.5	1.5	0.8	12.2	1.2	5.9	2.1
1981	1.6	1.0	1.1	9.9	1.0	4.6	1.7
1982	1.7	1.0	1.0	10.2	0.4	2.0	1.1

Sources: See Appendix C.

[a]Positive figures indicate reduction in net debt. Negative figures indicate reduction in net financial assets.

or deficit as a percentage of GDP, shown in Table 10.3. They permitted us to compare the unadjusted deficit (DF1), the "cyclically adjusted," structural, or high-employment deficit (DF2), and the cyclically adjusted deficit further adjusted for price changes (DF3).[2]

Figures for 1981 offer some interesting differences. For the United States, the cyclical adjustment turns a 1.0 percent (of GDP) deficit into a 1.2 percent surplus. The inflation adjustment raises this surplus to 3.0 percent. For Canada the cyclical adjustment turns a 1.5 percent deficit into a 0.8 percent surplus and the inflation adjustment raises that surplus to 2.4 percent. For France, a nominal actual deficit of 1.9 percent is moved to a cyclically and inflation-adjusted surplus of 4.3 percent, a far cry from the presumably over-stimulatory policies of the first year of Mitterrand's Socialist government. For Germany, viewed by some as following a tight fiscal policy, a largely modest deficit is reduced, but not wiped out by the adjustments.

For Italy and the United Kingdom, widely perceived as running highly expansionary budget deficits with perplexingly coexistent high unemployment, the inflation adjustments make a very great difference. In the case of Italy, a presumably huge nominal deficit equal to 11.7 percent of GDP is converted to an adjusted *surplus* of 0.6 percent. A 2.5 percent deficit in the United Kingdom is moved no less than 8.5 percentage points to an adjusted *surplus* of 6.0 percent. By contrast, *Japan, widely envied for its economic growth, had the largest structural deficit after adjustment for inflation, 2.7 percent, in 1981, and had the largest such deficit in all of the years back to 1976 as well.*

As with the United States, we have supplemented this simplified picture of deficits and growth with a more rigorous statistical analysis. For each of the seven countries we used the series of twelve observations from 1971 to 1982 to estimate relations between percentage changes in gross domestic product and previous high-employment surplus. A critical question: Was the surplus negatively related to changes in GDP, that is, did the deficits in these countries also promote growth?

With the official or noninflation-adjusted surplus, the relations were significantly negative only for the United States and France, as shown in Table 10.4. For two of the countries, Japan and the United Kingdom, the coefficients of HES, the cyclically adjusted or high-employment surplus, have the "wrong" sign, that

TABLE 10.3 Measures of the General Government Surplus or Deficit (−), 1970–82
(Annual Percentage of GDP)

(1) COUNTRY	(2) 1970	(3) 1971	(4) 1972	(5) 1973	(6) 1974	(7) 1975	(8) 1976	(9) 1977	(10) 1978	(11) 1979	(12) 1980	(13) 1981	(14) 1982
Canada													
DF1	0.9	0.1	0.1	1.0	1.9	−2.4	−1.7	−2.6	−3.1	−1.9	−2.1	−1.5	−5.5
DF2	1.5	0.1	−0.3	−0.2	0.9	−2.4	−2.0	−2.2	−2.7	−1.3	−0.5	0.8	1.3
DF3	1.7	0.6	0.2	0.5	1.5	−1.7	−1.5	−1.3	−1.7	−0.1	1.0	2.4	3.0
France													
DF1	0.9	0.7	0.8	0.9	0.6	−2.2	−0.5	−0.8	−1.9	−0.7	0.3	−1.9	−2.6
DF2	1.7	1.2	0.8	0.7	1.0	0.1	1.9	2.1	1.1	2.4	4.4	3.3	3.5
DF3	2.4	1.9	1.5	1.5	2.3	1.1	3.0	3.1	2.2	3.8	5.9	4.3	4.5
West Germany													
DF1	0.3	−0.1	−0.5	1.2	−1.3	−5.7	−3.4	−2.4	−2.5	−2.7	−3.2	−4.0	−3.9
DF2	−0.1	−0.1	−0.4	0.9	−0.8	−2.8	−1.5	−0.6	−0.8	−1.5	−1.4	−1.5	0.0
DF3	−0.2	−0.3	−0.5	0.8	−0.8	−2.6	−1.2	−0.3	−0.5	−0.8	−0.9	−0.4	1.1
Italy													
DF1	−5.0	−7.1	−9.2	−8.5	−8.1	−11.7	−9.0	−8.0	−9.7	−9.5	−8.0	−11.7	−12.0
DF2	−5.2	−6.5	−8.4	−8.4	−8.1	−9.7	−7.7	−6.4	−7.8	−8.0	−6.9	−9.3	−8.1
DF3	−3.3	−4.7	−5.3	−3.1	2.0	−4.6	2.9	0.2	−1.2	2.9	5.3	0.6	2.1
Japan													
DF1	1.9	1.4	0.4	0.5	0.4	−2.6	−3.8	−3.8	−5.5	−4.8	−4.5	−4.0	−4.1
DF2	1.7	1.6	0.4	0.1	0.5	−2.1	−3.1	−3.4	−5.3	−4.8	−4.3	−3.7	−3.6
DF3	1.1	1.3	0.0	−1.0	−0.7	−2.3	−2.9	−3.1	−4.9	−3.9	−3.1	−2.7	−3.2
U.K.													
DF1	3.0	1.5	−1.2	−2.7	−3.8	−4.6	−4.9	−3.2	−4.2	−3.2	−3.3	−2.5	−2.0
DF2	3.0	1.7	−0.6	−3.3	−3.1	−2.6	−3.0	−1.7	−4.0	−3.1	−1.4	1.4	3.2
DF3	8.0	6.6	3.5	1.7	6.2	7.7	3.3	3.7	0.1	4.0	4.5	6.0	5.2
U.S.													
DF1	−1.0	−1.7	−0.3	0.5	−0.2	−4.2	−2.1	−0.9	0.0	0.6	−1.3	−1.0	−3.8
DF2	−0.3	−0.9	−0.3	−0.4	0.5	−1.3	0.0	0.2	0.4	0.8	0.2	1.2	2.3
DF3	1.2	0.3	0.7	1.2	2.7	0.2	1.2	1.7	2.4	2.6	2.3	3.0	3.4

Sources: See Appendix C.

DF1 = unadjusted deficit   DF2 = cyclically adjusted deficit   DF3 = price- and cyclically adjusted deficit

TABLE 10.4 Own High-Employment Budgets, Unadjusted and Price-Adjusted, Time Series

$$\Delta GDP_{jt} = b_{0j} + b_{1j}\,HES_{j,t-1} + u_{jt} \qquad j = 1, \ldots, 7$$
$$\Delta GDP_{jt} = b_{p0j} + b_{p1j}\,PAHES_{j,t-1} + u_{pjt} \qquad t = 1971, \ldots, 1982$$

(1)	(2)	(3)	(4)	(5)	(6)	(7)	(8)	(9)
				REGRESSION COEFFICIENTS AND STANDARD ERRORS				
VARIABLE	Canada	France	W. Germany	Italy	Japan	U.K.	U.S.	All, Pooled
A. Unadjusted								
Constant	3.057	4.900	2.079	−0.671	4.910	2.046	2.710	—
	(1.135)	(0.895)	(0.990)	(5.594)	(1.022)	(0.936)	(0.659)	
HES_{t-1}	−0.184	−0.965	−0.201	−0.427	−0.121	0.383	−2.829	−0.067
	(0.748)	(0.431)	(0.765)	(0.718)	(0.330)	(0.360)	(0.982)	(0.195)
$\hat{R}^2$	−.093	.267	.092	.062	.085	.012	.399	.026
Σu^2	122.55	29.72	59.72	91.75	79.64	74.89	52.13	581.62[a]
Constants for all, pooled regressions	3.138	3.351	2.201	2.106	4.559	1.420	2.688	
	(0.810)	(0.866)	(0.818)	(1.698)	(0.877)	(0.843)	(0.799)	
B. Price-Adjusted								
Constant	3.283	5.982	1.628	2.259	5.218	0.879	6.334	—
	(0.974)	(1.033)	(0.875)	(0.710)	(1.117)	(1.866)	(1.174)	
$PAHES_{t-1}$	−0.700	−0.999	−0.987	−0.519	0.290	0.137	−2.264	−0.385
	(0.179)	(0.339)	(0.882)	(0.206)	(0.422)	(0.363)	(0.630)	(0.153)
$\hat{R}^2$	.005	.412	.022	.327	−.050	−.084	.520	.100
Σu^2	112.63	23.88	53.48	58.09	77.07	82.19	41.64	537.55[b]
Constants for all, pooled regressions	3.239	4.296	2.014	2.354	3.943	3.289	3.305	
	(0.768)	(0.875)	(0.774)	(0.775)	(0.818)	(1.042)	(0.806)	

F-ratios for differences of regressions:

[a] $F(6,70) = 1.63;\ F_{.05} = 3.72$

[b] $F(6,70) = 2.30;\ F_{.05} = 3.72$

119

is, are positive. The pooled time series regression coefficient, reflecting the average effect in all of the countries, is virtually zero.

When the price-adjusted, high-employment surplus ratio (*PAHES*) is used as a regressor, Italy joins the countries with a significant negative coefficient. Japan and the United Kingdom continue to show a small positive coefficient not differing significantly from zero. The pooled time series coefficient of *PAHES*, again reflecting the average effect in all countries, is small in absolute size but is significantly negative, with a value of -0.385. With the United States eliminated, that average coefficient (as shown in Table 10.8) is -0.318, which, with a standard error of 0.155, is still significantly negative, but barely so, at a .05 probability level. It would appear that there is some confirmation in the other countries of the relations found in the United States, but it is slight.

But what about effects of the *United States* budget deficit on the economies of the *other nations*? In search of at least a partial answer, we regressed real changes in gross domestic product in each country on previous changes in the high-employment surplus of the United States. A sharp negative relation is found in Table 10.5 for all of the other countries for both the unadjusted and the price-adjusted high-employment *United States* surpluses.

The closeness of fit of the relation or coefficient of determination—the value of $\hat{R}^2$—was distinctly greater for the price-adjusted than the unadjusted equations in all of the countries except Canada. There the coefficients of determination were both high (over .6) and about the same in the two equations. Pooling the time series for all countries except the United States yielded a regression coefficient of -2.186 with a standard error of 0.397, for the unadjusted surplus, and -1.798 with a standard error of only 0.260, for the price-adjusted surplus. The U.S. high-employment surplus thus showed a marked negative effect on the rates of growth of real domestic product in each of the other countries. But the relation was stronger and sharper with the price-adjusted high-employment surplus. The coefficient of determination there was .448, as against .348 in the regression involving the unadjusted surplus.

The dominance of the U.S. high-employment surplus or deficit is confirmed in regressions involving both the U.S. variable and each country's own high-employment surplus. As shown in Table 10.6, the pooled time series yields estimated parameters of

TABLE 10.5 U.S. High-Employment Budgets, Unadjusted and Price-Adjusted Time Series

$$\Delta GDP_{jt} = b_{0j} + b_{1j} USHES_{t-1} + u_{jt} \qquad j = 1, \ldots, 7$$
$$\Delta GDP_{jt} = b_{p0j} + b_{pij} USPAHES_{t-1} + u_{pjt} \qquad t = 1971, \ldots, 1982$$

(1)	(2)	(3)	(4)	(5)	(6)	(7)	(8)	(9)	(10)
VARIABLE	Canada	France	W. Germany	Italy	Japan	U.K.	U.S.	All, Pooled	All Except U.S., Pooled
				REGRESSION COEFFICIENTS AND STANDARD ERRORS					
A. Unadjusted									
Constant	3.216 (0.587)	3.253 (0.416)	2.280 (0.529)	2.636 (0.763)	4.693 (0.779)	1.525 (0.766)	2.710 (0.659)	—	—
$USHES_{t-1}$	−3.894 (0.874)	−2.100 (0.620)	−2.220 (0.787)	−2.153 (1.137)	−1.203 (1.161)	−1.547 (1.141)	−2.829 (0.982)	−2.278 (0.366)	−2.186 (0.397)
$\hat{R}^2$	.632	.488	.387	.190	.007	.071	.399	.354	.348
Σu^2	41.29	20.77	33.52	69.92	72.88	70.42	52.13	386.08[a]	332.10[b]
Constants for pooled regressions	3.203 (0.651)	3.255 (0.651)	2.281 (0.651)	2.639 (0.651)	4.702 (0.651)	1.531 (0.651)	2.706 (0.651)		
B. Price-Adjusted									
Constant	7.675 (1.176)	6.099 (0.617)	5.100 (0.955)	5.417 (1.448)	6.661 (1.465)	4.048 (1.378)	6.634 (1.174)	—	—
$USPAHES_{t-1}$	−2.788 (0.631)	−1.777 (0.331)	−1.762 (0.513)	−1.737 (0.777)	−1.228 (0.787)	−1.575 (0.740)	−2.264 (0.630)	−1.861 (0.240)	−1.798 (0.260)
$\hat{R}^2$	.627	.717	.496	.267	.115	.243	.520	.456	.448
Σu^2	41.78	11.50	27.59	63.35	64.91	57.37	41.64	324.85[c]	281.07[d]
Constants for pooled regressions	6.166 (0.710)	6.218 (0.710)	5.244 (0.710)	5.602 (0.710)	7.665 (0.710)	4.495 (0.710)	5.667 (0.710)		

F-ratios for differences of regressions:

[a] $F_{(6,70)} = 0.81$ [c] $F_{(6,70)} = 0.63$

[b] $F_{(5,60)} = 0.91$ [d] $F_{(5,60)} = 0.66$

TABLE 10.6 U.S. and Own High-Employment Budgets, Unadjusted and Price-Adjusted, Time Series

$$\Delta GDP_{jt} = b_{0j} + b_{1j} HES_{jt-1} + b_{2j} USHES_{t-1} + u_{jt} \qquad j = 1,\ldots,7$$
$$\Delta GDP_{jt} = b_{p0j} + b_{p1j} PAHES_{jt-1} + b_{p2j} USPAHES_{t-1} + u_{pjt} \qquad t = 1971,\ldots,1982$$

	(2)	(3)	(4)	(5)	(6)	(7)	(8)	(9)	(10)
(1)								All, Pooled	All Except U.S., Pooled
VARIABLES	Canada	France	W. Germany	Italy	Japan	U.K.	U.S.		
	REGRESSION COEFFICIENTS AND STANDARD ERRORS								
A. Unadjusted									
Constant	3.284 (0.695)	3.844 (0.908)	1.984 (0.770)	-1.343 (4.983)	4.540 (1.101)	1.989 (0.913)	2.710 (0.659)	—	—
HES_{t-1}	0.098 (0.461)	-0.345 (0.467)	-0.325 (0.596)	-0.517 (0.639)	-0.083 (0.398)	0.335 (0.353)	-2.829 (0.982)	-0.083 (0.159)	-0.068 (0.163)
$USHES_{t-1}$	-3.922 (0.928)	-1.737 (0.803)	-2.254 (0.819)	-2.222 (1.160)	-1.370 (1.459)	-1.425 (1.154)	—	-2.281 (0.368)	-2.200 (0.401)
$\hat{R}^2$	.593	.464	.341	.161	-.098	.061	.399	.348	.340
Σu^2	41.09	19.58	32.45	65.19	72.53	64.06	32.13	384.67[a]	331.21[b]
Constants for pooled regressions	3.146 (0.663)	3.399 (0.709)	2.205 (0.670)	1.997 (1.390)	4.547 (0.718)	1.416 (0.690)	2.707 (0.654)		
B. Price-Adjusted									
Constant	7.568 (1.232)	6.472 (0.735)	4.555 (1.109)	3.577 (2.170)	6.638 (1.530)	4.372 (2.407)	6.334 (1.174)	—	—
$PAHES_{t-1}$	-0.154 (0.473)	-0.297 (0.313)	-0.630 (0.645)	-0.363 (0.322)	-0.120 (0.514)	-0.056 (0.334)	-2.264 (0.630)	-0.173 (0.128)	-0.179 (0.122)
$USPAHES_{t-1}$	-2.722 (0.678)	-1.502 (0.442)	-1.675 (0.522)	-0.751 (1.164)	-1.358 (1.035)	-1.615 (0.814)	—	-1.806 (0.241)	-1.732 (0.262)
$\hat{R}^2$	.600	.714	.493	.286	.020	.162	.520	.466	.458
Σu^2	40.34	10.46	24.94	55.52	64.73	57.19	41.64	315.00[c]	272.03[d]
Constants for pooled regressions	6.056 (0.707)	6.591 (0.745)	4.989 (0.723)	5.338 (0.724)	7.188 (0.770)	5.212 (0.845)	5.830 (0.711)		

F-ratios for differences of regressions:

[a] $F(12,63) = 0.92$ [c] $F(12,63) = 0.66$

[b] $F(10,54) = 0.36$ [d] $F(10,54) = 0.40$

own *HES* close to zero for the unadjusted variable and a small negative value (-0.179) not statistically significant, in the case of the price-adjusted surplus, *PAHES*. The U.S. high-employment surplus has a highly significant negative parameter, in the neighborhood of -2, for both the unadjusted and price-adjusted variable. This means that each percentage point of U.S. high-employment *deficit* was associated, on the average, with two percentage points greater growth in gross domestic product in the other major OECD countries. The pooled or average regression for these other countries showed a higher coefficient of determination, though, in the relation involving the price-adjusted deficit, .458 as against .340 when there was no inflation adjustment.

The time series relations capture the extent to which growth in gross domestic product was higher *in each country* after years when deficits were larger than after years when they were smaller. They do not tell us whether countries with bigger deficits had greater growth in GDP. The cross section relations shown in Table 10.7 can answer that question. In fact, they reveal the extent to which the failure to adjust for differing rates of inflation obscures the differences associated with different national fiscal policies.

Thus, the estimated parameter of the *unadjusted,* own-country, high-employment surplus is virtually zero. This suggests that differences between countries in their deficits or surpluses had nothing to do with differences in their rates of growth. The cross section regression involving the price-adjusted high-employment surplus, *PAHES*, however, yielded a significantly negative coefficient, although one small in absolute amount. The overall regression, involving both cross section and time series variance and covariance, that is, differences between countries and differences over time in growth and deficits, showed a coefficient of -0.293. With a standard error of 0.105, this was clearly a *significantly* negative figure.

Adding the U.S. high-employment budget to the non-U.S. overall regressions greatly improved the fit, producing an adjusted coefficient of determination of .416. It also indicated the "robustness," that is, relative consistency with different approaches, of the estimate of the parameter of the own-country, price-adjusted, high-employment surplus. That estimate was now -0.231, some 2.7 times the standard error and thus again, in a statistical sense, significantly negative.

By way of summary, as shown in Table 10.8, year-to-year

TABLE 10.7 Own and U.S. High-Employment Budgets, Unadjusted and Price-Adjusted, Pooled Cross Sections and Overall Regressions

Unadjusted: $\Delta GDP_{jt} = b_{0t} + b_1 HES_{j,t-1} + b_2 USHES_{t-1} + u_{jt}$ $j = 1, \ldots, 6$

Adjusted: $\Delta GDP_{jt} = b_{p0t} + b_{p1} PAHES_{j,t-1} + b_{p2} USPAHES_{t-1} + u_{pjt}$ $t = 1971, \ldots, 1982$

REGRESSION COEFFICIENTS AND STANDARD ERRORS

| | Unadjusted | | | | Adjusted | | | |
| | CROSS SECTION | | OVERALL | | CROSS SECTION | | OVERALL | |
VARIABLE	(1)	(2)	(3)	(4)	(5)	(6)	(7)	(8)
Constant	—	2.972 (0.378)	2.834 (0.282)	2.956 (0.324)	—	3.127 (0.324)	5.797 (0.521)	5.827 (0.498)
$HES \atop PAHES \}_{t-1}$	0.017 (0.074)	0.031 (0.100)	—	0.012 (0.086)	−0.179 (0.078)	−0.293 (0.105)	—	−0.231 (0.084)
$USHES \atop USPAHES \}_{t-1}$	—	—	−2.186 (0.420)	−2.183 (0.424)	—	—	−1.798 (0.280)	−1.713 (0.270)
$\hat{R}^2$		−.013	.268	.258		.088	.361	.416
Σu^2	232.38	555.83	401.50	401.39	213.74	500.59	350.47	316.03
n	72	72	72	72	72	72	72	72

124

TABLE 10.8 Own and U.S. High-Employment Budgets, Unadjusted and Price-Adjusted, Pooled Time Series Excluding U.S.

$$\Delta GDP_{jt} = b_{0j} + b_1\,HES_{j,t-1} + b_2\,USHES_{t-1} + u_{jt} \qquad j = 1, \ldots, 6$$
$$\Delta GDP_{jt} = b_{p0j} + b_{p1}\,PAHES_{j,t-1} + b_{p2}\,USPAHES_{t-1} + u_{jpt} \qquad t = 1971, \ldots, 1982$$

	(1)	(2)	(3)	(4)	(5)	(6)	(7)
		REGRESSION COEFFICIENTS AND STANDARD ERRORS					
VARIABLE		*Unadjusted Budget (HES)*			*Adjusted Budget (PAHES)*		
b_{01}, Canada		3.191 (0.802)	3.202 (0.653)	3.156 (0.666)	3.229 (0.766)	6.065 (0.731)	5.985 (0.727)
b_{02}, France		3.220 (0.859)	3.254 (0.653)	3.371 (0.714)	4.110 (0.876)	6.117 (0.731)	6.503 (0.772)
b_{03}, W. Germany		2.270 (0.810)	2.180 (0.653)	2.218 (0.673)	2.058 (0.722)	5.143 (0.731)	4.922 (0.740)
b_{04}, Italy		2.691 (1.699)	2.638 (0.653)	2.117 (1.415)	2.400 (0.773)	5.509 (0.731)	5.272 (0.742)
b_{05}, Japan		4.701 (0.870)	4.702 (0.653)	4.575 (0.724)	4.097 (0.818)	7.564 (0.731)	7.129 (0.784)
b_{06}, U.K.		1.525 (0.836)	1.531 (0.653)	1.437 (0.695)	2.978 (1.048)	4.393 (0.731)	5.111 (0.876)
$b_1, \left\{\begin{matrix} HES \\ PAHES \end{matrix}\right\}_{t-1}$		0.009 (0.195)	—	−0.068 (0.163)	−0.318 (0.155)	—	−0.179 (0.122)
$b_2, \left\{\begin{matrix} USHES \\ USPAHES \end{matrix}\right\}_{t-1}$		—	−2.186 (0.397)	−2.200 (0.397)	—	−1.798 (0.260)	−1.732 (0.262)
$\hat{R}^2$		.044	.348	.340	.102	.448	.458
Σu^2		487.17	332.10	331.21	457.67	281.07	272.03
n		72	72	72	72	72	72

variation in their own *unadjusted* high-employment surplus had virtually nothing to do on the average with the year-to-year variation in rates of growth of real GDP in countries other than the United States. Their *price-adjusted* surpluses did show a slight negative relation with subsequent changes in real GDP, which is to say, of course, that price-adjusted deficits had a slight positive relation with growth in GDP.

The U.S. high-employment surplus, both adjusted for inflation and unadjusted, showed a strong negative relation with subsequent changes in real GDP in the other countries. The parameter of −1.798 for the U.S. price-adjusted high-employment surplus in the pooled time series regression means that each percentage point of U.S. deficit, measured as a ratio of GNP, was associated on the average with 1.8 percentage points more of the other nations' GDP growth. That figure of -1.798 for the other countries was in fact not markedly less in absolute value than the -2.264 for the United States (shown in Table 10.5). Our own budget deficits seem to have stimulated growth in output abroad almost as much as at home.

The extension of our analysis to Canada, France, West Germany, Italy, Japan, and the United Kingdom has thus offered some confirmation of the relation between inflation-adjusted budget deficits and subsequent economic growth. For countries outside the United States, their own cyclically adjusted budget deficits, when further adjusted for inflation, showed a positive, but very small relation with the next year's change in real gross domestic product. And where a country's price-adjusted and cyclically adjusted deficit was greater than that of other countries—or its surplus less—its growth in real GDP tended to be greater.

What then of the assertion that the experience of OECD nations argues for rejection of the notion that expansionary fiscal policy, as measured by budget deficits, fosters economic growth? Is it true that countries such as West Germany, with rapid growth, had tight fiscal policies while countries such as Italy, and particularly the United Kingdom, which did not fare nearly as well, had very large budget deficits?

The answers are that inflation adjustments turn that picture around. For cyclically adjusted budgets corrected for inflation were not in deficit but close to balance in Italy, and in substantial surplus in the United Kingdom, as may be confirmed in Table 10.9. West Germany's high-employment budget was close to bal-

TABLE 10.9   Unadjusted and Price-Adjusted High-Employment Budgets and Real Rates of Growth of GNP, Means and Standard Deviations by Country and Year, 1971–82

(1)	(2)	(3)	(4)
		MEANS AND STANDARD DEVIATIONS	
		High-Employment Surplus or Deficit $(-)$ as % of GDP, Lagged One Year	
COUNTRY OR YEAR	*GDP % Change*	UNADJUSTED	PRICE-ADJUSTED
A. *Country*			
Canada	3.184	-0.692	0.142
	(3.348)	(1.412)	(1.409)
France	2.236	1.725	2.750
	(2.014)	(1.206)	(1.375)

TABLE 10.9 *(continued)*

(1)	(2)	(3)	(4)
		MEANS AND STANDARD DEVIATIONS	
		High-Employment Surplus or Deficit (−) as % of GDP, Lagged One Year	
COUNTRY OR YEAR	GDP % Change	UNADJUSTED	PRICE-ADJUSTED
W. Germany	2.262 (2.338)	− 0.908 (0.963)	− 0.642 (0.790)
Italy	2.620 (2.938)	− 7.700 (1.273)	− 0.692 (3.527)
Japan	4.683 (2.709)	− 1.867 (2.575)	− 1.844 (1.982)
U.K.	1.512 (2.755)	− 1.392 (2.291)	4.608 (2.382)
U.S.	2.688 (2.944)	0.008 (0.701)	1.602 (0.983)
All	2.884 (2.804)	− 1.546 (3.160)	0.846 (2.842)
B. *Year*			
1971	3.974 (1.765)	0.329 (2.690)	1.509 (3.406)
1972	5.132 (2.284)	− 0.414 (2.851)	0.811 (3.338)
1973	6.661 (1.489)	− 1.257 (3.188)	0.026 (2.690)
1974	2.211 (2.369)	− 1.514 (3.339)	0.233 (1.714)
1975	− 0.457 (1.978)	− 1.300 (2.325)	1.890 (2.356)
1976	5.209 (0.739)	− 2.791 (3.129)	− 0.307 (3.996)
1977	3.134 (1.663)	− 2.200 (2.997)	0.687 (2.539
1978	3.919 (0.863)	− 1.714 (2.723)	0.579 (2.430)
1979	3.546 (1.250)	− 2.729 (3.218)	0.513 (2.499)
1980	1.407 (2.321)	− 2.214 (3.480)	1.219 (2.929)
1981	1.104 (2.148)	− 1.457 (3.553)	2.149 (3.348)
1982	− 0.239 (2.660)	− 1.114 (4.256)	1.876 (2.954)
All	2.884 (2.804)	− 1.546 (3.160)	0.846 (2.842)

ance. Japan, the country with the highest average growth rate, had the largest relative deficit.

But the most striking note is that the U.S. high-employment deficit, far from retarding growth in the other countries, was strongly associated with growth in their real GDP. And the role of U.S. fiscal policy in accounting for foreign rates of growth of gross domestic product emerges most sharply when the U.S. budget deficit is adjusted for inflation.

This empirical analysis, it must be noted, is still preliminary. Changes in the market value of debt due to interest rate variation have not yet been incorporated. The study may usefully be extended backward (and eventually forward) in time. We also have yet to include direct roles for money and interest rates. And for these other nations, as for the United States, we have still to go beyond single equations to full model specification and estimation.

But the bottom line so far is that the hand wringing in foreign capitals and at home is out of place. Neither U.S. budget deficits, nor their own properly measured, have been injuring OECD economies. And, as we anticipated earlier from their effects on American imports, the U.S. budget deficits have proved a marked stimulus to the economies of Canada, Western Europe, and Japan.

It has been said that when the United States sneezes the rest of the world catches a cold. American budgetary red ink would seem to be going a long way to putting the rest of the world in the black.

11

The Deficit,
the Cost of Capital,
and Wall Street

THE APPROPRIATE ANSWER of an academic economist asked to explain, let alone predict, stock prices is, "Consult the Psychology Department." That may be taken as an acknowledgement of our bewilderment. It does call attention to the uncertain human forces that seem to drive day-to-day and longer-term movements in financial markets in the United States and the world.

As Keynes aptly put it half a century ago:

> Professional investment may be likened to those newspaper competitions in which the competitors have to pick out the six prettiest faces from a hundred photographs, the prize being awarded to the competitor whose choice most nearly corresponds to the average preferences of the competitors as a whole; so that each competitor has to pick, not those faces which he himself finds prettiest, but those which he thinks likeliest to catch the fancy of the other competitors, all of whom are looking at the problem from the same point of view. It is not a case of choosing those which, to the best of one's judgment, are really the prettiest, nor even those which average opinion genuinely thinks the prettiest. We have reached the third degree where we devote our intelligences to anticipating what average opinion expects the average opinion to be. And there are some, I believe, who practise the fourth, fifth and higher degrees. (*The General Theory*, p. 156)

Current theory of financial markets, applying principles of rational expectations, argues that investors cannot "beat the market" with generally available information. If you try to react to news of the President's surgery, an outbreak of hostilities in the Middle East, or the latest pronouncements before a Congressional committee by the Chairman of the Federal Reserve Board or John Kenneth Galbraith, your actions will be too late to do you any good. If the "news" is thought likely to raise stock averages, for example, participants in market activity will react immediately by raising both bid and asked prices. An individual investor can only gain by getting the news *before* it reaches others.

All of this indicates that investors cannot beat the market if they have access only to information that other market participants have as well, and if all interpret the information in a similar fashion. *But what if the market is misinterpreting the information and bidding prices up or down on the basis of that misinterpretation?* The beauty contest described by Keynes suggests that for quite a while this may not matter. If almost everybody thinks that something is going to drive the market down, then everybody will think that everybody thinks the market will be driven down, and down indeed it will be driven.

Can the lower levels be maintained indefinitely? If the underlying information has been misinterpreted, will not underlying conditions, of profits and interest rates, for example, lead investors to a reappraisal which will bring stock prices back to their old "real" values? There is increasing evidence that, if investors as a whole are slow to see this, shrewd and bold individuals and groups will move in. By takeover bids, and threats of takeover bids, company by company, they bring about major changes in market values.

Modern investing is, of course, very largely a matter of timing. There is little point to buying a stock or stocks now because they will "inevitably" go up in three years. Big money is to be made by waiting two years or, if you can be that precise, two years and 364 days. But for those of us who cannot turn to a superhuman psychologist to learn exactly when "the market" will finally react to the "true" economic forces, there may yet be some gain to understanding those forces correctly. We can still come out substantially ahead by investing in two years. There may then be some advantage in understanding what impact budget deficits should ultimately have on financial markets.

The conventional wisdom is that deficits are bad for stock prices. When news breaks in Washington suggesting that deficits may after all be reduced, the stock market is expected to rise. Given the attitude of investors described by Keynes, it then generally does rise—only to fall again when the expectation of reduced deficits proves premature or unfounded.

To students of financial markets, it seems clear why deficits should tend to depress stock prices. Deficits generally imply Treasury borrowing. The supply of additional Treasury securities will tend to lower their prices, which means higher interest rates. The lure of high interest rates on Treasury securities will draw investors from competitive instruments such as corporate bonds, thus lowering prices and raising interest rates on these securities as well. But now investors in equity find the alternative yields on bonds higher and will be unwilling to invest in or hold stocks unless their prices are sufficiently lower for the expected yield on stocks to be again in line with the yields that can be gotten on bonds.

We have traced all this sequentially but, again given rational expectations, investors will act or try to act all at once. When they perceive the Treasury running a deficit, they know it must have to borrow and, understanding the chain of causation just described, will promptly bid down bond and stock prices generally. And of course, by this reasoning, the bigger the deficit the more will interest rates rise and bond and stock prices be lowered.

There are some important qualifications to this scenario. First, a deficit need not imply borrowing from the public. It can be financed by "printing money," or by the current more sophisticated procedure which amounts to that, selling Treasury bills or bonds to the Federal Reserve. In fact, the Federal Reserve does not buy newly issued Treasury securities. It can and does accomplish the same thing by buying existing Treasury bills.

We might try a brief explanation for those not up on the arcane process of money creation. First, we generally count as money the public's holdings of currency and its deposits in banks (or certain other "depository institutions"). Thus, purchases of Treasury securities by the Fed create money when sellers deposit their Federal Reserve checks in their banks. They indeed provide "high-powered money," as the banks take these checks and deposit them in *their* bank, the Federal Reserve Bank. These additional balances—or reserves—of the private banks then set off a further expansion of the "money supply," as banks with "excess" reserves make loans, and the proceeds of those loans are deposited. This goes on until the growth of deposits subject to reserve requirements raises required reserves—currently 12 percent of deposits considered "transactions balances"—to the new, higher level of actual reserves brought about by the Fed's purchase of securities.

But now, suppose the Fed buys securities in an amount equal to the deficit. The Fed's purchases match the Treasury's supply and hence prevent the Treasury borrowing from raising interest rates and depressing bond prices. The efforts of the private banks to make new loans out of their additional reserves, however, may be expected to *lower* interest rates and bid up bonds—and stock as well, in the wash.

If the Fed merely wanted to keep interest rates from rising in the face of a deficit, it need only buy Treasury securities equal to a fraction of the deficit. It could then rely upon the increased supply of money from the additional bank loans to generate public demand for that portion of additional Treasury securities outstanding which are not purchased by the Fed. Indeed, the banks might even use at least some of their excess reserves to buy Treasury securities themselves.

It would therefore seem that conventional deficits need not raise interest rates and lower bond and stock prices. It would also seem that federal budget deficits need not drain funds that would otherwise finance private borrowing and private investment. It would all depend upon monetary policy. If the Fed were willing to "monetize" at least part of the additional debt created by a deficit, the supply of funds to buy securities, or the supply of loanable funds, might be increased by as much as the Treasury deficit increases the demand.

To this line of reasoning, monetarists would have an answer. They would insist that increasing the money supply must raise prices. Understanding this, investors observing Federal Reserve monetization of even part of the deficit will expect prices to rise. The generation of an expectation of inflation, if this policy is seen continuing, will raise nominal interest rates. This implies a fall in bond prices and, again, a corresponding fall in the price of equity securities.

While this argument is widely advanced and accepted, there would appear to be a flaw in the logic. For if prices are expected to be rising, should that not affect the expected earnings of corporations? They will have purchased their capital and indeed have incurred their debt in the past when prices were lower. If prices rise, their revenues should rise without fully corresponding increases in costs.

As inflation continues, costs will of course rise. But since the capital invested now will be used to produce goods and services to be sold later, rising prices imply an increased spread between selling prices and costs, which should correspond to the higher rate of interest brought on by inflation.

All this should be translated into higher current and expected future corporate earnings sufficient to prevent stock prices from falling in response to higher rates of interest brought on by inflation. The notion that inflation brought on by increases in the money supply should lower stock prices has therefore bewildered thoughtful economists. This bewilderment indeed extends as well with regard to inflation brought on, in the more general Keynesian view, by any increases in aggregate demand, whether caused by increases in the money supply or other factors.

There is still another qualification to offer. We have earlier pointed out that the view that increases in aggregate demand must cause corresponding increases in prices rests on the implicit if not explicit assumption of full utilization of capacity or full employment. Otherwise increases in aggregate demand will generate increased output which may or may not be sold at higher prices.

The increased output must in turn imply higher real income and more saving. Thus, absent full employment, the increase in the money supply, brought about by Federal Reserve monetization of part of the deficit, will itself generate higher saving. This will come about as lower interest rates stimulate investment demand and raise real output and income. The greater supply of private saving may thus compensate or more than compensate for the public dissaving constituted by the federal budget deficit.

What is more, if the economy is not at full capacity or full employment, the stimulatory effects on GNP of the budget deficit, whether or not monetized by the Federal Reserve, must generate higher earnings and expected earnings for American business. The expectation of higher earnings should in turn raise stock prices.

We have thus come full circle. Budget deficits, when there is room for expansion in the economy, should cause the stock market to rise, not fall. Does this mean that Wall Street worries about budget deficits are entirely ill-founded?

Not entirely. The budget deficits themselves are not all that must be considered. One must also take into account Federal Reserve reactions to the deficits. If, correctly or not, the Federal Reserve response to larger deficits is a *tightening* of monetary policy out of real or imagined fear of inflation, results can be quite different. The tighter money supply will raise nominal interest rates, and will raise real interest rates as well by holding down expectations of future inflation. The higher nominal rates in themselves mean lower bond prices and, without fully compensating expectations of inflation, stock prices will fall. If the rise in real interest rates is so severe that its effects outweigh the stimulation of the budget deficit itself, real output will be lower than it would otherwise have been. This would cause stock prices to decline all the more.

All that we have indicated thus far relates to deficits that are really deficits. In line with our dominant theme, what happens if the reported deficits are mismeasured and are not really deficits?

First, suppose the deficit—in this case in the unified budget but not the federal sector of the National Income Accounts—results from lending by the government or federal credit agencies. These expenditures to buy loans or other debt obligations of the private sector may have to be financed by Treasury borrowing from the public. The Treasury borrowing does compete with private borrowing and that in itself might be expected to raise interest rates and lower bond and stock prices.

But by the same token, the loans to the public by the government or federal credit agencies satisfy a demand for funds which would otherwise be competing with the remaining demand for funds. Thus, while Treasury borrowing from the private sector will be greater as a consequence of this deficit, the deficit itself is financing private borrowing of an equal amount.

If, again, there is less than full employment, this deficit may stimulate the economy to the extent that the federally supported loans finance private spending which would not otherwise take place. With full employment, however, such deficit-financed loans cannot increase aggregate output. They can only generate inflation which, if unaccommodated by the money supply, will raise interest rates. The consequences for stock prices then depend, as in the earlier excess demand case, on reactions of the Federal Reserve. If monetary policy tightens, real interest rates will rise and stock prices should, in principle, be depressed. If the Federal Reserve is accommodative, there need be no adverse effects on the real value of market equity.

But now, finally, what are the tricks played by inflation? Suppose we have a nominal budget deficit, but that that deficit is offset by declines in the real value of net debt due to inflation and increases in interest rates. Suppose, that is, the *adjusted* budget is in balance.

Focus on the demand for loanable funds side of financial markets seems to indicate our much touted adjustments should not matter. If the Treasury has to borrow to finance a deficit, why should it matter whether the deficit is real or nominal? The federal borrowing will compete with other borrowing, raise interest rates and the cost of capital, and crowd out private investment. Or so it would seem.

But to argue thus is to be guilty of that cardinal sin of money illusion on the supply side of the loanable funds market. To see why, assume first that portfolio managers, whether business or individual, decide on the *real* value of Treasury securities that they wish to hold. If inflation and/or higher interest rates lower the real value of these securities, these managers will then have to increase their holdings to keep the real values intact. Thus, to the extent that the deficit is merely a nominal deficit, with no change in the real federal net debt, private investors may be expected, in an effort to maintain the real value of their security holdings, to raise their supply of funds to the level necessary to finance the deficit.

Let us assume further, as is reasonable, that the loss in real value of private holdings of net federal debt is equal to the loss in current wealth perceived by the private sector as a consequence of this inflation tax. As private savers and investors, alert to the mischief of money illusion, recognize this continuing taxation of their wealth, they strive to restore their preferred wealth position by additional saving out of disposable income. This is facilitated by the increase in measured nominal income because of the higher nominal interest receipts associated with inflation. Thus, while the nominal budget deficit turns up as public dissaving in our National Income and Product Accounts, it will be compensated for by increased private saving out of the larger nominal private disposable income. Private saving, as measured, is called forth to balance the public dissaving, as measured.

Another way to look at this is that, if private savers and investors are not guilty of money illusion, they count as part of their disposable income not nominal interest receipts but real interest receipts. Real interest receipts are nominal interest receipts minus the loss in real value of existing fixed-interest securities. With inflation which has become anticipated, nominal interest payments by the Treasury rise, creating, other things being equal, a nominal budget deficit. If nominal interest rates have risen no more than has the expected rate of inflation, however, there is no increase in real interest payments.

Thus, holders of the federal debt have no increase in real income. They therefore have no economic reason to increase their real consumption. This means there is no decrease in real private saving. But since the adjusted or real budget deficit is zero, there is also no public dissaving. Hence the nominal budget deficit which is not an adjusted real deficit has brought about no reduction in the private saving to finance private investment. These real economic measures thus lead us to the same conclusion as did a complete look at the nominal measures, where the apparent public dissaving was in fact matched by increased private saving out of disposable income.

What does this imply for the cost of capital? Will businesses trying to finance capital spending or households wanting mortgage loans for new homes be strapped? Will interest rates rise or funds prove unavailable?

The answer is, "Not to worry!" A nominal deficit that is not a real deficit does not increase the real supply of government debt competing for investment. Higher nominal interest payments will be invested in additional government securities so that holders can maintain the real value of their holdings. But then, what the Treasury taketh away from investable funds will be what it has just given.

True, nominal interest rates will rise with inflation, but real interest rates will not. The real cost of capital will be no higher. Indeed, given the full tax deductibility of nominal interest payments, it may be less. Borrowers should act accordingly.

To the extent then that official reported budget deficits are reduced by inflation corrections, they should not be expected to crowd out private investment, create an increased net demand for loanable funds, raise real interest rates, or depress the stock market. To the extent that deficits stimulate the economy and are associated with expectations of economic upturn, they should raise the stock market.

What does in fact happen?

In search of an answer, we have once more turned to statistical analysis, relating annual percentage changes in the Dow Jones Industrials to current and one-year lagged changes in federal budget surpluses (or deficits). The latter are again expressed as percentages of gross national product.

In line with rational expectations, we presume that stock values reflect whatever effects of budget surpluses (or deficits) market participants perceive. It is hence essentially changes in the budget which will bring about movements in the market.

This is why we have related changes in the Dow Jones average to changes in the budget, rather than the budget surplus itself. The question then is: Will changes in federal budget surpluses (or deficits) as a percentage of gross national product be positively or negatively associated with current and future changes in the Dow Jones industrial average?

We have analyzed the data from 1956 through 1984 and the history is remarkably clear; Figure 11.1 tells a dramatic story. The bigger the increase in the price-adjusted deficit, the more the Dow Jones average grew (or the less it fell)!

Precise measures of the relation may be seen first in Table 11.1. Looking at the regression coefficients of equation (11.1), we note that a constant federal budget deficit on national income account—the official, unadjusted budget—would be associated with a 1.8 percent annual increase in the Dow Jones. For each percentage point of GNP that this actual deficit increased, there would be a further increase in the Dow Jones of 6.45 percent in the current year and another 5.58 percent in the following year. While the precise numbers should hardly be taken too seriously, the coefficients of the budget variables are significantly positive. Increases in the deficit were clearly associated with favorable movements in the stock averages.

Similar regression results are presented in equation (11.2) for the price-adjusted national income account surplus. The price-adjusted surplus moved relatively less, but its impact was even sharper and clearer than that of the unadjusted surplus. Each percentage point increase in the price-adjusted deficit (as a percentage of GNP) was associated with a 5.71 percent increase in

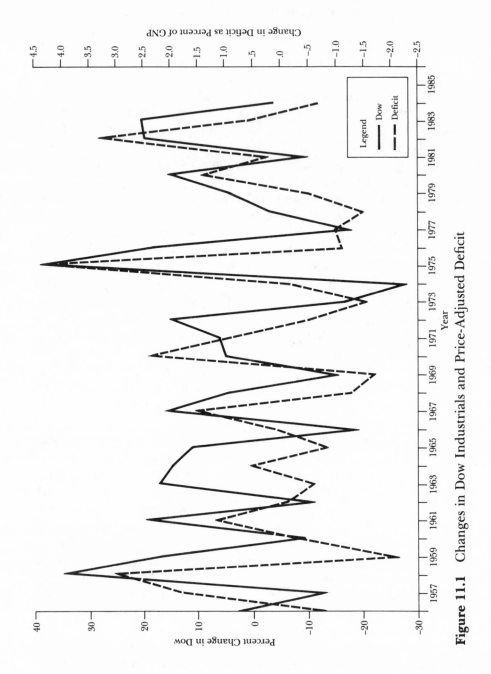

Figure 11.1 Changes in Dow Industrials and Price-Adjusted Deficit

TABLE 11.1   Deficits and the Dow Jones

$DOWCH_t = b_0 + b_1 SURCH_t + b_2 SURCH_{t-1}$ $t = 1957, \ldots, 1984$

(1)	(2)	(3)	(4)	(5)	(6)	(7)
	MEASURE OF SURPLUS	REGRESSION COEFFICIENTS[a]				
EQUATION	(OR DEFICIT)	*Constant* (b_0)	$SURCH_t$ (b_1)	$SURCH_{t-1}$ (b_2)	$\hat{R}^2$	D–W
(11.1)	OFNIS	1.806 (2.510)	−6.451 (1.753)	−5.580 (1.758)	.407	2.26
(11.2)	PANIS	1.805 (2.365)	−5.712 (1.463)	−5.221 (1.461)	.470	2.26
(11.3)	PIANIS	2.592 (2.620)	−2.238 (1.256)	−4.900 (1.251)	.345	2 54
(11.4)	OFHES	2.578 (2.886)	−9.026 (3.188)	−5.070 (3.183)	.210	2 23
(11.5)	PAHES	2.083 (2.572)	−9.030 (2.465)	−6.289 (2.421)	.372	2.27
(11.6)	PIAHES	2.964 (2.800)	−3.091 (1.855)	−6.251 (1.875)	.252	2.60
(11.7)[b]	PANISM	1.806 (2.322)	−10.933[b] (2.112)	—	.489	2.30

[a]Ordinary least squares; standard errors are shown in parentheses.

[b]$DOWCH_t = b_0 + b_1 [0.5(SURCH_t + SURCH_{t-1})]$

$DOWCH$ = percent change in Dow Jones Industrials
$SURCH$ = change in surplus as percent of GNP
$OFNIS$ = official National Income Account (NIA) surplus (actual) as percent of GNP
$PANIS$ = NIA surplus as percent of GNP adjusted for price effects
$PIANIS$ = NIA surplus as percent of GNP adjusted for price and interest effects
$OFHES$ = official high-employment surplus as percent of GNP
$PAHES$ = price-adjusted high-employment surplus as percent of GNP
$PIAHES$ = price- and interest-adjusted high-employment surplus as percent of GNP
$PANISM$ = mean of current and previous changes in price-adjusted NIA surplus as percent of GNP

the Dow Jones in the current year and a 5.22 percent increase in the following year. Both of these numbers (regression coefficients) were close to four times their standard errors and were statistically highly significant. The adjusted value of *R*-square, the coefficient of determination, was a substantial .470. And each one percentage point in the *two-year mean* increase in the price-adjusted deficit was associated with a 10.9 percent increase in the Dow, as shown in equation (11.7) and strikingly illustrated in Figure 11.2.

Relations involving the high-employment surpluses, both official, shown in equation (11.4), and price-adjusted, shown in equation (11.5) and illustrated in Figure 11.3, were similar in direction but coefficients of determination were considerably lower. We may conjecture that the economists' high-employment surplus

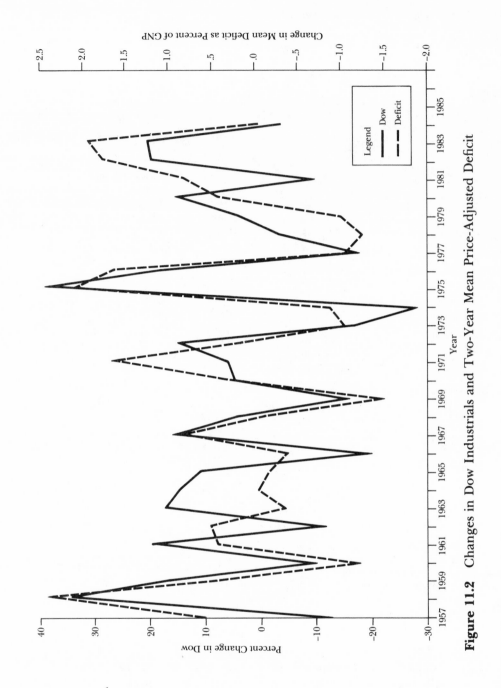

Figure 11.2 Changes in Dow Industrials and Two-Year Mean Price-Adjusted Deficit

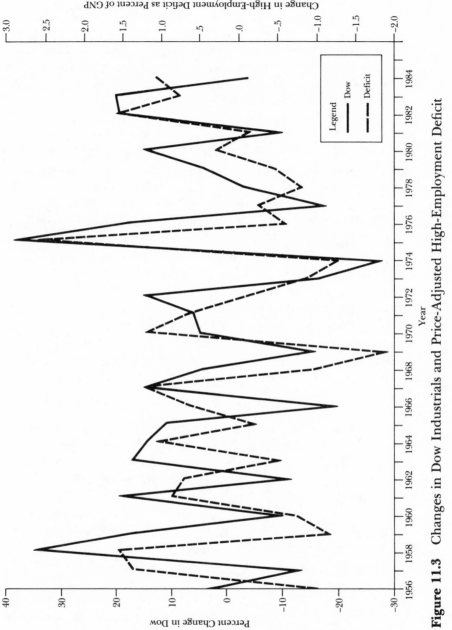

Figure 11.3 Changes in Dow Industrials and Price-Adjusted High-Employment Deficit

141

was relatively unknown to market participants, who did pay attention to the actual budget deficits and the effects these had on private wealth. It is also possible that the particular association of increases in actual deficits with recessions may, because recessions were expected to be followed shortly by recoveries, have strengthened their relation with Dow Jones.

Increases in the price- and interest-adjusted deficits showed, in equations (11.3) and (11.6), a similar but lesser association with current and future increases in the Dow Jones. It is not obvious why this relation is damped. But recall that the par-to-market adjustments of the value of debt, which we call the interest effect, are positive when interest rates are going up. They move federal budgets toward surplus by decreasing the value of government debt held by the public. The lower bond prices might be expected to bring lower equity values directly. And the lower value of the debt would reduce aggregate demand, slow the economy, and thus lower earnings and further lower stock prices.

But one may also observe that higher interest rates frequently stem from a brisk economy and booming real investment. With higher interest rates associated with higher investment and higher investment associated with generally profitable anticipations, we might then expect our interest effect, which stems from higher interest rates, to be in turn associated with *in*creases in stock averages.

We can hardly be sure that this is the explanation, but it does fit our findings. The interest effect, as may be seen in the markedly smaller absolute values of b_1 in equations (11.3) and (11.6), reduces the negative effects on the Dow Jones of reductions in budget deficits.

This interpretation gains support in Table 11.2. We see there the results of regressions of changes in the Dow Jones on changes in deficits and the current interest effect. Increases in deficits are again sharply associated with current and subsequent increases in the Dow Jones, while the interest effect, unlike the official surplus or the price effect of our adjusted budget, is positively related to the Dow Jones. In equation (11.9), with the price-adjusted national income surplus, the coefficient of the interest effect variable is statistically fairly significant.

We may note finally that in every case the fit of equations with the price-adjusted budget variables is markedly better, as indicated by values of $\hat{R}^2$, than equations with the official or unadjusted budgets.

TABLE 11.2 Deficits, Interest Effects, and the Dow Jones

$DOWCH_t = b_0 + b_1 SURCH_t + b_2 SURCH_{t-1} + b_3 IE_t \quad t = 1957, \ldots, 1984$

(1)	(2)	(3)	(4)	(5)	(6)	(7)	(8)
	MEASURE OF	REGRESSION COEFFICIENTS[a]					
EQUATION	SURPLUS (OR DEFICIT)	Constant (b_0)	$SURCH_t$ (b_1)	$SURCH_{t-1}$ (b_2)	IE_t (b_3)	$\hat{R}^2$	D–W
(11.8)	OFNIS	1.892 (2.444)	-6.975 (1.739)	-5.204 (1.729)	4.568 (2.956)	.438	2.22
(11.9)	PANIS	1.838 (2.217)	-6.651 (1.441)	-4.734 (1.388)	5.871 (2.783)	.534	2.21
(11.10)	OFHES	2.726 (2.912)	-9.088 (3.211)	-4.295 (3.343)	2.904 (3.570)	.199	2.15
(11.11)	PAHES	2.170 (2.515)	-9.888 (2.480)	-5.267 (2.466)	4.688 (3.188)	.400	2.14

[a]Ordinary least squares; standard errors are shown in parentheses.

$DOWCH$ = percent change in Dow Jones Industrials
$SURCH$ = change in surplus as percent of GNP
$OFNIS$ = official national income account surplus as percent of GNP
$PANIS$ = price-adjusted national income account surplus as percent of GNP
$OFHES$ = official high-employment surplus as percent of GNP
$PAHES$ = price-adjusted high-employment surplus as percent of GNP
IE = interest effect as percent of GNP

If current market participants do not understand all this, or in line with the beauty contest example of Keynes, all think that everybody else thinks that everybody else thinks that everybody else thinks . . . that this is not understood, stock prices might be depressed by mismeasured nominal budget deficits that are not real.

But then, if Abraham Lincoln was right in saying that you can't fool all of the people all of the time, those who are the first to understand that real budget deficits may raise the stock market would do well to buy in before—although not too long before—their slower associates stop being fooled.

12

Implications for Policy: Past, Present, and Future

YES, THE OFFICIALLY REPORTED U.S. federal debt has been growing at astronomical rates. Since Ronald Reagan took office in 1981, the gross public debt has more than doubled, from $930 billion to $1.9 trillion. The increase has reflected huge and repeated annual deficits, reaching $212 billion in fiscal 1985.

But no, this has not been all bad. Indeed, given the economic collapse of 1981–82, lesser deficits would have made the deep recession worse. Unemployment would have risen above the official 10.7 percent figure, which was already the highest since the Great Depression of the 1930s. Total production and business profits would have been less. Without the huge deficits, we would not have had the brisk recovery of 1983 and 1984. And the 1984 election results—whether regarded as good or bad—might well have been quite different.

Up to about 1966, when inflation was relatively minor, budget deficits really were budget deficits. In the period from 1966 on, however, when inflation became substantial, the officially balanced budget turned into one of surplus after inflation corrections were made. A balanced, inflation-adjusted high-employment budget would have been substantially expansionary,

145

producing high rates of growth of GNP and declines in unemployment. As late as 1981, however, we had a roughly balanced *official* high-employment budget, while the budget adjusted for inflation was substantially in surplus.

The Carter Administration, along with most outside critics, ignoring indications of sluggishness in the economy, interpreted the combination of apparent deficits and inflation as indicating excess demand. It initiated moves to combat the inflation by encouraging a tight money policy and, in its final years, striving to reduce budget deficits. This policy continued through the first year of the Reagan Administration as domestic spending was further restrained and more taxes rose than declined.

But in fact, fiscal policy was not stimulative. The high inflation and rising interest rates meant that budgets seemingly in deficit were actually in substantial surplus. Our statistical relations indicate strongly that these inflation-adjusted surpluses contributed significantly to the 1981–82 recession.

This suggests two important correctives to widespread views of fiscal and monetary policy. First, that recession cannot properly be interpreted as a triumph of all-powerful monetary constraints over relatively ineffective fiscal ease. Tight monetary policy *and* tight fiscal policy were its proximate causes.

Thus, those who acquiesced in tight money as "the only game in town" to slow a presumedly overheated, inflationary economy were wrong on two counts. First, the inflation had come from supply shocks, with critical energy prices up some 500 percent in a decade, rather than excess demand, an inference reinforced by the absence of real increases in fiscal thrust. And second, a strong-willed rejection of accommodative monetary policy, rather than balancing budget excesses, offered a near lethal combination of monetary and fiscal contraction.

But fiscal policy moved in a monumentally different direction in 1982. A combination of major tax cuts and increases in military expenditures, with a fall in inflation and interest rates, converted the *adjusted* high-employment budget from a very high surplus to a very high deficit. Indeed, the change of 3.46 percentage points, from a surplus of 1.45 percent of GNP in 1981 to a deficit of 2.01 percent in 1982, was one of the greatest such swings to expansion on record. Our estimated relations between budget deficits and changes in GNP and unemployment predicted a major swing to economic recovery and lower unemployment in 1983 and on into 1984, and that is of course precisely what occurred.

Prior to both the fiscal 1986 Congressional Budget Resolution and the Gramm–Rudman program to "balance the budget" by 1991, Congressional Budget Office estimates indicated very large and increasing budget deficits in the years ahead. As seen in Table 12.1, 1985 projections of the official *high-employment* budget, set at a 5.1 percent unemployment rate, show a deficit of $225 billion by 1990. This corresponds to an actual projected national income account deficit of $258 billion for that year.

Adjustment for price effects, however, brings the high-employment deficit down substantially,[1] to $58 billion in 1986, but shows it rising to $119 billion by 1990. The price- and interest-adjusted deficit in 1990 is projected at $116 billion.

We thus had projections of substantial high-employment deficits over the rest of this decade. The adjustments for anticipated inflation reduced those projected deficits, but still left them high. The projected adjusted deficits, therefore, while initially less than their 1982–84 peaks, were substantial, and turning higher.

Indeed, make no mistake about it. From a historical per-

TABLE 12.1 Projected High-Employment Budget Surplus or Deficit, and GNP without Deficit Reductions 1985–90[a]

(1)	(2)	(3)	(4)	(5)	(6)
			BUDGET SURPLUS OR DEFICIT (−)		
		Actual (National Income Accounts)		*High-Employment*	
				ADJUSTED FOR PRICE	ADJUSTED FOR PRICE AND
YEAR	GNP		OFFICIAL	EFFECTS	INTEREST EFFECTS
A. *Billions of Dollars*					
1985	3,906	− 169.9	− 103.7	− 45.3	− 72.4
1986	4,217	− 183.4	− 124.8	− 58.4	− 75.0
1987	4,548	− 200.2	− 146.8	− 70.7	− 81.8
1988	4,905	− 212.4	− 165.2	− 82.3	− 96.7
1989	5,289	− 237.4	− 197.1	− 102.4	− 103.0
1990	5,704	− 257.5	− 224.7	− 118.9	− 115.7
B. *As Percent of GNP*					
1985	100.0	− 4.35	− 2.66	− 1.16	− 1.85
1986	100.0	− 4.35	− 2.96	− 1.38	− 1.78
1987	100.0	− 4.40	− 3.23	− 1.55	− 1.80
1988	100.0	− 4.33	− 3.37	− 1.68	− 1.97
1989	100.0	− 4.49	− 3.73	− 1.94	− 2.46
1990	100.0	− 4.51	− 3.94	− 2.08	− 2.73

[a]GNP, national income account surplus, and "official" high-employment surplus from Congressional Budget Office projections in *The Economic and Budget Outlook: An Update* (1985). High-employment surpluses have been recalculated at 5.1 percent unemployment. Adjustments have been made on the basis of CBO projections of future prices and Treasury bill rates.

spective, these deficits are enormous. From 1986 to 1990 they would *average* 2.15 percent of GNP, while up to 1982 the largest inflation-adjusted deficit we had ever had, in any year since the high-employment series began in 1955, was 0.64 percent. From 1955 to 1981, the adjusted high-employment budget was, on the average, in *surplus* by 1.35 percent of GNP.

The huge deficits that had been projected, if they were large *real deficits,* could be expected to be highly expansionary, pushing the economy beyond its capacity. Plugging them into our equations of Chapter 9 offers revealing, if simplistic, confirmation. Even with the assumption that the monetary base increases only with inflation, real GNP is predicted to grow at rates of 5 and 6 percent per year for the rest of this decade. Our equations further predict unemployment in the 3 and 4 percent range by 1987 and in the 2 and 3 percent range for 1988. By 1990, officially measured unemployment would be close to zero or negative (!) according to the equations and, in any event, less than 2 percent.

Unlike some of my colleagues, I have never given up on the old "full-employment" goal of unemployment down to 4 percent. Without specific focus on problems of structural unemployment, however, approach of this goal seems likely to entail substantial wage inflation in the widening areas of scarce labor supply. Limitations on competition, including many set by government itself, would be likely to exacerbate the resulting price inflation. Clearly, the *very* low and negative unemployment rates which the equations project for 1989 and 1990 are unattainable.

Something then would have to give. We would have considerable inflation. Faced with this inflation, we can be virtually sure that the Federal Reserve would move sharply to curtail the supply of money and credit. This implies that our assumption of even a zero real increase in the monetary base is too liberal. We should rather anticipate real changes in the monetary base which are negative.

We would find ourselves on a collision course between the projected budget deficits and interest and inflation effects on the one hand, and the capacity of the economy on the other. If government expenditures, then, were not significantly cut or taxes raised, the inevitable economic forces of supply and demand would solve the problem and force the adjustments. For inflation would be rekindled and interest rates would rise, the latter all the more so as the Federal Reserve moved to curb the inflation by ever tighter monetary policy. The rising inflation and interest rates would bring sharper declines in the real value of outstanding government debt, an automatic increase in the "inflation tax." *Hence the real, adjusted deficits, but not the nominal or unadjusted deficits, would finally be eliminated by the very inflation and high interest rates which they had brought on.*

How can we appraise the consequences of continued large nominal deficits, along with more inflation and higher nominal and real interest rates, *after* they have contributed as much as they can to rekindling the economy and reducing unemployment? First, investment would be discouraged. Second, the higher interest rates would contribute again to a rising value of the dollar, current account deficits in our balance of international payments, and reduced U.S. investment abroad coupled with increased foreign purchases of both U.S. government securities and other private, American assets, thus reducing U.S. private net worth and wealth.

This course of events would hence bring on some combination of lesser U.S. investment at home and greater foreign investment in the United States. The output and income available to the American people would be less because we would have a less productive economy and because more of our product and earnings would be going to foreign owners of our productive assets and government securities.

There are costs to the American people in this. There can be no mistake about it. But how much are the costs and how do they compare with those of alternative policies?

The burden with respect to foreign borrowing can be reasonably well quantified. Our current account deficit, the shortfall of all the goods and services we sell abroad over what we buy plus what we give away, has recently run at an annual rate as high as $140 billion. Corresponding to that must be a capital import or reduction in our net capital position with the rest of the world of $140 billion. Each year that this continues we then reduce our net earnings abroad or add to our net payments abroad an amount equal to the product of the $140 billion and our net rate of return. Assuming that at about 5 percent, corresponding to a real not a nominal rate of interest, the added cost to the U.S. economy *each year that this continues* is some $7 billion.

Now, $7 billion may seem like a big number to an ordinary citizen, but in terms of the American economy, it is not really all that big. With a national income running well over $3 trillion per year, the $7 billion is approximately 0.2 percent of what we are earning. After five years of such deficits then, we would have increased our net payments on our "debt" to foreigners by about 1 percent of national income. One could say, "A percent here and a percent there and pretty soon we have a big number." But it is hard to argue that for the American people to suffer a 1 percent loss in the amount of their income that they can spend on themselves would be an unmitigated calamity.

The loss in future product as a result of lesser domestic investment is somewhat hard to quantify. But just to get some ballpark estimates, suppose the higher real interest rates crowded out 10 percent of our gross private domestic investment. This would come to some $60 billion per year at current rates. With calculations similar to those we have applied to our foreign debt, we can assume that the resultant reduction in real product, assuming a real rate of return again of 5 percent, would be in the order of $3 billion per year. Recalling that our national income is over $3 trillion, that implies a loss in product as a result of a lesser capital stock which might come to about 0.5 percent of national income in five years.

If we could add together our investment earnings lost to foreigners and our loss due to reduced domestic investment, we would still come only to something like 1.5 percent of national income per year after half a decade. That is, to put it another way, not peanuts. But neither is it quite the stuff of national bankruptcy or disaster.

But it is not even clear that we have two such losses to add. The foreign funds pouring into the United States are in fact enabling us to keep up domestic investment. To the extent that foreigners buy the Treasury bills, notes, and bonds created by our deficits, American private saving is available to finance investment. And as foreigners buy private assets or build factories in the United States, they finance our investment directly.

In fact, the current account deficit in our balance of payments means that foreigners are essentially financing our budget deficit. We are thus able to live high on the hog, enjoying a high level of consumption without sacrificing investment. To the extent that the budget deficit has brought on the trade deficit, it has permitted us to live better now, at the price of paying off foreigners later. There is thus a future cost, but we must not forget the current gain.

What are the costs of alternatives to the continuation of current deficits? That depends in a considerable part on the alternatives we have in mind. But a few general observations may be made.

Any cut in the deficit will *in itself* reduce aggregate demand. This means a lower growth in output, if not an actual dip, and less employment and more unemployment. These would appear to be safe inferences since the economy, despite our current huge deficits, does not show evidence of overheating. Rather, with the growth in gross national product slowing to some 2.5 percent in 1985, and our officially measured unemployment persisting at almost 7 percent, the economy shows disconcerting indications of slack. Hence it behooves us to be sure that any reductions in aggregate demand resulting from deficit reduction will be matched by increases which may be produced by an easier monetary policy. If the Federal Reserve keeps its supply of bank reserves and credit on the same course, reductions in aggregate demand and output imply some automatic monetary easing as the demand for credit falls. That, though, can only cushion the drop in output and employment, not prevent it. What would be needed is a shift by the Fed to greater monetary ease to compensate for the shift to greater fiscal tightness. Paul Volcker has given hints that he well understands this. It should be a firm departure point in national policy.

But aside from these broad considerations of aggregate demand, there are critical differences between particular policies that might be pursued in reducing budget deficits. If the latter could be viewed as a disease, we might yet conclude that many of the proposed cures are considerably worse.

First, there are problems of equity. We could reduce the deficit by abolishing veterans' benefits to all who fought in the wars that ended on odd days of the month or to all whose names began with even-numbered letters of the alphabet. We could indeed abolish all veterans' benefits, or medical services to the poor in affluent states, or even all medical services. These examples may seem outlandish. But how different are they from saying that we will reduce payments to the aged by "freezing" or delaying cost of living adjustments?

The point, simply enough, is that if Americans must sacrifice some of their after-tax income to reduce the deficit, why single out any particular group? The burden, it would seem, should be shared by all, perhaps adjusted for ability to sacrifice or pay. But

I have yet to hear the argument that the aged, as a group, are somehow more worthy of sacrifice. While there is no likely economic argument that cutting social security will hurt the nation as a whole—other than whatever the consequences may be of the perceived breaking of a social contract—it may well impress thoughtful people as well as those directly affected as patently unfair.

A method of reducing the deficit by a general increase in taxes does not raise much if anything in the way of equity considerations. Indeed, if current sacrifice is necessary to avoid the future costs of lesser domestic investment and a greater foreign debt, this would appear the obvious way to bring it about. A general increase in taxes would lower the taxable income of the majority of the population that pays taxes. It would induce them to consume less of both foreign goods and domestic goods since the income out of which they can spend would be reduced.

A general increase in tax rates, it is true, would have little or no effect on those currently paying no taxes. This would include some of the rich, taking advantage of our myriad tax shelters and loopholes, but it also includes many of those too poor to rate very high on the sacrifice list. And of course there could, in any event, be various measures, under the rubric of tax reform, which would broaden the tax base and make possible increased tax revenues without increasing tax rates.

The tax increase route does have some further appeal as a direct antidote to the major cause of current deficits. For while the 1985 fiscal year deficit has been calculated at $212 billion, the tax cuts of the last four years have reduced current tax receipts by some $150 billion. Merely rescinding one-third of those tax cuts would bring the deficit into the range to which our political representatives and leaders have been struggling, thus far without success, to get it. Rescinding one monumental change in business taxation alone, the so-called accelerated cost recovery system (ACRS) which so increased tax depreciation deductions, would net some $60 billion per year in increased tax revenues. The 1985 tax reform bill passed by the House of Representatives in December would eliminate ACRS, but would give up the added tax revenues by lowering tax rates. A similar amount could be gained by the move to "economic depreciation" in the Treasury's proposal of November 1984 (unfortunately gutted in President Reagan's recommendations of May 1985).

In general, income tax increases would result most directly in reduction of current consumption. The main effect of reducing tax depreciation allowances would be to lower the value and hence the stock prices of corporations gaining particular advantage from these provisions. This, too, would reduce consumption. It would presumably have some effect in reducing business investment, but there is substantial evidence that this effect would be much less than many like to claim (Chirinko and Eisner, 1982, 1983; Eisner, 1983b). Further, the business investment that would be lost would generally be that which was insufficiently productive to be undertaken without the tax advantage. It is difficult to see much loss in future productivity or output as a consequence.

The most frequently proposed solution, at least from the Reagan Administration, is to cut nondefense spending. But what spending and with what consequences? Consider a partial list of the domestic programs that were to be frozen, cut, or eliminated in the original Reagan budget for fiscal 1986:

- Black lung benefits
- Food stamps
- Child nutrition
- Library grants
- Employment and training programs
- Jobs Corps
- Legal services
- Urban mass transit
- Sewer grants
- Grants for disadvantaged and handicapped children
- Aid to vocational and science and math education
- Women, Infants and Children Nutrition
- Head Start and child welfare

- Older American services, centers and jobs
- Handicapped rehabilitation services
- Agricultural research and extension
- National Science Foundation
- National Institutes of Health and other health research
- Public lands and parks
- Law enforcement
- Environmental Protection Agency
- Medicare
- Medicaid
- Peace Corps
- Coast Guard.[2]

Some may applaud such a hit list as an opportunity to undo half a century of New Deal, Fair Deal, Great Society, and Big Government. But others, with some justification, may see in it mindless cruelty, however unintentional, and a reckless reduction in investment in the human and public capital on which our future well-being depends.

Recall that the argument against budget deficits—and government spending in general—is that they crowd out private investment, thus reducing our stock of capital and future output. But suppose the government spending which contributes to the deficit does itself involve investment. Capital formation includes far more than what we traditionally measure in business spending for plant and equipment or the somewhat wider but still narrow category of gross private domestic investment. It also includes investment in tangible capital by government and government enterprises, households and nonprofit institutions. Government construction of roads or airport runways is as much investment, and in some instances more productive, than acquisition of additional vehicles and aircraft by trucking firms and airlines. Government expenditures for research and development and the development of national resources also entail the accumulation of capital, and frequently more productive capital than the acquisition of additional tangible goods.

And most important, investment in health and education and the basic skills and capacity of human labor involves some of the most fundamental accumulation of the capital necessary for output and economic growth. In extensive work in developing a new "Total Incomes System of Accounts," I have indeed found that narrowly defined business investment in plant and equipment—the private investment with which many have been so concerned—has been no more than some 14 percent of total capital formation of the United States in recent years (Eisner, 1985). It makes little sense to try to increase private investment by reducing the budget deficit in ways that cut public investment, and frequently more productive public investment, all the more.

We are left with one final fiscal initiative for reducing the deficit, relating to the other major cause of the deficit. The fiscal 1981 budget, inherited from the Carter Administration, ended $58 billion in deficit. Military spending four years later was some $120 billion higher, with massive further increases scheduled. The $120 billion increase in military spending may well be compared with the $160 billion increase in the deficit since 1981.

For those who feel that the huge increase in military spending has brought us much valuable security or those who, defying the laws of economics, refuse to "put a price tag" on the military, the issue may well be closed. But for those who suspect that too much military spending contributes to an arms race which reduces our security, as well as those who hard-headedly apply a cost–benefit approach to *all* public and private spending, military expenditures would appear a prime target for significant reductions in budget deficits. Such reductions would have the advantage of freeing resources for both consumption and investment. We could eat more cake now and still have more later, if of course some foreign devils don't take advantage of our lowered guard and steal it all away.

We should mention a few beguiling approaches to federal deficit reduction which are likely to have no more than cosmetic value, if that. The first is to take advantage of certain bizarre federal accounting practices and reduce the deficit with no reduction in real government spending or increase in taxes. This can be done, as we suggested earlier, by selling off public property. It can also be done by selling government financial assets. We might, for example, sell the Treasury's gold for some $90 billion at current market prices. This would cut the deficit by more than a third, in the year it was done. We would of course have a problem of what to do for an encore once the gold was gone.

A proposal to have the government sell its loan portfolios has been sponsored recently by Senator Daniel Patrick Moynihan. Given the risks involved in many of the loans to distressed farmers, small businessmen, students, and low-income homeowners, they would probably sell at bargain prices. This might mean some ultimately substantial gains by the enterprising investors, but it would also bring in some tidy sums—again a once-only gain—to the U.S. Treasury. In December 1985 it was revealed that the Reagan Administration was planning to recommend the sale of the Federal Housing Administration, an agency with an estimated value of $3 billion. As reported in *The New York Times,* the FHA "has provided mortgage insurance for more than 51 million home buyers, enabling many to get mortgages they might otherwise not have been able to obtain."[3]

Such actions would technically reduce the current deficit. Indeed, the federal government and associated credit agencies have several hundred billion dollars of financial assets that they could sell. But they would also reduce future government revenues as the interest payments on the loans would be going to their new private owners. Further, aside from the accounting differences, one may well wonder how it could help the economy for the government to bring in money by selling other people's I.O.U.'s rather than its own.

Another in the genre of cosmetic deficit-reduction policies

embodies the "palm-it-off-on-somebody-else" approach. This indeed has been warmly advocated by the Reagan Administration and in considerable part adopted by the Congress. It involves essentially reducing the federal budget deficit by passing the burden on to states and localities. For example, reduction or elimination of federal revenue sharing with states and cities would have the first-order effect of reducing state and local government surpluses or increasing their deficits, dollar for dollar with any reduction of the federal deficit. The total government deficit— the sum of federal, state, and local deficits—would be unaffected. Since it is this total deficit that ultimately affects the economy, we have merely transferred the hot potato from one hand to the other.

There may of course be further, second-order effects of considerable consequence. State and local governments may raise taxes to restore their surpluses or reduce their deficits. While avoiding increased taxes at the federal level, we would then have brought on increased taxes at state and local levels. It is hard to see what difference this would make to taxpayers or to the economy. An increase in taxes is after all an increase in taxes.

State and local governments might, on the other hand, feel impelled to reduce their own spending. But is there anything more desirable about reducing state and local spending than reducing federal spending? Conservatives have generally argued that government spending decisions should be brought closer to home and that more should be done at the state and local levels as opposed to the federal level of government. Where this argument is not a smokescreen for having government in general do less, it would appear to have some merit.

Why then force cuts in nonfederal government spending? The question seems all the more pointed in view of the widespread conviction that more rather than less is needed in the way of major state and local services in the areas of health, sanitation, sewerage, highways, bridges, police protection, and education. And all of this goes beyond direct allocation of federal revenues to states. It applies as well to such federal tax-raising proposals as the elimination of the federal tax deduction for state and local taxes. For this would remove a federal subsidy to state and local taxpayers and hence make it more difficult for the states and localities to collect their taxes.

A federal budget deficit may also be reduced by passing expenditures off to the private sector. Thus, instead of government spending to protect our environment of land, air, and water, we can tighten controls on private businesses and force them to spend more to conserve our resources and reduce pollution. This would reduce the budget deficit but it would help the economy only if such forced private spending were more efficient than the government spending it replaced.

We might bring about reductions in the official budget deficit by inducing the Federal Reserve to follow an easier money policy. Easing of credit would be a good idea in itself, as it would reduce monetary barriers to investment. And by increasing aggregate demand, it would reduce the danger of unemployment from budget cuts. Its appeal with regard to the budget deficit is that lower interest rates will reduce federal net interest payments, currently running at some $140 billion per year.

It should be noted, however, that lower interest rates will reduce the official or measured budget deficit, but there are significant offsets in our adjusted budget. Lower interest rates increase the market value of the outstanding government debt. In terms of effects upon aggregate demand, this adds to the perceived net wealth of the private sector and thus tends to encourage private spending. To the extent that deficit reduction is intended to reduce potentially inflationary demand, easier monetary policy has two counts against it. The easier credit and lower interest rates in themselves will encourage investment spending. And the increase in the market value of government debt may further add to private spending as much as or even more than the fall in interest receipts reduces it. But by this same token, easier monetary policy is an ideal way to reduce the official deficit without jeopardizing economic recovery.

We shall pass over a variety of other cosmetic devices for reducing the deficit. These would include delaying expenditures temporarily, thus reducing the current deficit while building in a greater future deficit. Analogously, tax receipts can be accelerated in the short run at the expense of future tax receipts. One variety of this is the set of depreciation schedules in President Reagan's tax proposal of May 1985, which claimed little or no loss of tax revenue from 1986 through 1990. It omitted estimates of the effects in later years of inflation adjustment which, by the year 2000, would be costing some $20 billion a year at current tax rates.

Still another device, along the lines of the one mentioned above of forcing private industry to undertake expenditures previously made by government, is to substitute, for government loan programs, government guarantees or even subsidies of private loans. The effects on the economy would be similar, but the loan expenditures would be taken out of the budget.

By contrast, there are certain real deficit reduction proposals whose effects their sponsors sometimes seek to mask. Among this genre are the delay, freezing, suspension, or skipping of cost of living adjustments on government payments such as those for social security or retirement benefits of federal employees. With inflation at even, say, a modest 4 percent, skipping one year of cost of living adjustments, for example, would entail much more than a one-year loss to benefit recipients. It would rather reduce future benefits in all years by 4 percent. Making cost of living adjustments every two years instead of every year, as was proposed in the summer of 1985 as a "compromise" on social security reductions, again assuming an inflation rate of 4 percent, would lower all future payments by an average of 2 percent.

What is really dominating the deficit struggle is what may well be characterized as a game of "chicken" at fairly high stakes. Conservatives have long advocated reducing the role of government in the American economy, at least in matters other than, perhaps euphemistically labeled, defense expenditures. Their efforts to implement their antigovernment program have not, at least in their view, been crowned with success as regards federal spending.

Unable to cut expenditures directly, they finally came to a strategy of seeking to reduce tax revenues first. Then, with revenues down, it was reasoned that fear of continuation of budget deficits would generate irresistible pressure to cut expenditures. As Senator Moynihan has reminded us,[4] the strategy was hardly hidden. On February 5, 1981, in his first television address to the nation, President Reagan said:

> There are always those who told us that taxes couldn't be cut until spending was reduced. Well, you know, we can lecture our children about extravagance until we run out of voice and breath. Or we can cure their extravagance by simply reducing their allowance.

There were curiously divergent arguments in the justification of this cut-taxes-first program for expenditure reduction. The new, so-called "supply-side" theorists said, as we did with regard to the effects of nominal deficits that are not real, "Not to worry!" The tax reduction would stimulate so great an increase in the supply of labor and capital that the resultant higher incomes would generate more taxes than before. Pure monetarists did not necessarily accept the supply siders' arguments but insisted that the deficits would not be inflationary because only the quantity of money affected prices. And those taken with Barro's reincarnation of the Ricardian Equivalence Theorem also argued that the deficits would have no impact on aggregate demand or prices because we would all realize that the cut in taxes now would have to be matched by a corresponding increase in taxes later. We were only postponing our tax burden, not eliminating it. Among potential Democratic critics of the Republican-sponsored tax reductions, what was left of Keynesian thought argued that a deficit brought on by tax reduction warranted support as a means of reviving a sluggish economy.

As the tax reductions legislated in 1981 came into effect, contrary to the predictions of some of the extreme supply siders, the deficit increased sharply. The pressure to cut spending then intensified.

There were then as now three real ways to reduce the deficit: cutting military spending, cutting nonmilitary spending, or rescinding some of the tax cuts. The Administration insisted that military spending had to increase and had its way. After accepting some significant tax increases in 1982, President Reagan, rejecting the advice of Martin Feldstein, the Chairman of his own Council of Economic Advisers, became increasingly adamant in rejecting further tax increases or cancelling any more of the earlier cuts. And the indexing of tax rates to inflation was to deprive the Treasury, from 1985 on, of the automatic increases in tax revenues which it had been enjoying for many years without legislated tax increases.

Then, in the presidential campaign of 1984, political circumstance led President Reagan to seemingly unequivocal opposition to tax increases. This opposition was qualified by the acknowledgment that such increases might be accepted as a last resort, but this apparently meant only after the political opposition had forced them by failing to make appropriate reductions in expenditures. The evidence that Walter Mondale's insistence that he would raise taxes contributed to his massive defeat essentially consigned proposals for tax increases to political oblivion.

Hence the game of chicken! Both the Administration and

the opposition profess acceptance of the conventional wisdom that continued deficits are a disaster. Both insist that the disaster must be avoided. The Administration says we must avoid it by further cuts in domestic programs. The opposition, somewhat timidly, says it must be avoided in some other way, such as restraining military spending increases or, *sotto voce,* allowing some increase in taxes. And each side waits for the other to give in.

The failure of either side to surrender is conventionally viewed as an extreme example of political irresponsibility. David A. Stockman, President Reagan's Budget Director for four and a half years, stated:

> The basic fact is that we are violating badly, even wantonly, the cardinal rule of sound public finance: governments must extract from the people in taxes what they dispense in benefits, services and protections. . . . Indeed, if the [Securities and Exchange Commission] had jurisdiction over the Executive and Legislative branches, many of us would be in jail.

But another interpretation may be more to the point. For at least half a century, politicians, most prominently until recently Republican conservatives, have been declaiming budget deficits. While generally nodding agreement, the electorate has rarely been much moved. One may infer that to most of the public there can be worse things than deficits. Despite all the prophets of gloom and doom, the sky has somehow not fallen.

Perhaps, deep down, at least to the extent that they are responsive to the really heartfelt concern of their constituents, our political representatives sense this too. Hence, when the choice comes down to reducing the deficit by cutting or eliminating a program which seems otherwise worthy of support, the balance seems to be tipped against deficit reduction. That, of course, is the argument for the Gramm–Rudman program of automatic proportional cuts in nonexempt expenditures if deficit reduction targets are not met by Congress and the President.

One recent technical paper, after a statistical analysis of expenditures and tax data from 1955 through 1982, concludes that changes in tax receipts have not in the past forced changes in government expenditures (von Furstenberg, Green, and Jeong, 1985). Is that a guarantee that they will not do so in the future?

The answer may well depend upon the relative strength of conviction and dedication among the citizenry and the conflicting groups in the body politic. For the fact is that for those who believe that "to dismantle fifty years' social legislation" would scar and disfigure the America of which they are proud, the true cost of continued large deficits is less. And, I must acknowledge, for those who are convinced that restraining our massive military buildup, let alone cutting it back, would threaten the destruction of our nation, the cost of continued large budget deficits is also relatively small.

The bottom line then is that budget deficits still matter and that in an economy approaching full capacity utilization, it may be well to reduce them. It does appear likely that prospective future deficits would, in that situation, prove too large. They would contribute to inflation and a costly, restrictive monetary policy. The cost of continuing the deficits, however, may be outweighed by the costs of various actions that might reduce them.

The ultimate argument, therefore, should be on the merits and demerits of expenditure programs and tax proposals. If cutting domestic programs is really in the interest of the economy and the nation, it should be done aside from deficit considerations. If military spending has reached the point where its contributions to our national interest and security are minimal or actually negative, they should be reduced, also aside from deficit considerations. And if tax reform is justified by considerations of economic efficiency and equity, it should be undertaken. Budget hysteria has no proper place in the argument.

New ingredients were recently put into the picture. First, we had the deficit reductions pledged in the Joint Congressional Budget Resolution for fiscal 1986 and its projections for future years. While there was much complaint that this action did not go far enough, prospective deficits were actually cut substantially. And now we have the Gramm–Rudman Act, which would "balance the budget" by fiscal 1991. It is instructive to consider the likely results of these deficit-reduction packages.

Taking up first the Budget Resolution, Table 12.2 shows projected budget surpluses and deficits on national income accounts, actual and high-employment, official and adjusted, for calendar years 1986 to 1990. Comparisons with Table 12.1 reveal the magnitude of the proposed cuts. The actual deficit on national income account in 1990 would be reduced from 4.51 percent of GNP to 1.48 percent. The official high-employment deficit would

TABLE 12.2   Projected High-Employment Budget Surplus or Deficit and
GNP, on Basis of Fiscal 1986 Congressional Budget Resolution,[a] 1985–90

(1)	(2)	(3)	(4)	(5)	(6)
			BUDGET SURPLUS OR DEFICIT (−)		
		Actual	*High-Employment*		
		(National Income Accounts)		ADJUSTED FOR PRICE EFFECTS	ADJUSTED FOR PRICE AND INTEREST EFFECTS
YEAR	GNP		OFFICIAL		
A. *Billions of Dollars*					
1985	3,906	− 161.3	− 95.9	− 36.8	− 62.7
1986	4,217	− 138.8	− 80.6	− 15.6	− 25.8
1987	4,548	− 125.5	− 72.3	− 0.2	− 1.8
1988	4,905	− 104.0	− 57.6	17.5	15.9
1989	5,289	− 96.8	− 57.2	24.1	13.9
1990	5,704	− 84.6	− 51.7	33.7	19.7
B. *As Percent of GNP*					
1985	100.0	− 4.13	− 2.43	− 0.94	− 1.60
1986	100.0	− 3.29	− 1.91	− 0.37	− 0.61
1987	100.0	− 2.76	− 1.59	0.00	− 0.04
1988	100.0	− 2.12	− 1.18	0.36	0.32
1989	100.0	− 1.83	− 1.08	0.46	0.26
1990	100.0	− 1.48	− 0.91	0.59	0.34

[a]GNP, national income account surplus, and "official" high-employment surplus from Congressional
Budget Office projections in *The Economic and Budget Outlook: An Update* (1985). High-employment
surpluses have been recalculated at 5.1 percent unemployment. Adjustments have been made on the
basis of CBO projections of future prices and Treasury bill rates and net debt consistent with actual
deficits.

be cut from 3.94 percent to 0.91 percent. And the fully inflation-
adjusted deficit of 2.73 percent would become a surplus of 0.34
percent.

Substitution of the new projections into our equations brings
quite different results for GNP growth and unemployment from
those for the no-deficit-reduction projections. The projected growth
of GNP is reduced and unemployment, after declining substantially, levels off at about 5½ percent if no real money growth is
assumed, but around 4 percent if monetary policy is eased. These
projections do not necessarily imply accelerated inflation, particularly since they may be overoptimistic regarding GNP and employment. Our equations should of course be taken as merely
suggestive,[5] but they apparently underestimated the negative drag
of surging imports. GNP growth for 1985 was actually about 2.5
percent rather than in the 4 to 5 percent range of our forecasts.
And unemployment averaged 7.3 percent rather than our equation prediction of 6.8 percent.

What about the Gramm–Rudman Act to balance the official budget by fiscal 1991? As originally proposed, it would reduce the deficit from $180 billion in fiscal 1986—actually somewhat higher than the earlier Budget Resolution[6]—in $36 billion annual chunks, thus reaching zero in five years. Table 12.3 indicates what this will amount to.

First, the budget on national income accounts would be slightly in surplus by calendar 1990. Second, and probably more important, the high-employment budget would then be in surplus by some $39 billion. And third, and most significant, the budget adjusted for inflation would move to *substantial* surplus. *We would have an inflation-adjusted, high-employment surplus of well over $100 billion, about 2 percent of projected gross national product.*

Results of plugging the G–R projected deficits—and inflation-adjusted surpluses by 1987—into our equations are sobering. The rate of real GNP growth falls to about 2 percent by 1990 with a relatively easy monetary policy, and to 1 percent if the real

TABLE 12.3 Projected High-Employment Budget Surplus or Deficit and GNP, on Basis of Gramm–Rudman[a]

(1)	(2)	(3)	(4)	(5)	(6)
			BUDGET SURPLUS OR DEFICIT (−)		
		Actual		*High-Employment*	
		(National Income Accounts)		ADJUSTED FOR PRICE EFFECTS	ADJUSTED FOR PRICE AND IN-TEREST EFFECTS
YEAR	GNP		OFFICIAL		
A. *Billions of Dollars*					
1985	3,906	− 161.9	− 95.7	− 37.5	− 64.3
1986	4,217	− 138.2	− 79.5	− 14.5	− 24.6
1987	4,548	− 102.7	− 49.3	22.3	23.8
1988	4,905	− 63.2	− 16.0	57.3	60.8
1989	5,289	− 31.2	9.1	86.1	84.2
1990	5,704	6.2	39.0	116.6	114.4
B. *As Percent of GNP*					
1985	100.0	− 4.14	− 2.45	− 0.96	− 1.62
1986	100.0	− 3.28	− 1.89	− 0.34	− 0.58
1987	100.0	− 2.26	− 1.08	0.49	0.52
1988	100.0	− 1.29	− 0.33	1.17	1.24
1989	100.0	− 0.59	0.17	1.63	1.59
1990	100.0	0.11	0.68	2.04	2.01

[a]GNP from Congressional Budget Office projections in *The Economic and Budget Outlook: An Update* (1985). High-employment surpluses have been recalculated at 5.1 percent unemployment. Adjustments have been made on the basis of CBO projections of future prices and Treasury bill rates and net debt consistent with actual deficits.

monetary base is not allowed to grow. Unemployment would rise 1 or 2 percent from 1987 to 1990. And while, as we have cautioned, our equations are hardly to be taken too seriously, it should be recalled that they have been erring thus far in the direction of being too optimistic. If we adjusted for their errors already apparent for 1985, projections of future GNP growth would be revised sharply downward, and unemployment would rise to deep recession levels, and beyond.

Once we get over the notion that deficits are an automatic sin, and once we learn to measure them correctly, a lot of the easy answers have to be rejected. It is not true that deficits must always be reduced. The current mix of fiscal and monetary policy, with high real interest rates and a huge trade imbalance accountable to an expensive dollar is far from ideal. Our budget priorities may be all wrong. But the knee-jerk reaction that wiping out all of the overall official deficit will solve our problems is hard to sustain.

It may rather make them worse!

13

Implications for the Disarray in Macroeconomics

REACTIONS TO BUDGET DEFICITS have a long history as a political litmus test. To many, those who accept and condone them are reckless spendthrifts irresponsibly courting disaster for the economy and the country. Few present a principled defense of deficits. At best, deficits are viewed as temporary necessities brought on by unusual expenditures, as for wars, or declines in revenues due to recessions. The goal of a budget balanced over at least the long run, with boom surpluses matching recession deficits, is rarely questioned.

Yet, advocacy of "deficit financing" of government expenditures is a fairly central policy implication of a major body of economic thought. Its modern origin can be traced to the then "new economics" of John Maynard Keynes half a century ago. The categorical rejection of budget deficits, as at best irrelevant and at worst deeply injurious, is the common theme of both pre-Keynesian, neoclassical economic thought and the new, anti-Keynesian counterrevolution of monetarists and "rational expectationalists" who seek to explain economic fluctuations within the framework of market-clearing equilibrium.

It must be said that the counterrevolution in macroeconomic

theory has been powerful. It has fascinated—perhaps seduced—some of the best and most rigorous theorists among the generation of young economists who came of age in the last decade.

The macroeconomic, rational expectations revolution, or counterrevolution, is well associated with the outstanding University of Chicago economist, Robert Lucas. It is instructive to note his own explanation of economic evidence that led him to question and reject the Keynesian model to which he had initially sought to contribute, and to build his own substitute paradigm. It was, simply enough, that the Keynesian theory led to the policy conclusion that government budget deficits and easy money would bring about the curbing and reduction of unemployment, and that conclusion was contradicted by the facts. Keynesians had conceded that the fiscal and monetary stimulus might cause some inflation, but this would be accompanied, it was argued, by lesser unemployment. Lucas observed, with Thomas Sargent, that the lesson of the 1970s was that "massive government budget deficits and high rates of monetary expansion" were accompanied not by decreasing unemployment but by *growing* unemployment *and* growing inflation (see, for example, Lucas, 1981, p. 2, and Lucas and Sargent, 1981, pp. 295–296).

I will not tackle here the imposing superstructure that Lucas and others have built on this rejection of Keynesian theory as falsified by events. It is important to recognize though the force of Lucas' reading of recent economic history. For the history that he perceives, and that many others think they see, does indeed have damaging implications for the Keynesian theory that had so long dominated macroeconomic theory as well as policy in most capitalist economies. In correcting that history we can lay a new groundwork for neoclassical support of the basic Keynesian model. To show how, we shall retrace the controversy between Keynes and his neoclassical critics.

Pre-Keynesian economists, faced with large-scale and persistent unemployment, attributed it to technological limitations, interferences with free markets by government or labor unions, or preferences for idleness by the workers themselves. Unemployment might exist because some workers were simply unfit for productive labor in a sophisticated, modern economy. They were insufficiently educated or skilled and there were no employers who would find them worth hiring. Perhaps, like the horse, they had been made largely obsolete by machines.

Unemployment might also be brought on and made to persist by government interferences in the form of minimum wage laws and similar restrictions, or by labor unions that insisted upon wages in excess of the productivity of many workers. Economic theory indicates that, in competitive markets, suppliers can always sell all the product they can profitably produce if they are willing to accept the market price. If there is an excess of the quantity supplied over the quantity demanded, that excess will be eliminated by a fall in the price, increasing the quantity demanded and reducing the quantity supplied.

That argument was assumed to apply in labor markets. Hence, unemployment could only exist when wages, the price of labor, were kept above their market-clearing level. Virtually all of us, after all, would find that nobody would wish to employ us if we insisted upon too high a wage or salary.

Of course, there may also be amongst us those too shiftless or lazy to work. And many do not want to work all of the time. If each worker left his job for two weeks of the year to look for another job, or for any other reason, average unemployment would be almost 4 percent (2 divided by 52) on this account alone.

All of the unemployment, by this line of thought, was "voluntary," the choice of the unemployed themselves. Either they insisted upon or acquiesced in the setting of too high a wage, were too lazy to work, chose to take time between jobs, or, taking a longer view, chose not to acquire education and skills which would make them employable.

We should add, particularly in recent formulations, a rigorous explanation of unemployment in terms of search theory. Employers do not fill openings until they find the right worker and workers may not accept a job until they are convinced that the cost of waiting or further search in hope of finding a better job is not worth the cost of further idleness. All unemployment though, in any event, aside from that occasioned by essential human inadequacy, is frictional or voluntary.

It is this conclusion that Keynes challenged. He did not deny the existence of frictional or voluntary unemployment or the possibility that some people might lack the ability or training to be productive. He insisted though that this was only a part of the story, and frequently a relatively small part. Much unemployment—and persistent unemployment—was not voluntary, not frictional, and not due to the fact that wages were too high.

This involuntary unemployment stemmed from an essential

fact of modern economies, that there is frequently, if not chronically, insufficient effective demand—in lay language, purchasing power—for the goods and services that could be produced in a full-employment economy. And most critically, there may be nothing in the way of equilibrating forces in a free market which would, by themselves, correct this situation. Hence some government action was necessary.

Keynes saw domestic demand, in the absence of government, coming from consumers who bought goods and services for current use, and business which invested in capital goods to be used in future production. The market value of production, net of capital depreciation, must equal the national income, which consists of all of the wages, rent, and interest paid to the owners of factors of production, and the remainder which is profits. If we were always willing to spend all of our national income on current consumption, there would be no problem from the demand side in attaining and maintaining full employment. To the extent people wanted to work, they would work and buy all of what they produced.

The problem of insufficient demand develops because we do not generally spend all of our income on current consumption. We save some of our income, presumably to meet future consumption needs.

To the classical or neoclassical economist, the answer is that this is not a problem. If we do not want to buy all that can be produced because we want to save some of our income to consume later, business will demand (invest in) new plant and equipment or additional inventories to provide for that future consumption. In fact, there is a market price which equates the supply of saving with investment demand, and that price is the rate of interest. If consumers want to refrain from buying more output (save more) than the output that business wants to buy (invest), the rate of interest will fall. With the lower return to saving, households will save less and consume more. And with the lower interest cost of investment, businesses will invest more, that is buy more capital goods. Whatever consumers do not want to buy, business will, and there can thus be no shortage of demand.

The objection to this by Keynes was twofold. First, there is a limit or lower bound to the rate of interest. Keynes presented a sophisticated argument that savers would not lend their money to business investors if they thought rates of interest would rise sufficiently for their capital loss from lower bond prices to out-weigh their interest return. Since at lower rates of interest, the likelihood and amount of loss from higher rates would be greater and the interest return itself less, savers would be unwilling to lend at rates of interest below what historical experience and their expectations suggested was prudent.

But the critical sticking point is that the lowest rate of interest attainable might still be too high to make business want to invest as much as consumers want to save. Hence the gap created by the fact that we do not want to use all of our income for con-sumption will not necessarily be filled by businesses buying in-vestment goods equal to the amount that we save.

Since output must go somewhere, what consumers do not buy must be acquired by business. What business acquires is in-vestment. Saving then, what consumers do not buy, is identically equal to investment. But if business investment *demand* is less than investment, business will cut production so as to eliminate the expense of goods which it cannot sell and does not want. As it cuts production it cuts employment, which in turn reduces in-come and therefore reduces saving (as well as consumption). In this manner, saving is brought into equality with investment de-mand, but it is accomplished by laying off workers and creating unemployment.

It has been objected that the argument by Keynes that savers will not lend at a sufficiently low rate of interest because they expect interest rates will rise is logically inconsistent with the equi-librium he thought to depict. For in the long run, if interest rates did not rise, rational individuals would stop expecting them to rise and would be willing to lend at however low a rate were necessary for investment demand to absorb all the saving that would be forthcoming at full employment.

We need not here fall back on the retort, "in the long run we are all dead." For simply enough, we can dispense with this particular argument by recognizing that, in a monetary economy, people would not want to lend their saving at a rate of interest less than zero. Rather than give a business investor $1,000 with a promise that he would return $990, they can always put the $1,000 under the mattress, or in a checking account, with the knowledge that they can get the full $1,000 back when they want it.

That leads to the other part of the Keynesian problem. Businesses may not see enough investment projects on which they expect to show a rate of profit sufficient to cover interest costs. If the rate of interest is zero, this means that businesses may not see sufficient investment that they can expect to show any positive return after they meet all of their costs, including depreciation. By sufficient we mean as much as the saving that would be forthcoming out of the income earned in an economy with full employment.

This insufficiency may stem from underlying problems of the technology of production. There may be a limit to the amount of additional plant and equipment that would in fact contribute as much to future production as its own cost.

Even if there is not a basic technological bar, "rational expectations," as Keynes might have interpreted the term, would not necessarily lead business to undertake sufficient investment. Rational expectations implies that economic agents act on views of the future which are based upon the efficient use of all current available information. The fact is that when consumers decide to save now and consume later, business may have no way of knowing what or when they will consume later. There simply do not exist futures markets or any other mechanism that will guarantee that businesses will anticipate future prices and returns that will make them want to invest an amount equal to what consumers want to save.

Keynes' insistence that it might not be possible for the rate of interest to get low enough to bring forth sufficient investment demand seemed to rule out lower wages as a solution to the problem of unemployment. Keynes pointed out that any fall in wages as a consequence of unemployment, because it would lower costs of production, would in a competitive economy bring corresponding declines in prices. Hence the nominal fall in wages would not imply a decline in real wage costs and would not directly induce employers to hire the unemployed.

But if unemployment is allowed to bring lower wages and prices, with any given nominal supply of money, the real quantity of money would increase. If the real quantity of money increased, real interest rates would decline and investment demand would increase. Here, though, we again confront directly that lower bound to the rate of interest. No matter how low prices get—and no matter how high, therefore, the real quantity of money—the rate of interest, which cannot get below zero, may not be low enough.

Keynes added tartly that, to the extent lower wages and prices would help by increasing the real quantity of money and lowering rates of interest, it was a foolish solution to pursue. Falling wages might well cause havoc in labor relations, and falling prices, if expected to continue, might only reduce demand by causing would-be buyers to delay their purchases. If a greater real quantity of money can help, the much simpler and nondamaging way to get it is through the monetary authority. Increasing the real quantity of money is something better left to the Chairman of the Federal Reserve than to the President of the AFL–CIO.

The argument that lower prices could solve the problem of full-employment saving exceeding investment demand led the neoclassical economists to a theoretical contribution that rocked the pure Keynesian model. This contribution to the debate by Gottfried Haberler and A. C. Pigou, while not so intended, in turn leads to the relations between government debt, deficits, and inflation which are central to our current analysis.

What Haberler and Pigou pointed out was that, if prices were lower, people who had money would feel wealthier. If they felt wealthier, as we argued early in this work, they would have less need to save and would consume more; indeed they would consume more now and plan to consume more later as well. If we assume free markets and concede therefore that unemployment will drive wages and hence prices down, unemployment will generate its own cure. For, as long as there is unemployment, prices will keep falling. Eventually, if only when what now costs a dollar has a price of a penny, we will feel so wealthy that we will consume so much out of our current income—perhaps all of it—that saving, which is of course income minus consumption, will no longer exceed, even at full employment, whatever investment demand is forthcoming.

We need not dwell on the counterarguments to these counterarguments to Keynes. They include the one already raised that falling prices will generate expectations of further declines which will lower current purchases and demand all the more. There is also the objection that lower prices will tend to bankrupt businesses with fixed contractual obligations, particularly on debt. Thus, even if at some lower level of prices saving would be sufficiently low to solve our problem, the economy would have to go through an impossible wringer to get there. There is even a potential problem that, while lower prices would increase consumption and reduce saving (called the "Pigou effect" by Don Patinkin), it does not necessarily follow that people's propensities are such that they will save enough less to guarantee full employment (dubbed by Patinkin the "Pigou theorem").

But the Haberler–Pigou argument, that lower prices would increase consumption and reduce saving by adding to the public's real monetary wealth, would not really apply to money per se. For money in our economy is essentially deposits or bank liabilities (including currency in the form of Federal Reserve notes). These bank liabilities are in turn backed by bank assets in the form of loans or bonds, which are others' liabilities. Thus, while lower prices increase the real wealth of money holders, they cause exactly equal increases in the real liabilities, and hence reductions in the real net worth, of debtors. This is true, at least, to the extent that all money is backed by private debt.

The neoclassical argument of Haberler and Pigou is saved by the existence of government debt. Whether the government debt is held by the public or constitutes the assets which match the liabilities of private banks or the Federal Reserve, it is that government debt which makes possible a greater net worth of the private sector when prices are lower. If all monetary assets were offset by equal private monetary liabilities, lower prices would prove a wash in affecting the perceived net worth or wealth of the private sector as a whole.

This old anti-Keynesian argument thus brings us full circle. It purports to demonstrate that the "underemployment equilibrium" of Keynes cannot exist in a free economy where prices are permitted to fall when there is excess supply of labor, or anything else. But the argument rests on the recognition that the debt of government is perceived by the public to be its asset. The greater the wealth of the private sector in terms of government debt, the greater will be private consumption. The anti-Keynesian argument that the economic system does have within it a mechanism to bring it to full employment thus depends upon the existence of a government debt.

We might add that, for practical purposes, the government debt would have to be very large, for any reasonable fall in prices to do much good. If prices were to fall as much as they did with the mass unemployment of the Great Depression, that is, by about 25 percent, the real value of even the current federal net debt would rise by only $400 billion. This might raise consumption by, say, $40 billion per year, which is not trivial. But that is still only 1 percent of output, and recall that it took four years in the Great Depression, with unemployment at perhaps 30 percent, for prices to decline 25 percent.

But suppose we believe, with Haberler and Pigou, that lower prices will be associated with greater consumption and aggregate demand because they increase the real value of the government's debt to the private sector. Why not increase that real value directly by increasing the debt? That is accomplished, of course, by running a budget deficit.

Now we have married Keynes and Pigou! Keynes argued that aggregate demand might be insufficient to sustain full employment and the economy unaided could not correct this. Demand could be increased by fiscal policy and, specifically, by having the government spend more to increase demand directly, or by giving household income out of which to spend, or by cutting taxes, thus giving the private sector more after-tax income out of which to spend.

Haberler and Pigou argue that, in principle, lower prices would increase aggregate demand by increasing private wealth in the form of government debt (money or interest-bearing). But if that increase is impossible, difficult, or too slow to obtain by waiting for prices to fall, we can accomplish the same purpose by running a budget deficit.

While Keynesian formulations stress the advantage of budget deficits in contributing to the flow of current after-tax income and purchasing power, the neoclassical, and more fundamental formulation sees *changes in wealth* as affecting current and future demand. This, as we have noted earlier, is consistent with the life cycle theory of consumption advanced by Modigliani and the permanent income theory of Milton Friedman. The neoclassical formulation implies that the budget deficit that will matter for aggregate demand is the one that increases the real net debt of the government to the public.

We come thus to the point, in this review of past arguments in economic theory, which is fundamental to the arguments of today. The implications of the neoclassical formulation of the wealth effect are that budget deficits will increase aggregate demand to the extent that, and *only to the extent that,* they correspond to the increases in the *real net debt* of the government to the public.

That finally brings us back to the Lucas explanation of how he was led to reject the Keynesian model. He charged that the budget deficits which, according to Keynesian theory, should have reduced unemployment, were in fact associated with increasing unemployment. But budget deficits that reduced unemployment would have to be real budget deficits that increase the real value of net debt. The deficits that Lucas—and Keynesians—saw in the seventies, were not real deficits. The combination of rising interest rates which lowered the market value of the debt held by the public, and the inflation lowering the real value all the more, converted the nominal budget deficits into real surpluses. Since Keynesian theory—and neoclassical theory as well, as we have noted—would predict that these surpluses would depress aggregate demand and hence increase unemployment, there is nothing in this economic history which can properly motivate rejection of the Keynesian model.

There remain a number of questions to resolve and *obiter dicta* that may be suggested. First, the evidence of real budget surpluses and hence tight fiscal policy challenges the conventional view that the inflation of the 1970s was due to excess demand. This points us all the more to the conclusion that explanation of the inflation was rather to be found on the supply side, in particular, from huge increases in the cost of energy brought on by skyrocketing oil prices, as well as sharp rises in the cost of agricultural products and other raw materials on world markets.

This then leads to a new view of the seemingly shifting and unstable Phillips curves originally thought to show a negative relation between inflation and unemployment. The acceleration of inflation over a number of years should not have been attributed to movement up the vertical Phillips curve at the "natural rate of employment." For if demand was insufficient, employment was below its "natural" rate and the causes of the acceleration of inflation were to be found elsewhere.

The relevance, if not the reasonableness, of the new "equilibrium" macroeconomics is also called into question. If increasing unemployment is found again to be associated with inadequate aggregate demand because of real, if unrecognized, budget surpluses, there seems less point in the equilibrium explanations. It becomes all the harder to believe that unemployment grew because workers increasingly decided that the real wages being offered them were inadequate. And similarly we need not explain reductions in unemployment in terms of workers, not recognizing that prices are rising as rapidly as wages, being fooled into thinking that the real wage is higher and hence accepting work at jobs that they would otherwise reject.

In short, correct perception of what has been happening to debt and deficits over the past decade should restore the demand side to its proper and major place in economic analysis. Economists can and should confidently open both eyes so that they can understand, and manipulate where necessary, both blades of the Marshallian scissors.

14

Where It All Gets Us: A Summing Up

THE FEDERAL BUDGET DEFICIT has become in some circles the hottest political issue since Vietnam. Democrats and Republicans echo each others' proclamations of disaster and largely restrict their differences to their proposed remedies, and the casting of blame. Scoring political points has replaced almost all efforts at sober economic analysis.

Thus, we have the spectacle of the Senate of the United States, after no hearings, adopting by an overwhelming 75–21 vote a deficit-elimination bill which would revolutionize the fiscal process. And then they ask staff aides to try to figure out what they have done. The way federal budgets are put together, they may never know.

The message of this book is simple. Deficits do matter. But to know how and how much you have to measure them correctly. And deficits can be good as well as bad.

The tricks played by inflation have been critical. Moderate deficits have been made to appear huge. Real surpluses have been made to look like deficits.

Misunderstanding facts, we have foolishly courted and deepened recessions. We have confused economic and financial analysis. We have encouraged economic theorists off on a tangent to our central concerns.

Of fundamental importance, the federal budget deficit is someone else's surplus. The federal debt, however, frequently viewed as a burden to the government or to future taxpayers, is wealth to those who own it. And the more wealth people have, the more they try to spend, now and in the future.

Since federal deficits add to federal debt, which adds to private wealth, deficits are expected to increase aggregate demand and spending. If there is slack in the economy, the result is increased output. If we are at full employment and there is no slack, the increased demand raises prices and encourages inflation.

But for the deficit to matter it must be a *real* deficit. A real deficit is one which increases the real debt outstanding and hence increases the real wealth of those who hold that debt. Hence the vital importance of the inflation correction!

Inflation in effect generates an "inflation tax," as it eats away the real value of the public's holdings of Treasury bills, notes, and bonds, or the cash which they back.

As inflation accelerated in the years of the Carter Administration, the real value of outstanding public debt declined sharply. Higher interest rates reduced the market value of Treasury securities and higher prices further cut their real worth. The declines in the real market value of debt held by the public more than offset the increases in public holdings resulting from the nominal deficits. In real terms, corresponding to the total change in the real market value of debt, the federal budget was not in deficit but in surplus.

The false perception of a real deficit led to restrictive monetary *and* fiscal policies and the worst recession since the Great Depression of the 1930s.

The major tax reductions of 1982 and 1983, coupled with reduction in the inflation tax, then propelled the 1983–84 recovery. Jack Kemp and the other supply-side tax cutters were right, for the wrong reasons. The economy reacted to classic demand-side stimulus.

This is made clear by a new look at the statistical data, incorporating inflation-corrected measures of budget deficits. Without corrections, even cyclically adjusted or high-employment budgets seem to be in deficit, and increasing deficit, through the sluggish and rising-unemployment decade of the 1970s. That could be taken to mean that deficits, fiscal policy, and demand did not matter. Hence the reversion to monetarism and supply siders!

Adjusted for inflation, the "deficits" become surpluses and the demand-oriented explanation of stagnation re-emerges. Inflation-adjusted high-employment budget deficits show a remarkably close relation with subsequent growth in real gross national product and reductions in unemployment.

What is more, the corrected budget deficits maintain their strong relation with real economic growth and reduction in unemployment when monetary variables are included in the statistical relations. Changes in the monetary base are also positively related to increases in real GNP and negatively related to unemployment. We have new confirmation that monetary and fiscal policy both matter, but there is evidence that the corrected budget deficits may well be the more potent.

The adjusted deficits cast further light on important currents within the economy. Their expansionary effect on output as a whole is such that, widespread belief to the contrary notwithstanding, deficits are positively associated with private investment. We have "crowding in" rather than "crowding out."

The budget deficits are, however, associated with subsequent increases in imports and decreases in net exports. They would appear thus to have contributed substantially to our large current trade deficit.

There is further evidence that inflation-corrected, cyclically adjusted budget deficits have similar effects in major OECD countries. The United Kingdom, with the slowest economic growth, turns up with inflation-adjusted budget surpluses, while high-growth Japan has had the largest deficits. And the United States budget deficit, whatever problems, real or imagined, it may pose for other nations, has been highly correlated with *their* growth in output.

Statistical analysis also offers some possible surprises for Wall Street. Increases in deficits turn out to be associated with increases in Dow Jones stock averages. This probably relates in part to the stimulatory effect of deficits on demand and output and hence on profits. It also relates to the fact that nominal deficits which are not real do not increase the cost of capital.

Armed with more meaningful measures we should be able to guide future policy better. Recognizing the variety of possible measures of budget deficits, we may be particularly wary of so-called "balanced-budget" constitutional amendments. Recognizing that the federal government, unlike private business and most state and local governments, has no separate capital budget, we should be especially resistant to deficit reducers who would destroy the nation's wealth.

Our future and our children's future is always a proper concern. The public has feared that budget deficits add to their own debt burden and that of future generations.

What we really bequeath to the future, however, is our physical and human capital. A "deficit" which finances construction and maintenance of our roads, bridges, harbors, and airports is an investment in the future. So are expenditures to preserve and enhance our natural resources, or to educate our people and keep them healthy. Federal budgets which are balanced by running down our country's capital or mindlessly selling public assets to private exploiters are real national deficits.

As for that bottom line on what to do about the current federal deficit, it depends. If we were to realize the projections of the fiscal 1986 Joint Congressional Budget Resolution, and we are seriously committed to a high-employment economy, we would have probably gone far enough in overall budget cutting. The increase in debt for the last five years has been such that even our slower rate of inflation generates a substantial inflation tax. The inflation tax rate is less, but the public debt on which it is paid is more.

Inflation-adjusted budget deficits, assuming that the budget resolution projections are realized, would not be unduly large. For those of us who highly prize economic growth and low unemployment, the risk of insufficient fiscal stimulus must be weighted heavily. One cannot properly counsel budget balancing in an economy with unemployment still near 7 percent and real economic growth well below its potential. The politics of Gramm–Rudman notwithstanding, a budget balanced by current federal rules of accounting is an invitation to economic disaster. If achieved solely by expenditure cuts, it would be likely to devastate public investment. And, however accomplished, by reducing aggregate demand and purchasing power, it would threaten the worst recession or depression in half a century.

The budget mix is another matter. We may well wish to spend more on investment in our public infrastructure and human capital and less on subsidies and support to those with the most political clout. We may also wish to devote more to our nation's welfare and less to warfare. And we may wish to finance our expenditures with a more equitable tax system.

With a sound and balanced fiscal policy, we should look all the more to a monetary policy which permits the economy to move at full speed. No artificial shortage of money should be allowed to so distort the value of the dollar as to cripple the significant sectors of the American economy which do and should compete in world markets.

And as for economics itself, the lesson is to think again. Our theory and analysis of the last half century have not been all wrong. Many of our numbers have. Supply and demand are *both* going strong.

As with any science, economics can be expected to be always changing. New facts help new theories supplant the old. We are properly moved by new currents, and learn from the experience. We need not be carried away.

We have listened to new monetarists, supply siders, and the market-clearing apostles of rational expectations. We have been challenged and have learned in the process. We can now return confidently to what has been the mainstream of economic thinking. A competitive, market-oriented economy is capable of stunning successes. But there remains a major role for government policy to insure the aggregate demand necessary for full employment and maximum growth. With correct measures, the macroeconomic theory of the past half century can continue to point the path.

Appendices

A

Appendix to Chapter 7

CRITICAL ARGUMENTS REGARDING the effects of deficits, explicit federal debt and "contingency obligations" such as social security may be presented in a simple macroeconomic model in which output is a function of effective demand up to the point of full employment. Where aggregate demand exceeds full-employment output, prices rise until a real-balance effect, directly and/or through higher rates of interest, reduces real demand to full-employment output. We can reduce this system to its barest essentials in the following equations:

$$C/P = C(Y/P, K, GD/P, M_x/P, i) \tag{A.1}$$
$$0 < C_1 < 1, \ C_2, C_3, C_4 > 0, \ C_5 \gtreqqless 0$$
$$I/P = I[C(t)/P(t), i]; \ I_1 > 0, \ I_2 < 0, \ -C_5 \tag{A.2}$$
$$M/P = L(Y/P, K, GD/P, i); \ L_1, L_2, L_3 > 0, \ L_4 < 0 \tag{A.3}$$
$$Y/P \equiv C/P + I/P \tag{A.4}$$
$$Y/P \gtreqqless (Y/P)_f \tag{A.5}$$

where: C = nominal consumption
Y = nominal income or output
K = real capital
GD = government debt to the private sector
M_x = outside money
M = total quantity of money, inside and outside
P = the price level
i = the rate of interest
I = nominal investment
$C(t), P(t)$ = the expected paths of nominal consumption and prices
$(Y/P)_f$ = full-employment output

and numerical subscripts indicate partial derivatives with respect to arguments of the behavioral functions.

Thus, real consumption is a function of real output, of wealth in the form of real capital, of outside money and government debt to the private sector, and of the rate of interest (A.1). Real investment is a function of the rate of interest and of the expected path of real consumption (A.2). The rate of interest is determined by the condition that the real supply of money equals the demand for money, which is a function of real output, of the stock of nonmonetary wealth, and of the rate of interest (A.3). Finally, real output equals real consumption plus real investment (A.4), but is bounded by the supply constraint of full employment (A.5).

We have made the customary assumptions regarding partial derivatives. The only crucial one for our argument is that the partial derivative of real consumption with respect to wealth in the form of real government debt to the private sector, C_3, is positive. We thus reject the Barro equivalence effect, by which government debt is not perceived, either in whole or in part, as a net asset.

Deficits increase government debt, GD, or outside money, M_x, to the extent the deficit is financed by printing money. High values of GD or M_x increase both current consumption and planned future consumption (thus expected future consumption). The greater the deficit, the greater the increase in consumption and hence the greater the growth in output. Inflation, by raising the value of P, lowers the real value of the government debt, GD/P. It hence reduces consumption, both current and planned, or reduces the rate of growth of consumption associated with a given nominal deficit. Increases in current and planned consumption will in turn generate investment, thus further adding to output.

The system may be extended by the introduction of net social security wealth, defined as the difference perceived by current households between the present value of the expected social security benefits and the present value of the taxes that they are paying and expect to pay for social security. We may then write (A.1) as

$$C/P = C(Y/P, K, GD/P + SSWN/P, M_x/P, i) \qquad (A.1')$$

where $SSWN$ = net social security wealth. We should then similarly rewrite (A.3) as

$$M/P = L(Y/P, K, GD/P + SSWN/P, i) \qquad (A.3')$$

Thus, consumption demand would be higher if households perceive greater wealth in their holdings of either explicit government debt or implicit government debt in the form of the present value of the excess of social security commitments over social security taxes. Now, if the introduction of net social security wealth increases the total government debt to the private sector, explicit and implicit, consumption demand will rise. If real output is less than full-employment output, investment may also rise, accommodated of course by a marginal propensity to consume of less than one. Just how investment will change will depend upon interest elasticities and the reaction of the money supply. Since, in accordance with the life cycle hypothesis, increased wealth will generate higher planned consumption not only currently but over the entire life cycle, rational firms will strive to invest more in anticipation of greater future consumption.

What is the effect of an explicit deficit, or the effect of any implicit deficit brought on by the increase in net contingency obligations, such as for social security, if we assume full (or fixed) employment? The answer, at least for the equilibrium or steady-state case, can be remarkably simple. According to equations (A.1) or (A.1'), at the existing price level the demand for real consumption would increase. The anticipation that real consumption would increase would generate increased investment demand according to (A.2). But since real output cannot increase, the price level, P, will rise. If the money supply, M, is not increased, the new equilibrium will entail a higher rate of interest (associated with a lower ratio of money to total government debt), less investment, and more consumption.

But this result, it should be clear, stems only from the assumption that the money supply is not accommodative. In the case of expansion of social security, if the initial real value of the explicit government debt, GD/P, is sufficiently high, at least higher than the addition of real (indexed) social security wealth, there would appear to be no reason why the price level, the money supply, and all nominal variables cannot be increased in some proportion, δ, such that the sum of explicit and implicit government debt, $GD/\delta P + \delta SSWN/\delta P$, will equal the original explicit debt, GD/P. Since, with the usual assumption of no money illusion, all real functions are homogeneous of degree zero in nominal variables and the price level, if the initial system can be full-employment equilibrium, there is no reason why there cannot be a corresponding new equilibrium with prices, the money supply (including outside money), and total government debt all proportionately higher, but the interest rate, real consumption, real investment, real output, and the stock of real capital all unchanged.[1] We are indeed abstracting from the possibility that parameters of GD/P and $SSWN/P$ in both the consumption and liquidity preference functions would be different, but this would seem, at worst, to ignore minor, second-order effects.

B

Additional Tables

TABLE B.1 Assets, Liabilities, and Net Worth, Total Government, 1945–84
(Billions of Dollars)

(1)	(2)	(3)	(4)	(5)	(6)	(7)
		ASSETS		TOTAL	NET DEBT	NET WORTH
YEAR	*Tangible*	*Financial*	*Total*	LIABILITIES	(3) − (5)	(4) − (5)
1945	261.2	115.0	376.1	349.0	234.0	27.2
1946	254.2	92.3	346.6	323.3	231.0	23.2
1947	246.1	101.4	347.5	314.4	213.1	33.0
1948	231.2	109.4	340.6	314.6	205.2	26.0
1949	207.8	105.7	313.5	318.4	212.7	−4.9
1950	226.1	116.6	342.6	321.6	205.1	21.0
1951	247.0	125.9	372.9	323.0	197.1	49.9
1952	269.6	130.5	400.0	334.4	203.9	65.7
1953	268.5	133.9	402.4	347.9	214.0	54.4
1954	322.3	131.5	453.8	356.0	224.5	97.8
1955	352.1	137.2	489.3	357.9	220.7	131.4
1956	384.4	138.4	522.8	353.2	214.8	169.6
1957	401.5	142.1	543.6	365.4	223.3	178.2
1958	416.5	141.5	558.0	374.6	233.1	183.4
1959	428.8	151.4	580.2	387.2	235.8	193.0
1960	442.9	157.5	600.4	406.0	248.5	194.5
1961	461.6	164.1	625.7	420.1	256.1	205.5
1962	486.6	175.2	661.8	442.5	267.3	219.4
1963	512.9	187.8	700.7	455.2	267.4	245.5
1964	542.5	199.5	742.0	474.6	275.1	267.4
1965	574.7	212.1	786.8	486.3	274.3	300.5
1966	613.5	229.9	843.4	510.6	280.7	332.8
1967	658.1	240.8	898.9	533.0	292.2	365.9
1968	713.9	259.1	973.0	561.4	302.2	411.7
1969	783.8	273.2	1057.0	566.2	293.0	490.8
1970	854.4	303.5	1157.9	633.9	330.4	524.0
1971	925.4	331.6	1257.0	700.8	369.2	556.2
1972	1009.1	361.3	1370.4	741.7	380.4	628.7
1973	1179.5	419.9	1599.4	788.7	368.8	810.7
1974	1341.2	480.4	1821.6	834.0	353.6	987.6
1975	1461.4	499.8	1961.2	957.4	457.5	1003.8
1976	1574.4	545.5	2119.9	1090.7	545.2	1029.2
1977	1765.3	599.6	2365.0	1167.5	567.8	1197.5
1978	2018.5	694.7	2713.2	1253.0	558.4	1460.1
1979	2330.5	850.2	3180.7	1342.0	491.8	1838.7
1980	2663.6	926.6	3590.2	1437.3	510.7	2152.9
1981	2870.7	960.1	3830.9	1568.9	608.8	2262.0
1982	2958.4	1061.2	4019.6	1929.2	868.0	2090.5
1983	3118.3	1117.1	4235.4	2143.0	1026.0	2092.4
1984	3231.3	1232.3	4463.5	2478.7	1246.5	1984.8

TABLE B.2 Assets, Liabilities, and Net Worth, Federal, 1945–84
(Billions of Dollars)

(1)	(2)	(3)	(4)	(5)	(6)	(7)
		ASSETS		TOTAL	NET DEBT	NET WORTH
YEAR	*Tangible*	*Financial*	*Total*	LIABILITIES	(3) − (5)	(4) − (5)
1945	186.2	102.8	289.0	332.6	229.8	−43.7
1946	169.9	79.8	249.7	307.1	227.3	−57.5
1947	148.9	87.2	236.1	297.0	209.7	−60.9
1948	127.3	93.9	221.2	294.6	200.7	−73.5
1949	110.5	89.3	199.8	295.8	206.4	−96.0
1950	111.7	98.7	210.4	295.0	196.3	−84.6
1951	118.6	107.1	225.7	294.5	187.3	−68.7
1952	134.7	109.8	244.5	302.2	192.4	−57.6
1953	127.0	111.2	238.1	311.8	200.6	−73.6
1954	175.1	106.7	281.8	313.4	206.7	−31.6
1955	187.2	111.5	298.7	310.7	199.2	−12.0
1956	198.9	112.7	311.6	303.7	191.0	7.9
1957	200.5	115.7	316.2	310.9	195.1	5.4
1958	202.9	114.4	317.4	314.7	200.3	2.6
1959	202.8	121.7	324.5	320.9	199.2	3.5
1960	205.8	124.7	330.4	331.8	207.1	−1.3
1961	208.4	129.9	338.3	340.3	210.4	−2.1
1962	215.5	138.1	353.6	355.3	217.2	−1.7
1963	222.7	146.8	369.5	362.7	215.9	6.8
1964	230.1	154.9	385.0	374.8	219.9	10.1
1965	236.6	162.8	399.4	380.5	217.7	18.9
1966	244.0	176.3	420.3	398.9	222.6	21.4
1967	254.9	184.1	439.0	415.7	231.6	23.3
1968	267.8	197.4	465.2	435.0	237.7	30.2
1969	287.8	211.7	499.5	437.5	225.8	62.0
1970	304.6	232.8	537.4	484.3	251.5	53.1
1971	323.7	251.8	575.5	528.9	277.1	46.6
1972	345.0	266.7	611.7	551.5	284.8	60.2
1973	383.7	310.6	694.3	586.0	275.3	108.3
1974	414.7	361.8	776.5	628.0	266.2	148.5
1975	457.8	378.0	835.8	736.3	358.2	99.6
1976	493.6	411.2	904.8	841.8	430.5	63.1
1977	549.6	443.7	993.3	904.3	460.6	89.1
1978	614.9	518.7	1133.3	981.1	462.7	152.2
1979	709.1	657.1	1366.2	1058.6	401.5	307.6
1980	822.5	720.9	1543.4	1161.6	440.7	381.8
1981	892.4	742.4	1634.9	1301.1	558.7	333.7
1982	965.2	801.7	1766.9	1591.3	789.6	175.6
1983	1049.4	821.6	1871.0	1764.9	943.3	106.1
1984	1118.0	887.4	2005.4	2063.3	1175.9	−57.9

TABLE B.3   Assets, Liabilities, and Net Worth, State and Local, 1945–84
(Billions of Dollars)

(1)	(2)	(3)	(4)	(5)	(6)	(7)
	ASSETS			TOTAL	NET DEBT	NET WORTH
YEAR	*Tangible*	*Financial*	*Total*	LIABILITIES	(3) − (5)	(4) − (5)
1945	75.0	12.2	87.2	16.3	4.2	70.8
1946	84.4	12.5	96.9	16.2	3.7	80.7
1947	97.2	14.1	111.3	17.4	3.3	93.9
1948	104.0	15.5	119.4	20.0	4.5	99.5
1949	97.3	16.4	113.7	22.7	6.3	91.0
1950	114.4	17.8	132.2	26.6	8.8	105.6
1951	128.4	18.8	147.2	28.6	9.8	118.6
1952	134.8	20.7	155.5	32.2	11.5	123.3
1953	141.5	22.7	164.2	36.1	13.4	128.1
1954	147.2	24.8	172.0	42.6	17.8	129.3
1955	164.9	25.7	190.6	47.3	21.5	143.4
1956	185.5	25.7	211.2	49.5	23.8	161.7
1957	201.0	26.4	227.4	54.6	28.2	172.8
1958	213.5	27.1	240.6	59.8	32.7	180.8
1959	226.1	29.7	255.8	66.3	36.6	189.4
1960	237.2	32.8	270.0	74.2	41.4	195.8
1961	253.2	34.1	287.4	79.8	45.7	207.6
1962	271.1	37.1	308.2	87.1	50.0	221.1
1963	290.2	41.0	331.2	92.5	51.5	238.7
1964	312.5	44.6	357.1	99.8	55.2	257.3
1965	338.2	49.3	387.4	105.9	56.6	281.6
1966	369.5	53.6	423.1	111.7	58.1	311.4
1967	403.2	56.6	459.8	117.3	60.6	342.6
1968	446.1	61.8	507.9	126.4	64.6	381.5
1969	496.0	61.5	557.5	128.8	67.2	428.8
1970	549.8	70.7	620.5	149.6	78.9	470.9
1971	601.7	79.8	681.4	171.9	92.1	509.5
1972	664.1	94.6	758.7	190.2	95.6	568.5
1973	795.8	109.3	905.1	202.7	93.5	702.4
1974	926.5	118.7	1045.1	206.0	87.4	839.1
1975	1003.6	121.8	1125.4	221.1	99.3	904.3
1976	1080.8	134.3	1215.1	248.9	114.7	966.1
1977	1215.7	156.0	1371.7	263.2	107.2	1108.4
1978	1403.6	176.3	1579.9	271.9	95.7	1307.9
1979	1621.4	193.0	1814.4	283.4	90.3	1531.1
1980	1841.1	205.8	2046.8	275.8	70.0	1771.1
1981	1978.3	217.7	2196.0	267.8	50.1	1928.2
1982	1993.2	259.5	2252.7	337.8	78.3	1914.8
1983	2068.9	295.5	2364.4	378.1	82.6	1986.3
1984	2113.3	344.9	2458.2	415.5	70.6	2042.7

TABLE B.4   Assets, Liabilities, and Net Worth, Total Government, Current
Dollars Divided by GNP Price Deflator, 1945–84
(Billions of 1972 Dollars)

(1)	(2)	(3)	(4)	(5)	(6)	(7)
		ASSETS		TOTAL	NET DEBT	NET WORTH
YEAR	*Tangible*	*Financial*	*Total*	LIABILITIES	(3) − (5)	(4) − (5)
1945	638.7	281.2	919.9	853.4	572.2	66.5
1946	535.1	194.3	729.4	680.5	486.2	48.9
1947	475.9	196.0	671.9	608.0	412.0	63.9
1948	435.1	205.8	641.0	592.0	386.2	48.9
1949	397.6	202.2	599.9	609.3	407.0	−9.4
1950	404.3	208.5	612.8	575.2	366.8	37.6
1951	428.9	218.7	647.6	561.0	342.3	86.6
1952	459.5	222.4	681.8	569.9	347.5	111.9
1953	454.6	226.7	681.3	589.1	362.4	92.2
1954	536.9	219.1	756.0	593.1	374.1	162.9
1955	571.0	222.6	793.6	580.6	358.0	213.1
1956	600.2	216.1	816.3	551.5	335.4	264.8
1957	613.0	216.9	829.9	557.9	340.9	272.1
1958	623.9	212.0	835.9	561.1	349.1	274.8
1959	628.6	221.9	850.5	567.6	345.7	282.9
1960	642.7	228.5	871.2	589.0	360.5	282.2
1961	660.0	234.6	894.6	600.7	366.1	293.9
1962	683.0	245.9	929.0	621.0	375.1	307.9
1963	709.7	259.9	969.6	629.9	370.0	339.8
1964	738.5	271.6	1010.0	646.1	374.5	364.0
1965	762.9	281.5	1044.4	645.6	364.1	398.8
1966	786.6	294.7	1081.3	654.6	359.9	426.7
1967	816.1	298.6	1114.7	660.9	362.4	453.7
1968	845.0	306.8	1151.8	664.5	357.7	487.3
1969	878.1	306.1	1184.2	634.4	328.3	549.9
1970	911.7	323.9	1235.6	676.4	352.5	559.1
1971	943.7	338.2	1281.9	714.7	376.5	567.2
1972	987.1	353.4	1340.5	725.5	372.1	615.0
1973	1075.9	383.0	1458.9	719.4	336.4	739.5
1974	1107.2	396.6	1503.8	688.5	291.9	815.3
1975	1130.0	386.5	1516.6	740.3	353.8	776.3
1976	1159.6	401.8	1561.3	803.3	401.6	758.0
1977	1224.4	415.9	1640.3	809.7	393.8	830.6
1978	1287.6	443.1	1730.7	799.3	356.2	931.4
1979	1369.4	499.6	1869.0	788.6	289.0	1080.4
1980	1419.9	494.0	1913.9	766.2	272.2	1147.7
1981	1415.3	473.4	1888.7	773.5	300.1	1115.2
1982	1398.3	501.6	1899.9	911.8	410.2	988.1
1983	1421.3	509.2	1930.5	976.8	467.6	953.7
1984	1419.8	541.5	1961.3	1089.2	547.7	872.1

TABLE B.5   Assets, Liabilities, and Net Worth, Federal, Current Dollars
Divided by GNP Price Deflator, 1945–84
(Billions of 1972 Dollars)

(1)	(2)	(3)	(4)	(5)	(6)	(7)
		ASSETS		TOTAL	NET DEBT	NET WORTH
YEAR	*Tangible*	*Financial*	*Total*	LIABILITIES	(3) − (5)	(4) − (5)
1945	455.3	251.5	706.7	813.5	562.0	− 106.8
1946	357.6	167.9	525.5	646.4	478.5	− 120.9
1947	287.9	168.7	456.6	574.3	405.6	− 117.7
1948	239.5	176.7	416.2	554.4	377.7	− 138.2
1949	211.4	170.9	382.3	565.9	395.0	− 183.6
1950	199.8	176.6	376.4	527.6	351.0	− 151.2
1951	206.0	186.0	392.0	511.4	325.3	− 119.3
1952	229.7	187.1	416.8	515.0	327.9	− 98.2
1953	215.0	188.2	403.2	527.9	339.6	− 124.7
1954	291.8	177.8	469.5	522.1	344.4	− 52.6
1955	303.6	180.9	484.4	503.9	323.0	− 19.5
1956	310.6	175.9	486.5	474.2	298.3	12.3
1957	306.1	176.7	482.8	474.6	297.9	8.2
1958	304.0	171.4	475.4	471.5	300.1	3.9
1959	297.2	178.4	475.6	470.4	292.0	5.2
1960	298.6	180.9	479.5	481.4	300.5	− 1.9
1961	297.9	185.7	483.7	486.6	300.9	− 3.0
1962	302.5	193.9	496.4	498.7	304.9	− 2.4
1963	308.2	203.1	511.3	501.9	298.8	9.4
1964	313.2	210.8	524.0	510.2	299.4	13.8
1965	314.0	216.1	530.1	505.0	289.0	25.1
1966	312.9	226.0	538.9	511.4	285.4	27.4
1967	316.1	228.3	544.4	515.5	287.2	28.9
1968	317.0	233.6	550.6	514.9	281.3	35.7
1969	322.4	237.2	559.6	490.1	252.9	69.5
1970	325.0	248.4	573.5	516.8	268.4	56.6
1971	330.1	256.8	586.9	539.4	282.6	47.6
1972	337.5	260.9	598.4	539.5	278.6	58.9
1973	350.0	283.4	633.3	534.5	251.2	98.8
1974	342.3	298.7	641.0	518.4	219.8	122.6
1975	354.0	292.3	646.3	569.3	277.0	77.0
1976	363.6	302.9	666.4	620.0	317.1	46.5
1977	381.2	307.7	688.9	627.2	319.5	61.8
1978	392.2	330.7	722.9	625.8	295.2	97.1
1979	416.7	386.1	802.8	622.1	235.9	180.8
1980	438.5	384.3	822.8	619.2	234.9	203.5
1981	440.0	366.0	806.0	641.5	275.4	164.5
1982	456.2	378.9	835.2	752.2	373.2	83.0
1983	478.3	374.5	852.8	804.5	430.0	48.3
1984	491.2	389.9	881.1	906.6	516.7	− 25.4

TABLE B.6   Assets, Liabilities, and Net Worth, State and Local, Current
Dollars Divided by GNP Price Deflator, 1945–84
(Billions of 1972 Dollars)

(1)	(2)	(3)	(4)	(5)	(6)	(7)
		ASSETS		TOTAL	NET DEBT	NET WORTH
YEAR	*Tangible*	*Financial*	*Total*	LIABILITIES	(3) − (5)	(4) − (5)
1945	183.4	29.7	213.2	39.9	10.2	173.2
1946	177.6	26.4	203.9	34.1	7.7	169.9
1947	188.0	27.3	215.3	33.7	6.4	181.6
1948	195.6	29.1	224.8	37.6	8.4	187.2
1949	186.2	31.3	217.6	43.4	12.0	174.2
1950	204.5	31.9	236.4	47.6	15.8	188.8
1951	222.9	32.7	255.6	49.6	17.0	205.9
1952	229.8	35.2	265.0	54.9	19.7	210.1
1953	239.6	38.5	278.1	61.2	22.7	216.9
1954	245.2	41.3	286.5	71.0	29.7	215.5
1955	267.5	41.7	309.2	76.6	34.9	232.5
1956	289.6	40.2	329.8	77.3	37.1	252.5
1957	306.9	40.2	347.1	83.3	43.0	263.8
1958	319.9	40.6	360.4	89.6	49.0	270.8
1959	331.4	43.5	374.9	97.2	53.7	277.7
1960	344.1	47.6	391.7	107.7	60.0	284.1
1961	362.1	48.8	410.9	114.1	65.3	296.8
1962	380.5	52.1	432.6	122.3	70.2	310.3
1963	401.5	56.8	458.3	128.0	71.2	330.3
1964	425.3	60.7	486.0	135.8	75.1	350.2
1965	448.9	65.4	514.3	140.5	75.1	373.8
1966	473.7	68.7	542.4	143.2	74.5	399.2
1967	500.0	70.2	570.2	145.4	75.2	424.8
1968	528.0	73.1	601.2	149.6	76.4	451.6
1969	555.7	68.9	624.7	144.2	75.3	480.4
1970	586.7	75.5	662.1	159.6	84.2	502.5
1971	613.6	81.4	695.0	175.3	93.9	519.7
1972	649.6	92.5	742.1	186.0	93.5	556.1
1973	725.9	99.7	825.6	184.9	85.3	640.7
1974	764.9	98.0	862.8	170.1	72.1	692.8
1975	776.0	94.2	870.2	171.0	76.8	699.3
1976	796.0	98.9	894.9	183.4	84.5	711.6
1977	843.2	108.2	951.4	182.6	74.4	768.8
1978	895.3	112.4	1007.8	173.5	61.0	834.3
1979	952.8	113.4	1066.2	166.5	53.1	899.7
1980	981.5	109.7	1091.2	147.0	37.3	944.1
1981	975.3	107.3	1082.7	132.0	24.7	950.6
1982	942.1	122.7	1064.7	159.7	37.0	905.1
1983	943.0	134.7	1077.7	172.3	37.7	905.3
1984	928.6	151.5	1080.1	182.6	31.0	897.6

TABLE B.7　　Actual Budget Surplus, 1955–84 (Billions of Dollars)

(1)	(2)	(3)	(4)	(5)
		SURPLUS OR DEFICIT (−) ON NATIONAL INCOME ACCOUNTS		
YEAR	Official	Adjusted for Price Effects	Adjusted for Interest Effects	Adjusted for Price and Interest Effects
1955	4.4	10.5	8.3	14.3
1956	6.1	14.3	9.9	18.2
1957	2.3	7.1	− 3.3	1.5
1958	− 10.3	− 6.1	− 4.4	− 0.2
1959	− 1.1	3.6	3.0	7.8
1960	3.0	5.3	− 6.8	− 4.5
1961	− 3.9	− 0.6	− 1.5	1.8
1962	− 4.2	0.0	− 6.6	− 2.3
1963	0.3	3.6	3.0	6.3
1964	− 3.3	0.6	− 3.6	0.2
1965	0.5	6.4	3.7	9.5
1966	− 1.8	6.3	− 3.5	4.6
1967	− 13.2	− 5.2	− 8.7	− 0.8
1968	− 6.0	5.5	− 5.0	6.5
1969	8.4	21.9	16.0	29.4
1970	− 12.4	− 0.2	− 26.4	− 14.2
1971	− 22.0	− 9.5	− 25.9	− 13.4
1972	− 16.8	− 4.5	− 12.5	− 0.1
1973	− 5.5	15.7	− 2.1	19.1
1974	− 11.5	19.7	− 13.5	17.7
1975	− 69.3	− 46.0	− 71.8	− 48.6
1976	− 53.1	− 32.0	− 65.7	− 44.6
1977	− 45.9	− 16.6	− 29.8	− 0.6
1978	− 29.5	13.7	− 10.3	32.9
1979	− 16.1	27.5	− 11.5	32.1
1980	− 61.2	− 6.1	− 47.5	7.6
1981	− 64.3	− 14.6	− 68.0	− 18.3
1982	− 148.2	− 114.8	− 210.6	− 177.2
1983	− 178.6	− 143.5	− 136.3	− 101.2
1984	− 175.8	− 133.6	− 196.3	− 154.1

TABLE B.8.   High-Employment Surplus, 1955–84 (Billions of Dollars)

(1)	(2)	(3)	(4)	(5)
		SURPLUS OR DEFICIT ($-$) ON NATIONAL INCOME ACCOUNTS		
YEAR	*Official*	*Adjusted for Price Effects*	*Adjusted for Interest Effects*	*Adjusted for Price and Interest Effects*
1955	5.2	11.2	9.0	15.1
1956	7.9	16.1	11.8	20.0
1957	6.1	10.9	0.5	5.3
1958	0.0	4.2	5.9	10.1
1959	5.4	10.2	9.6	14.3
1960	12.1	14.4	2.3	4.5
1961	7.1	10.4	9.5	12.8
1962	3.0	7.3	0.7	4.9
1963	7.4	10.7	10.2	13.5
1964	1.1	4.9	0.8	4.6
1965	0.9	6.8	4.0	9.9
1966	-5.6	2.5	-7.3	0.8
1967	-15.1	-7.1	-10.7	-2.7
1968	-11.0	0.5	-9.9	1.6
1969	4.9	18.3	12.4	25.9
1970	-4.6	7.6	-18.6	-6.4
1971	-11.3	1.2	-15.2	-2.7
1972	-12.1	0.3	-7.8	4.6
1973	-9.5	11.8	-6.1	15.2
1974	-0.3	30.9	-2.3	28.9
1975	-29.1	-5.9	-31.6	-8.4
1976	-17.4	3.7	-30.0	-8.9
1977	-20.4	8.8	-4.3	24.9
1978	-15.9	27.3	3.2	46.4
1979	-2.0	41.6	2.6	46.2
1980	-17.1	38.0	-3.4	51.8
1981	-3.2	46.5	-6.9	42.8
1982	-32.6	0.8	-95.0	-61.7
1983	-59.7	-24.6	-17.4	17.7
1984	-108.6	-66.4	-129.1	-87.0

TABLE B.9.   Actual Budget Surplus, 1955–84 (Billions of 1972 Dollars)

(1)	(2)	(3)	(4)	(5)
		SURPLUS OR DEFICIT (−) ON NATIONAL INCOME ACCOUNTS		
YEAR	Official	Adjusted for Price Effects	Adjusted for Interest Effects	Adjusted for Price and Interest Effects
1955	7.2	17.0	13.4	23.2
1956	9.5	22.4	15.5	28.4
1957	3.5	10.9	− 5.1	2.3
1958	− 15.4	− 9.1	− 6.5	− 0.3
1959	− 1.7	5.3	4.4	11.4
1960	4.4	7.7	− 9.9	− 6.6
1961	− 5.6	− 0.8	− 2.1	2.6
1962	− 6.0	0.0	− 9.3	− 3.3
1963	0.4	4.9	4.2	8.7
1964	− 4.4	0.8	− 4.9	0.3
1965	0.7	8.5	4.9	12.6
1966	− 2.3	8.1	− 4.5	5.9
1967	− 16.4	− 6.5	− 10.8	− 0.9
1968	− 7.2	6.5	− 5.9	7.7
1969	9.5	24.5	17.9	32.9
1970	− 13.3	− 0.2	− 28.2	− 15.2
1971	− 22.5	− 9.7	− 26.4	− 13.7
1972	− 16.8	− 4.5	− 12.5	− 0.1
1973	− 5.0	14.4	− 1.9	17.5
1974	− 9.5	16.2	− 11.2	14.6
1975	− 53.6	− 35.6	− 55.5	− 37.6
1976	− 39.1	− 23.6	− 48.4	− 32.8
1977	− 31.8	− 11.5	− 20.7	− 0.4
1978	− 18.8	8.8	− 6.6	21.0
1979	− 9.5	16.2	− 6.7	18.9
1980	− 32.6	− 3.3	− 25.3	4.1
1981	− 31.7	− 7.2	− 33.5	− 9.0
1982	− 70.0	− 54.3	− 99.5	− 83.8
1983	− 81.4	− 65.4	− 62.1	− 46.1
1984	− 80.8	− 61.4	− 90.2	− 70.9

TABLE B.10.   High-Employment Surplus, 1955–84 (Billions of 1972 Dollars)

(1)	(2)	(3)	(4)	(5)
		SURPLUS OR DEFICIT (−) ON NATIONAL INCOME ACCOUNTS		
YEAR	*Official*	*Adjusted for Price Effects*	*Adjusted for Interest Effects*	*Adjusted for Price and Interest Effects*
1955	8.4	18.2	14.7	24.4
1956	12.3	25.2	18.4	31.3
1957	9.3	16.7	0.7	8.1
1958	0.0	6.2	8.9	15.1
1959	7.9	14.9	14.0	21.0
1960	17.6	20.8	3.3	6.6
1961	10.2	14.9	13.6	18.4
1962	4.2	10.2	0.9	6.9
1963	10.2	14.8	14.0	18.6
1964	1.5	6.7	1.0	6.3
1965	1.2	9.0	5.4	13.1
1966	−7.2	3.2	−9.4	1.0
1967	−18.7	−8.8	−13.2	−3.3
1968	−13.0	0.6	−11.8	1.8
1969	5.5	20.5	13.9	29.0
1970	−4.9	8.1	−19.8	−6.8
1971	−11.5	1.2	−15.5	−2.8
1972	−12.1	0.3	−7.8	4.6
1973	−8.7	10.7	−5.6	13.8
1974	−0.2	25.5	−1.9	23.9
1975	−22.5	−4.5	−24.5	−6.5
1976	−12.8	2.7	−22.1	−6.6
1977	−14.1	6.1	−3.0	17.3
1978	−10.1	17.4	2.1	29.6
1979	−1.2	24.5	1.5	27.2
1980	−9.1	20.3	−1.8	27.6
1981	−1.6	22.9	−3.4	21.1
1982	−15.4	0.4	−44.9	−29.1
1983	−27.2	−11.2	−7.9	8.1
1984	−49.9	−30.5	−59.3	−40.0

TABLE B.11.   Actual Budget Surplus, 1955–84 (as Percent of GNP)

(1)	(2)	(3)	(4)	(5)
		SURPLUS OR DEFICIT (−) ON NATIONAL INCOME ACCOUNTS		
YEAR	Official	Adjusted for Price Effects	Adjusted for Interest Effects	Adjusted for Price and Interest Effects
1955	1.10	2.61	2.06	3.58
1956	1.44	3.39	2.35	4.31
1957	0.51	1.60	−0.75	0.34
1958	−2.28	−1.36	−0.97	−0.04
1959	−.23	0.75	0.62	1.60
1960	0.60	1.04	−1.34	−0.90
1961	−0.74	−0.11	−0.28	0.35
1962	−0.75	0.00	−1.17	−0.41
1963	0.04	0.60	0.50	1.06
1964	−0.51	0.09	−0.57	0.04
1965	0.08	0.93	0.53	1.38
1966	−0.24	0.84	−0.47	0.61
1967	−1.65	−0.65	−1.09	−0.10
1968	−0.69	0.62	−0.57	0.75
1969	0.89	2.32	1.69	3.11
1970	−1.25	−0.02	−2.66	−1.43
1971	−2.04	−0.88	−2.41	−1.25
1972	−1.42	−0.38	−1.05	−0.01
1973	−0.42	1.19	−0.16	1.44
1974	−0.80	1.37	−0.94	1.23
1975	−4.47	−2.97	−4.63	−3.13
1976	−3.09	−1.86	−3.82	−2.60
1977	−2.39	−0.87	−1.55	−0.03
1978	−1.36	0.63	−0.48	1.52
1979	−0.67	1.14	−0.48	1.33
1980	−2.33	−0.23	−1.81	0.29
1981	−2.17	−0.49	−2.30	−0.62
1982	−4.83	−3.74	−6.86	−5.77
1983	−5.40	−4.34	−4.12	−3.06
1984	−4.80	−3.65	−5.36	−4.21

Table B.12 Federal Government Net Worth, 1945–84
(Billions of Dollars)

	1945	1946	1947	1948	1949	1950	1951	1952	1953	1954
Tangible Assets	186.2	169.9	148.9	127.3	110.5	111.7	118.6	134.7	127.0	175.1
Reproducible assets	179.3	162.5	140.9	119.0	105.1	102.2	108.4	123.9	116.2	163.6
Residential structures	2.2	2.6	2.7	2.3	2.1	2.2	1.9	2.0	1.9	1.9
Nonresidential structures	28.9	33.1	37.4	38.6	37.3	39.1	43.8	47.2	18.9	49.6
Equipment	88.3	75.4	57.9	45.0	37.1	34.4	35.7	43.2	51.3	56.1
Inventories	59.9	51.5	43.0	33.2	28.6	26.5	26.9	31.6	44.1	55.9
Land	6.8	7.4	7.9	8.3	5.4	9.5	10.3	10.8	10.8	11.5
Financial Assets	102.8	79.8	87.2	93.9	89.3	98.7	107.1	109.8	111.2	106.7
Currency, demand & time deposits	31.3	8.8	8.3	9.5	9.9	9.7	10.0	12.5	11.1	10.9
Gold	20.1	20.7	22.9	24.4	24.6	22.8	22.9	23.3	22.1	21.8
Foreign exchange & SDRs	0.0	-0.2	0.9	1.3	1.5	1.4	1.4	1.5	1.4	1.2
U.S. government securities	31.5	30.0	27.9	29.0	24.8	26.2	27.0	27.7	29.5	28.5
Treasury issues	31.5	30.0	27.9	29.0	24.8	26.2	27.0	27.7	29.5	28.5
Agency issues	0.0	0.0	0.0	0.0	0.0	0.0	0.0	0.0	0.0	0.0
Mortgages	2.5	2.0	1.8	1.9	2.4	2.8	3.4	4.0	4.4	4.7
Other loans	4.7	8.1	12.8	14.3	15.1	16.0	17.0	18.1	19.4	19.0
Taxes receivable	9.6	8.2	10.6	11.4	9.1	16.5	21.6	18.0	18.5	15.5
Miscellaneous assets	3.1	2.2	2.1	2.1	2.0	3.2	3.9	4.7	4.7	5.2
Total Assets	289.0	249.7	236.1	221.2	199.8	210.4	225.7	244.5	238.1	281.8
Liabilities										
Treasury currency & SDR ctfs.	2.3	2.4	2.4	2.4	2.4	2.4	2.4	2.4	2.5	2.5
Demand deposits & currency	31.1	30.4	29.3	29.4	28.5	28.2	28.6	29.9	29.8	29.9
Bank reserves & vault cash	19.0	19.1	20.8	22.5	18.6	19.9	22.8	22.7	22.7	21.3
Credit market instruments	264.5	240.4	228.9	223.1	227.9	224.5	218.6	223.6	231.2	233.9
Treasury issues	220.4	194.9	181.2	173.4	176.8	173.1	168.3	172.8	179.7	181.7
Agency issues	0.9	1.2	1.3	1.6	1.5	1.8	2.0	2.1	2.1	2.1
Savings bonds	43.2	44.4	46.4	48.1	49.6	49.5	48.2	48.7	49.4	50.1
Insurance, retirement reserves	6.5	8.0	9.5	10.5	11.6	12.7	13.6	14.6	15.2	15.3
Misc. liabilities	9.2	6.8	6.1	6.8	6.7	7.4	8.6	8.9	10.4	10.5
Total Liabilities	332.6	307.1	297.0	294.6	295.8	295.0	294.5	302.2	311.8	313.4
Net Debt	229.8	227.3	209.7	200.7	206.4	196.3	187.3	192.4	200.6	206.7
Net Worth	-43.7	-57.5	-60.9	-73.5	-96.0	-84.6	-68.7	-57.6	-73.6	-31.6

197

TABLE B.12 (continued)

	1955	1956	1957	1958	1959	1960	1961	1962	1963	1964
Tangible Assets	187.2	198.9	200.5	202.9	202.8	205.8	208.4	215.5	222.7	230.1
Reproducible assets	175.0	185.5	186.1	187.7	186.2	187.4	187.8	193.4	199.8	204.6
Residential structures	1.9	2.0	2.1	2.4	2.9	3.2	3.7	4.1	4.4	4.4
Nonresidential structures	52.6	56.7	58.4	59.0	59.9	60.8	62.7	65.0	67.5	70.2
Equipment	60.3	64.9	65.1	64.7	64.7	65.6	68.1	71.1	74.1	76.2
Inventories	60.2	61.8	60.5	61.6	58.7	57.7	53.2	53.2	53.9	53.8
Land	12.2	13.4	14.4	15.2	16.6	18.4	20.6	22.1	22.9	25.5
Financial Assets	111.5	112.7	115.7	114.4	121.7	124.7	129.9	138.1	146.8	154.9
Currency, demand & time deposits	10.6	10.4	10.5	11.0	11.7	12.8	13.0	14.0	13.6	13.9
Gold	21.8	22.1	22.9	20.6	19.5	17.8	16.9	16.1	15.6	15.5
Foreign exchange & SDRs	1.0	1.6	2.0	2.0	2.0	1.6	1.8	1.2	1.2	1.2
U.S. government securities	28.7	29.3	30.3	32.1	32.6	35.2	36.6	39.9	44.6	48.2
Treasury issues	28.7	29.3	30.3	32.1	32.6	35.1	36.6	39.9	44.5	48.1
Agency issues	0.0	0.0	0.0	0.0	0.0	0.0	0.0	0.0	0.1	0.1
Mortgages	5.2	5.9	7.3	7.7	9.8	11.2	12.0	12.3	11.4	11.7
Other loans	20.0	20.2	21.1	22.5	24.6	25.1	27.2	30.5	34.1	37.8
Taxes receivable	18.2	16.4	14.4	12.0	14.1	12.7	13.2	13.7	15.5	15.7
Miscellaneous assets	6.0	6.8	7.2	6.7	7.4	8.4	9.2	10.4	10.8	10.9
Total Assets	298.7	311.6	316.2	317.4	324.5	330.4	338.3	353.6	369.5	385.0
Liabilities										
Treasury currency & SDR ctfs.	2.5	2.5	2.6	2.6	2.6	2.7	2.7	2.8	2.8	2.8
Demand deposits & currency	30.0	30.1	30.1	30.3	30.8	30.6	31.4	32.1	34.9	36.9
Bank reserves & vault cash	21.7	22.3	22.4	21.8	21.2	20.4	21.1	22.0	21.3	22.4
Credit market instruments	231.7	222.8	229.7	231.8	237.3	246.7	251.8	263.0	267.3	274.1
Treasury issues	178.4	169.5	175.0	179.3	185.0	192.5	196.8	205.6	208.0	213.3
Agency issues	3.5	3.8	6.1	5.4	7.3	7.8	8.3	10.0	11.4	11.8
Savings bonds	49.8	49.5	48.6	47.2	45.0	46.5	46.7	47.4	48.0	48.9
Insurance, retirement reserves	15.8	17.0	17.5	18.5	19.5	20.5	21.5	22.6	23.9	25.3
Misc. liabilities	8.9	8.9	8.6	9.8	9.5	10.9	11.8	12.9	12.4	13.3
Total Liabilities	310.7	303.7	310.9	314.7	320.9	331.8	340.3	355.3	362.7	374.8
Net Debt	199.2	191.0	195.1	200.3	199.2	207.1	210.4	217.2	215.9	219.9
Net Worth	−12.0	7.9	5.4	2.6	3.5	−1.3	−2.1	−1.7	6.8	10.1

TABLE B.12 (continued)

	1965	1966	1967	1968	1969	1970	1971	1972	1973	1974
Tangible Assets	236.6	244.0	254.9	267.8	287.8	304.6	323.7	345.0	383.7	414.7
Reproducible assets	209.3	214.5	223.4	234.3	250.5	259.8	269.9	281.6	310.9	338.2
Residential structures	4.5	4.8	4.8	5.1	5.3	5.7	6.7	8.3	10.7	12.4
Nonresidential structures	73.7	77.7	81.6	86.9	93.4	100.2	107.5	114.9	138.5	156.2
Equipment	78.4	82.1	85.0	88.0	90.5	95.3	97.1	100.3	103.6	111.5
Inventories	52.7	49.9	52.0	54.3	61.2	58.6	58.7	58.1	58.1	58.1
Land	27.3	29.5	31.5	33.5	37.3	44.8	53.8	63.4	72.8	76.5
Financial Assets	162.8	176.3	184.1	197.4	211.7	232.8	251.8	266.7	310.6	361.8
Currency, demand & time deposits	12.6	12.9	14.6	12.5	14.2	17.6	21.6	22.4	22.1	18.3
Gold	13.8	13.2	12.1	13.2	12.1	12.0	12.8	18.0	31.1	53.7
Foreign exchange & SDRs	1.6	1.6	2.8	4.8	5.1	3.4	2.0	2.7	2.7	4.2
U.S. government securities	52.5	58.8	64.4	66.4	68.3	77.5	88.7	88.9	98.3	104.3
Treasury issues	52.4	57.3	63.0	65.0	68.0	77.4	87.9	87.3	96.1	98.8
Agency issues	0.1	1.5	1.4	1.5	0.3	0.2	0.8	1.5	2.2	5.5
Mortgages	12.8	16.1	18.6	21.9	26.7	32.6	36.7	40.2	45.6	58.6
Other loans	41.4	45.5	47.4	51.7	60.2	65.2	65.4	71.3	82.4	93.5
Taxes receivable	17.0	15.7	10.5	11.6	8.4	5.7	7.1	6.4	8.0	7.8
Miscellaneous assets	11.1	12.5	13.8	15.2	16.6	18.9	17.4	16.8	20.3	21.4
Total Assets	399.4	420.3	439.0	465.2	499.5	537.4	575.5	611.7	694.3	776.5
Liabilities										
Treasury currency & SDR ctfs.	3.1	4.0	4.6	5.1	5.3	6.0	6.4	7.0	7.4	7.7
Demand deposits & currency	38.8	41.2	44.1	45.6	48.9	52.0	56.4	60.4	65.0	71.9
Bank reserves & vault cash	23.3	25.2	27.0	29.1	29.4	31.2	35.3	34.3	37.7	37.5
Credit market instruments	274.6	284.1	288.8	300.8	299.7	338.5	374.3	390.7	411.3	441.4
Treasury issues	211.9	215.3	220.6	228.1	221.8	246.1	276.0	285.9	289.1	299.4
Agency issues	13.5	18.5	17.6	22.0	28.7	39.3	42.3	46.9	62.4	79.0
Savings bonds	49.3	50.3	50.6	50.8	49.2	53.1	56.0	58.0	59.7	63.1
Insurance, retirement reserves	26.7	28.1	29.5	30.8	32.4	34.9	37.8	40.9	43.3	46.1
Misc. liabilities	13.9	16.3	21.7	23.6	21.7	21.8	18.6	18.1	21.3	23.3
Total Liabilities	380.5	398.9	415.7	435.0	437.5	484.3	528.9	551.5	586.0	628.0
Net Debt	217.7	222.6	231.6	237.7	225.8	251.5	277.1	284.8	275.3	266.2
Net Worth	18.9	21.4	23.3	30.2	62.0	53.1	46.6	60.2	108.3	148.5

199

TABLE B.12 *(continued)*

	1975	1976	1977	1978	1979	1980	1981	1982	1983	1984
Tangible Assets	457.8	493.6	549.6	614.9	709.1	822.5	892.4	965.2	1049.4	1118.0
Reproducible assets	377.4	403.1	444.1	494.6	571.6	648.1	717.3	784.6	854.4	915.2
Residential structures	12.6	13.3	14.9	17.7	18.9	20.9	22.7	22.4	22.3	24.5
Nonresidential structures	167.6	177.9	192.7	210.7	241.5	262.9	283.0	285.7	292.8	299.6
Equipment	123.9	132.7	148.0	165.8	191.7	228.6	262.3	304.0	350.0	395.6
Inventories	73.3	79.2	88.5	100.4	119.5	135.7	149.3	172.5	189.3	195.5
Land	80.4	90.5	105.5	120.3	137.5	174.4	175.1	180.7	195.0	202.8
Financial Assets	378.0	411.2	443.7	518.4	657.1	720.9	742.4	801.7	821.6	887.4
Currency, demand & time deposits	22.2	27.2	27.1	31.8	33.8	31.3	33.2	41.2	33.6	40.7
Gold	38.7	37.2	45.9	62.6	135.6	155.9	118.9	105.2	101.0	81.0
Foreign exchange & SDRs	4.6	7.1	7.6	7.0	7.8	15.6	18.9	22.8	22.6	23.8
U.S. government securities	112.0	122.4	123.4	124.7	129.7	129.8	139.3	155.1	160.5	172.3
Treasury issues	105.4	114.6	115.0	117.0	121.0	120.6	129.8	144.3	151.3	162.7
Agency issues	6.5	7.7	8.4	7.8	8.7	9.2	9.5	10.8	9.2	9.6
Mortgages	72.0	75.2	83.1	97.5	114.7	132.3	143.5	171.9	190.2	202.6
Other loans	97.1	105.2	118.6	147.0	174.7	201.5	238.3	251.2	253.8	288.1
Taxes receivable	5.5	11.1	9.6	12.5	20.0	7.1	-2.9	-15.5	-12.2	-16.2
Miscellaneous assets	25.9	25.9	28.3	35.4	40.9	47.3	53.1	69.6	72.0	94.9
Total Assets	835.8	904.8	993.3	1133.3	1366.2	1543.4	1634.9	1766.9	1871.0	2005.4
Liabilities										
Treasury currency & SDR ctfs.	8.7	9.9	10.2	10.7	12.3	13.6	14.8	16.5	16.9	17.5
Demand deposits & currency	82.6	93.2	98.0	104.3	112.5	121.5	132.4	142.5	155.5	171.4
Bank reserves & vault cash	38.3	37.3	40.8	46.7	48.3	47.3	43.9	46.0	42.4	40.5
Credit market instruments	531.3	615.7	660.7	710.1	760.8	841.9	956.8	1214.1	1361.6	1613.7
Treasury issues	380.5	451.0	492.3	523.9	555.2	625.1	714.2	930.9	1083.3	1296.8
Agency issues	82.9	90.2	91.9	108.9	129.3	148.4	177.2	214.4	206.3	240.8
Savings bonds	67.9	74.5	76.5	77.3	76.3	68.4	65.3	68.8	72.0	76.1
Insurance, retirement reserves	49.9	54.6	61.3	68.5	76.7	85.5	95.5	107.5	121.7	139.8
Misc. liabilities	25.5	31.1	33.3	40.8	48.1	51.8	57.8	64.8	66.7	80.4
Total Liabilities	736.3	841.8	904.3	981.1	1058.6	1161.6	1301.1	1591.3	1764.9	2063.3
Net Debt	358.2	430.5	460.6	462.7	401.5	440.7	558.7	789.6	943.3	1175.9
Net Worth	99.6	63.1	89.1	152.2	307.6	381.8	333.7	175.6	106.1	-57.9

TABLE B.13 State and Local Government Net Worth, 1945–84
(*Billions of Dollars*)

	1945	1946	1947	1948	1949	1950	1951	1952	1953	1954
Tangible Assets	75.0	84.4	97.2	104.0	97.3	114.4	128.4	134.8	141.5	147.2
Reproducible assets	60.0	68.1	79.8	85.8	85.6	93.5	105.8	111.1	113.3	117.0
Residential structures	0.9	1.2	1.5	1.7	2.0	2.4	3.1	3.7	4.2	4.5
Nonresidential structures	57.3	65.1	76.1	81.4	80.4	87.2	98.3	102.3	103.4	106.1
Equipment	1.7	1.7	2.1	2.6	3.1	3.7	4.3	5.0	5.6	6.2
Inventories	0.1	0.1	0.1	0.1	0.1	0.1	0.1	0.1	0.1	0.1
Land	15.0	16.2	17.4	18.1	11.7	20.9	22.5	23.7	28.2	30.2
Financial Assets	12.2	12.5	14.1	15.5	16.4	17.8	18.8	20.7	22.7	24.8
Currency, demand & time deposits	4.2	5.3	6.2	6.9	7.3	7.9	8.4	8.8	9.5	10.4
Security RPs	0.0	0.0	0.0	0.0	0.0	0.0	0.0	0.0	0.0	0.0
U.S. government securities	5.6	5.3	5.8	6.3	6.5	6.8	7.1	8.5	9.6	10.6
Treasury issues	5.4	5.1	5.7	6.1	6.3	6.6	6.9	8.2	9.0	9.9
Agency issues	0.2	0.2	0.2	0.2	0.2	0.2	0.2	0.3	0.6	0.7
State and local obligations	1.8	1.5	1.4	1.4	1.7	2.1	2.1	2.1	2.3	2.5
Mortgages	0.0	0.0	0.0	0.1	0.2	0.2	0.3	0.4	0.5	0.6
Taxes receivable	0.5	0.5	0.6	0.7	0.7	0.8	0.9	0.9	0.9	0.8
Total Assets	87.2	96.9	111.3	119.4	113.7	132.2	147.2	155.5	164.2	172.0
Liabilities										
State and local obligations	15.2	14.9	16.0	18.3	21.1	24.9	26.5	29.7	33.9	40.6
Short-term	0.3	0.3	0.5	0.7	0.9	1.3	1.6	1.8	1.9	2.1
Other	14.9	14.6	15.5	17.6	20.2	23.6	24.9	28.0	32.0	38.5
U.S. government loans	0.5	0.5	0.5	0.6	0.5	0.6	0.8	1.1	0.8	0.4
Trade debt	0.6	0.8	0.9	1.1	1.1	1.2	1.2	1.3	1.4	1.6
Total Liabilities	16.3	16.2	17.4	20.0	22.7	26.6	28.6	32.2	36.1	42.6
Net Debt	4.2	3.7	3.3	4.5	6.3	8.8	9.8	11.5	13.4	17.8
Net Worth	70.8	80.7	93.9	99.5	91.0	105.6	118.6	123.3	128.1	129.3

TABLE B.13 (continued)

	1955	1956	1957	1958	1959	1960	1961	1962	1963	1964
Tangible Assets	164.9	185.5	201.0	213.5	226.1	237.2	253.2	271.1	290.2	312.5
Reproducible assets	129.0	144.9	154.5	162.1	169.7	176.6	186.9	199.2	212.2	227.9
Residential structures	4.8	5.1	5.3	5.7	6.1	6.4	6.8	7.5	7.6	8.1
Nonresidential structures	117.0	131.5	139.9	146.9	154.1	160.6	170.5	182.0	194.5	209.2
Equipment	7.0	8.1	9.2	9.3	9.2	9.3	9.4	9.5	9.8	10.3
Inventories	0.2	0.2	0.2	0.2	0.2	0.3	0.3	0.3	0.3	0.3
Land	35.9	40.6	46.5	51.4	56.4	60.6	66.3	71.9	78.0	84.6
Financial Assets	25.7	25.7	26.4	27.1	29.7	32.8	34.1	37.1	41.0	44.6
Currency, demand & time deposits	10.3	9.8	9.6	10.2	11.4	12.8	13.6	14.7	17.2	20.2
Security RPs	0.0	0.0	0.0	0.0	0.0	0.0	0.0	0.0	0.0	0.0
U.S. government securities	11.3	11.7	12.3	12.1	13.1	14.4	14.6	16.1	17.4	17.7
Treasury issues	10.7	11.2	11.6	11.3	12.2	13.2	13.0	14.3	14.8	14.8
Agency issues	0.6	0.6	0.7	0.9	0.9	1.3	1.5	1.9	2.6	2.8
State and local obligations	2.4	2.4	2.5	2.6	2.6	2.7	2.8	2.6	2.3	2.2
Mortgages	0.6	0.7	0.9	1.1	1.4	1.6	1.9	2.1	2.3	2.6
Taxes receivable	1.0	1.1	1.1	1.0	1.2	1.3	1.3	1.5	1.7	1.9
Total Assets	190.6	211.2	227.4	240.6	255.8	270.0	287.4	308.2	331.2	357.1
Liabilities										
State and local obligations	45.1	47.1	51.8	56.7	62.8	70.4	75.6	82.3	87.1	93.9
Short-term	2.1	2.2	2.3	2.8	3.1	3.4	3.7	3.7	4.1	4.8
Other	43.0	45.0	49.5	53.9	59.7	67.0	71.9	78.6	83.1	89.0
U.S. government loans	0.5	0.5	0.7	0.9	1.0	1.2	1.5	2.0	2.2	2.5
Trade debt	1.8	1.9	2.1	2.3	2.4	2.5	2.7	2.9	3.1	3.4
Total Liabilities	47.3	49.5	54.6	59.8	66.3	74.2	79.8	87.1	92.5	99.8
Net Debt	21.5	23.8	28.2	32.7	36.6	41.4	45.7	50.0	51.5	55.2
Net Worth	143.4	161.7	172.8	180.8	189.4	195.8	207.6	221.1	238.7	257.3

TABLE B.13   (*continued*)

	1965	1966	1967	1968	1969	1970	1971	1972	1973	1974
Tangible Assets	338.2	369.5	403.2	446.1	496.0	549.8	601.7	664.1	795.8	926.5
Reproducible assets	248.1	271.6	298.9	335.4	379.7	428.3	473.4	520.1	626.5	735.5
Residential structures	8.5	9.3	10.0	11.3	12.5	13.8	15.4	17.0	19.4	21.8
Nonresidential structures	228.3	250.1	274.9	307.9	348.7	393.2	434.3	476.8	576.8	675.1
Equipment	10.9	11.8	13.6	15.7	17.9	20.6	22.9	25.4	29.3	37.3
Inventories	0.4	0.4	0.4	0.5	0.6	0.7	0.8	0.9	1.0	1.3
Land	90.1	97.9	104.3	110.7	116.3	121.5	128.3	144.0	169.3	190.9
Financial Assets	49.3	53.6	56.6	61.8	61.5	70.7	79.8	94.6	109.3	118.7
Currency, demand & time deposits	22.0	23.8	26.9	29.3	25.4	34.3	42.4	49.6	56.3	61.4
Security RPs	0.0	0.0	0.0	0.0	0.0	0.0	0.0	0.0	2.4	6.0
U.S. government securities	20.4	22.6	22.3	24.2	27.2	26.1	25.6	31.0	34.2	31.5
Treasury issues	17.3	19.8	18.7	18.2	20.5	22.5	21.6	25.4	24.2	18.9
Agency issues	3.0	2.7	3.6	6.1	6.8	3.6	4.0	5.6	10.0	12.5
State and local obligations	2.1	2.1	2.0	2.1	2.0	2.3	2.1	1.8	2.1	2.4
Mortgages	2.7	2.9	3.0	3.1	3.5	4.4	5.6	7.0	8.5	10.8
Taxes receivable	2.0	2.3	2.5	3.1	3.5	3.6	4.1	5.1	5.8	6.5
Total Assets	387.4	423.1	459.8	507.9	557.5	620.5	681.4	758.7	905.1	1045.1
Liabilities										
State and local obligations	99.3	104.0	108.9	117.0	118.2	138.4	159.6	177.0	189.3	190.1
Short-term	5.4	6.1	7.9	8.0	10.7	13.1	15.6	15.6	15.8	18.4
Other	93.8	97.9	101.0	109.0	107.5	125.3	144.0	161.5	173.5	171.7
U.S. government loans	2.8	3.4	3.6	4.0	4.7	4.8	5.2	5.5	4.9	5.6
Trade debt	3.8	4.3	4.8	5.4	5.8	6.4	7.1	7.6	8.5	10.3
Total Liabilities	105.9	111.7	117.3	126.4	128.8	149.6	171.9	190.2	202.7	206.0
Net Debt	56.6	58.1	60.6	64.6	67.2	78.9	92.1	95.6	93.5	87.4
Net Worth	281.6	311.4	342.6	381.5	428.8	470.9	509.5	568.5	702.4	839.1

TABLE B.13 (continued)

	1975	1976	1977	1978	1979	1980	1981	1982	1983	1984
Tangible Assets	1003.6	1080.8	1215.7	1403.6	1621.4	1841.1	1978.3	1993.2	2068.9	2113.3
Reproducible assets	791.4	838.2	925.4	1043.5	1187.5	1328.9	1394.7	1391.0	1419.1	1437.4
Residential structures	23.1	25.4	28.5	33.3	36.5	40.0	43.6	44.2	45.9	48.0
Nonresidential structures	724.5	764.1	843.0	950.2	1084.4	1216.5	1272.8	1265.6	1290.0	1303.9
Equipment	42.2	46.9	51.9	57.9	64.4	70.1	75.8	78.5	80.3	82.4
Inventories	1.6	1.8	2.0	2.1	2.2	2.3	2.5	2.7	2.9	3.1
Land	212.2	242.6	290.3	360.1	433.9	512.2	583.6	602.2	649.9	675.9
Financial Assets	121.8	134.3	156.0	176.3	193.0	205.8	217.7	259.5	295.5	344.9
Currency, demand & time deposits	60.3	61.5	69.2	76.3	73.8	71.3	72.0	74.3	67.4	72.4
Security RPs	7.0	7.0	8.0	10.0	14.0	14.0	16.5	16.6	19.6	19.6
U.S. government securities	30.0	35.1	45.0	54.2	63.0	69.1	71.2	101.5	130.8	164.6
Treasury issues	17.6	20.2	29.1	33.7	36.3	41.7	41.0	59.7	85.6	114.0
Agency issues	12.4	14.8	15.9	20.5	26.7	27.4	30.2	41.8	45.2	50.6
State and local obligations	4.7	7.5	8.1	7.1	6.5	6.0	5.8	8.3	9.2	9.7
Mortgages	12.7	13.9	14.5	16.7	22.2	30.9	36.7	44.8	52.5	58.2
Taxes receivable	7.1	9.3	11.1	11.9	13.5	14.5	15.5	14.1	16.0	20.4
Total Assets	1125.4	1215.1	1371.7	1579.9	1814.4	2046.8	2196.0	2252.7	2364.4	2458.2
Liabilities										
State and local obligations	203.7	229.0	242.4	251.0	260.6	250.1	239.8	307.9	346.3	375.1
Short-term	18.3	14.3	11.4	11.8	12.7	14.3	15.4	21.3	14.9	7.8
Other	185.4	214.8	231.1	239.2	247.9	235.8	224.3	286.6	331.4	367.3
U.S. government loans	5.8	7.8	8.0	6.5	6.7	7.6	8.8	9.8	10.9	18.5
Trade debt	11.6	12.1	12.8	14.5	16.1	18.1	19.2	20.1	20.9	21.9
Total Liabilities	221.1	248.9	263.2	271.9	283.4	275.8	267.8	337.8	378.1	415.5
Net Debt	99.3	114.7	107.2	95.7	90.3	70.0	50.1	78.3	82.6	70.6
Net Worth	904.3	966.1	1108.4	1307.9	1531.1	1771.1	1928.2	1914.8	1986.3	2042.7

TABLE B.14   Market-to-Par Indices: Treasury Bills, Notes, and Bonds;
Mortgages; and State and Local Bonds
(Billions of Dollars)

(1)	(2)	(3)	(4)	(5)	(6)	(7)
	U.S. GOVERNMENT SECURITIES				FEDERAL	STATE &
YEAR	*Total*	*Bills*	*Notes*	*Bonds + Notes*	MORTGAGES	LOCAL BONDS
1945	102.59	99.95	100.66	103.47	102.20	102.54
1946	102.71	99.95	100.47	103.58	100.33	100.32
1947	101.05	99.89	100.35	101.27	98.99	98.16
1948	101.26	99.84	100.57	101.54	99.48	99.20
1949	102.66	99.85	100.64	103.46	100.06	100.05
1950	100.94	99.82	99.99	101.09	100.92	102.05
1951	99.25	99.72	98.24	98.67	100.06	99.88
1952	99.14	99.68	99.06	98.70	99.83	98.22
1953	99.90	99.81	100.15	99.77	98.35	98.19
1954	100.26	99.86	100.31	100.38	99.34	99.96
1955	98.33	99.65	99.11	97.90	99.02	98.15
1956	96.06	99.61	98.75	94.65	98.18	95.11
1957	98.79	99.60	100.88	98.02	97.88	96.35
1958	95.98	99.47	98.85	93.78	98.37	95.54
1959	94.07	98.80	98.00	91.73	97.77	95.83
1960	98.54	99.40	101.82	98.01	99.08	99.53
1961	97.61	99.27	100.48	97.03	100.51	99.68
1962	98.84	99.30	100.93	98.44	101.03	101.42
1963	97.71	99.10	99.65	97.05	101.30	100.30
1964	97.87	98.86	99.73	97.51	101.05	101.13
1965	96.39	98.64	99.14	95.52	100.81	99.02
1966	97.02	98.55	100.09	96.22	99.28	98.15
1967	95.13	98.49	98.72	93.66	98.36	95.60
1968	94.80	98.12	97.87	93.31	97.15	94.70
1969	92.05	97.69	94.99	89.23	95.77	87.96
1970	97.18	98.59	102.02	96.43	96.97	95.56
1971	98.99	98.91	102.97	99.03	99.58	98.67
1972	97.92	98.57	100.51	97.52	100.12	100.86
1973	96.73	97.96	98.97	95.92	97.53	100.73
1974	97.17	98.06	99.62	96.52	96.55	93.55
1975	98.48	98.48	100.75	98.78	99.35	94.65
1976	101.01	98.68	103.42	102.72	99.16	101.70
1977	98.31	98.10	99.64	98.43	99.45	102.30
1978	95.30	97.15	95.80	94.38	97.55	98.27
1979	94.44	96.64	95.47	93.38	94.82	95.40
1980	92.86	96.00	94.34	91.29	92.78	85.94
1981	93.46	96.45	95.74	91.93	89.65	80.65
1982	101.25	97.52	100.65	103.30	97.52	94.70
1983	98.23	97.14	100.65	98.75	101.42	96.11
1984	99.84	97.54	102.19	100.83	101.26	97.29

TABLE B.15 Percentage Changes in Dow Industrials and Changes in Budget Surplus as Percentage of GNP, 1956–84[a]

(1)	(2)	(3)	(4)	(5)	(6)	(7)	(8)
		BUDGET SURPLUS AS PERCENTAGE OF GNP					
		National Income Account			High-Employment		
YEAR	DOW INDUSTRIALS	OFFICIAL	PRICE-ADJUSTED	PRICE- AND INTEREST-ADJUSTED	OFFICIAL	PRICE-ADJUSTED	PRICE AND INTEREST-ADJUSTED
1956	2.27	0.33	0.78	0.73	0.57	1.02	0.97
1957	-12.77	-0.92	-1.79	-3.97	-0.50	-1.36	-3.54
1958	33.96	-2.80	-2.96	-0.38	-1.37	-1.54	1.04
1959	16.40	2.05	2.11	1.64	1.11	1.16	0.70
1960	-9.34	0.83	0.30	-2.50	1.28	0.75	-2.05
1961	18.71	-1.34	-1.15	1.25	-1.04	-0.85	1.55
1962	-10.81	-0.01	0.11	-0.76	-0.82	-0.70	-1.58
1963	17.00	0.79	0.59	1.47	0.71	0.51	1.38
1964	14.57	-0.56	-0.51	-1.02	-1.07	-1.02	-1.53
1965	10.88	0.59	0.83	1.34	-0.04	0.20	0.71
1966	-18.94	-0.31	-0.09	-0.77	-0.87	-0.64	-1.33
1967	15.20	-1.41	-1.49	-0.70	-1.15	-1.22	-0.44
1968	4.27	0.96	1.27	0.84	0.63	0.95	0.51
1969	-15.19	1.59	1.69	2.37	1.78	1.88	2.56
1970	4.82	-2.15	-2.34	-4.55	-0.98	-1.17	-3.38
1971	6.11	-0.79	-0.86	0.18	-0.59	-0.66	0.39
1972	14.58	0.63	0.51	1.23	0.03	-0.09	0.64
1973	-16.58	1.00	1.56	1.45	0.30	0.87	0.76
1974	-27.57	-0.39	0.18	-0.21	0.70	1.27	0.87
1975	38.32	-3.67	-4.34	-4.37	-1.86	-2.53	-2.55
1976	17.86	1.38	1.11	0.54	0.87	0.59	0.02
1977	-17.27	0.70	0.99	2.56	-0.05	0.25	1.82
1978	-3.15	1.03	1.50	1.55	0.33	0.80	0.85
1979	4.19	0.70	0.50	-0.19	0.65	0.46	-0.23
1980	14.93	-1.66	-1.37	-1.04	-0.57	-0.28	0.06
1981	-9.23	0.15	-0.26	-0.91	0.54	0.13	-0.52
1982	19.60	-2.65	-3.25	-5.16	-0.95	-1.55	-3.46
1983	20.27	-0.58	-0.60	2.71	-0.75	-0.77	2.54
1984	-3.74	0.61	0.69	-1.15	-1.16	-1.07	-2.91

[a]Minus signs for changes in surplus indicate movement toward deficit, that is, reduction in surplus, move from surplus to deficit, or increase in deficit, as percentage of GNP. Positive numbers indicate decreases in deficit, movement from deficit to surplus, or increase in surplus, as percentage of GNP.

TABLE B.16   Monetary Base, GNP, and Unemployment, 1955–84

(1)	(2)	(3)	(4)	(5)	(6)	(7)	(8)
	MONETARY BASE	GNP	UNEMPLOYMENT (% OF LABOR FORCE)	CHANGES IN			
YEAR				Real Monetary Base		Real GNP	Unemployment (% of Labor Force)
	(1972$ Billions)			(%)	(% OF GNP)		
1955	—	657.5	4.4	—	—	6.7	−1.2
1956	—	671.6	4.1	—	—	2.1	−0.3
1957	—	683.8	4.3	—	—	1.8	0.1
1958	—	680.9	6.8	—	—	−0.4	2.5
1959	63.7	721.7	5.5	—	—	6.0	−1.3
1960	63.0	737.2	5.5	−1.1	−0.09	2.1	0.1
1961	63.6	756.6	6.7	0.9	0.08	2.6	1.2
1962	64.2	800.3	5.5	0.9	0.08	5.8	−1.2
1963	66.3	832.5	5.7	3.3	0.27	4.0	0.1
1964	68.4	876.4	5.2	3.2	0.25	5.3	−0.5
1965	70.3	929.3	4.5	2.8	0.22	6.0	−0.7
1966	70.6	984.8	3.8	0.3	0.02	6.0	−0.7
1967	72.5	1011.4	3.8	2.8	0.20	2.7	0.1
1968	74.0	1058.1	3.6	2.0	0.15	4.6	−0.3
1969	73.5	1087.6	3.5	−0.6	−0.04	2.8	−0.1
1970	74.4	1085.6	4.9	1.1	0.08	−0.2	1.4
1971	75.8	1122.4	5.9	1.9	0.13	3.4	1.0
1972	80.8	1185.9	5.6	6.5	0.44	5.7	−0.3
1973	79.8	1254.3	4.9	−1.2	−0.08	5.8	−0.7
1974	78.1	1246.3	5.7	−2.1	−0.13	−0.6	0.8
1975	77.9	1231.6	8.5	−0.3	−0.02	−1.2	2.8
1976	79.8	1298.2	7.7	2.4	0.15	5.4	−0.8
1977	81.5	1369.7	7.1	2.1	0.13	5.5	−0.6
1978	81.7	1438.6	6.1	0.2	0.01	5.0	−1.0
1979	81.6	1479.4	5.8	−0.1	0.00	2.8	−0.2
1980	80.1	1475.0	7.1	−1.8	−0.10	−0.3	1.3
1981	78.0	1512.2	7.6	−2.7	−0.15	2.5	0.5
1982	80.4	1480.0	9.7	3.1	0.16	−2.1	2.1
1983	84.5	1534.7	9.6	5.1	0.28	3.7	−0.1
1984	91.0	1638.8	7.5	7.6	0.42	6.8	−2.1

C

Sources and Methods*

A. *Balance Sheet Sources*

The major basic sources of U.S. data are the Bureau of Economic Analysis of the Department of Commerce and the Flow of Funds section at the Board of Governors of the Federal Reserve System.

Bureau of Economic Analysis revised series on reproducible tangible assets of government are estimated replacement costs net of depreciation, taken from *Fixed Reproducible Tangible Wealth in the United States, 1925–79* and from "Fixed Reproducible Tangible Wealth in the United States, 1980–83" (Musgrave, 1984). Their accuracy as indicators of market values is dependent upon the accuracy of the price indices and deflators used to obtain both gross values and accumulated depreciation. Data for 1984 and for government inventories are from unpublished series provided by John Musgrave of the Bureau's National Income and Wealth Division.

Land estimates for 1952 through 1968 originated with Grace Milgram in Goldsmith (1973). Federal land estimates were extrapolated backward and state and local estimates were extrapolated backward and forward on the basis of total private land estimates taken from the Flow of Funds. Federal land estimates for the years 1969 through 1981 are from Boskin et al. (1984), with later years extrapolated by the Flow of Funds private land estimates.

Federal government data were totals for the government of the United States, federally sponsored credit agencies, and the monetary

*Paul J. Pieper, of the University of Illinois at Chicago, has joined me in the preparation and writing of the Sources and Methods section.

208

authority. Current assets in federal employee and retirement funds were treated as offset by current liabilities. The state and local data excluded state and local retirement funds. Except in the separate presentation of Treasury estimates of federal contingent liabilities, we did not consider future retirement obligations or associated future receipts at either the federal or state and local levels.

B. Par-to-Market Conversion

ASSETS

Currency, demand and time deposits. Taken at face value.

Gold. Prior to 1968, we accepted the official gold price of $35 per ounce. From 1968 through 1980, market values for the last trading day of the year were taken from "Daily market prices of industrial gold in the United States, quoted by Engelhard Minerals and Chemical Corporation, Murray Hill, New Jersey," in the 1968 through 1980 issues of the U.S. Treasury's *Report of the Director of the Mint.* Data from 1981 through 1984 were taken from the *Wall Street Journal.* The value of gold holdings was calculated as the value of the stock of gold at the official price, multiplied by the ratio of the market price to the official price.

U.S. government securities. Indices for U.S. government securities were taken or derived from data prepared by W. Michael Cox (1985). For agency issues we took a weighted average of the Cox index for Treasury bonds and Treasury notes.

The Cox indexes were used to construct a market-to-par index for Treasury issues held by the Federal Reserve as follows:

$$MP_t^{FED} = \frac{\sum_{i=1}^{4} MP_{it} PV_{it}^{FED}}{\sum_{i=1}^{4} PV_{it}^{FED}} \tag{C.1}$$

where: MP^{FED} = market-to-par index for Treasury issues held by the Federal Reserve and federal credit agencies and trust funds,

PV_i^{FED} = par value of U.S. Treasury marketable debt in maturity class i held by the Federal Reserve and federal credit agencies and trust funds, and

MP_i = Cox market-to-par index for maturity class i, and
the t subscript, here and elsewhere, denotes the
year to which the valuables relate.

The four maturity classes are: less than one year; one to four years; five
to nine years; and ten years and over. The data source for PV_i^{FED} is the
Treasury Bulletin, Table TSO-2. This table was discontinued after the
second quarter of 1982. The maturity distribution of debt was assumed
not to change subsequently.

State and local obligations. For short-term state and local obligations, that
is, those of less than one year, we used the Cox index for U.S. Treasury
bills. For other state and local obligations, we constructed an index on
the assumption that the maturity was ten years, that the coupon rate
for each quarter was equal to the long-term yield on state and local
government securities as shown in Standard and Poor's, that interest
payments were made once a year, and that market values at the end of
the quarter varied in accordance with the Standard and Poor yields as
applied to the stock of bonds issued over the forty most recent quarters.
Data sources for bond issues and yields were *Banking and Monetary Statistics, 1941–70; Business Statistics, 1979;* and the *Survey of Current Business.*
    Our procedure in constructing a price index of state and local
securities may then be described algebraically as follows:

$$MV_{t,\tau} = PV_{t,\tau}(1 + r_t)^{-\frac{40-\tau}{4}} + r_{t,\tau}PV_{t,\tau} \sum_{i=1}^{40-\tau} (1 + r_t)^{i/4} \quad (C.2)$$

which may be rewritten as

$$MV_{t,\tau} = PV_{t,\tau}\left[(1 + r_t)^{\frac{\tau-40}{4}} + r_{t,\tau} \sum_{i=1}^{40-\tau} (1 + r_t)^{-i/4}\right]$$

where: $MV_{t,\tau}$ = market value at the end of period t of securities
issued τ quarters earlier,

$PV_{t,\tau}$ = par value at the end of period t of securities issued τ
quarters earlier,

$r_{t,\tau}$ = coupon rate (and initial yield) of securities issued in
the quarter $t - \tau$, and

r_t = market rate of interest or yield at the end of period t.

It may be noted that the first term in (C.2) represents the present
value of principal, and the second term the present value of interest
payments, on securities with $40 - \tau$ quarters left to maturity.
    The value of all securities is, of course, the sum of the values of

securities of all vintages. Hence, the market-to-par price index for state and local securities at the end of the period t is defined as:

$$P_{t,SL} = \sum_{\tau=1}^{40} MV_{t,\tau} \bigg/ \sum_{\tau=1}^{40} PV_{t,\tau} \qquad (C.3)$$

Mortgages. This is the sum of mortgages held by the U.S. government, and residential mortgages and farm mortgages held by federal credit agencies. We constructed a market-to-par index using methodology similar to that employed for the state and local bond index. After conversations with economists at the Federal National Mortgage Association, we decided to assume a twelve-year life. For a rate of discount we took the Federal Home Loan Board series on new home mortgage yields, extrapolated for the years prior to 1949 on the basis of Moody's Baa corporate bond rate. The precise algebraic description of our par-to-market calculations for mortgages is as follows.

The flow of payments of interest and amortization of principal relating to each year's gross investment is calculated as:

$$F_t = I_t^G \bigg/ \sum_{i=1}^{12} (1 + r_t)^{-i} \qquad (C.4)$$

where: F_t = yearly payments on mortgages issued in year t,

I_t^G = gross investment or new acquisitions of mortgages in year t, and

r_t = average annual mortgage yield in year t.

The market and par values of the mortgages are discounted flow of payments of mortgages acquired over the previous twelve years:

$$MV_t = \sum_{\tau=0}^{11} \sum_{i=1}^{12-\tau} \frac{F_{t,\tau}}{(1 + r_t')^i} \qquad (C.5)$$

and

$$PV_t = \sum_{\tau=0}^{11} \sum_{i=1}^{12-\tau} \frac{F_{t,\tau}}{(1 + r_{t,\tau})^i} \qquad (C.6)$$

where r_t' = end-of-year-t mortgage yield. Then, MV_t/PV_t = the market-to-par index for mortgages for the year t.

Gross mortgage acquisitions were calculated as the sum of net investment I^N, and retirements, R:

$$I_t^G = I_t^N + R_t \qquad (C.7)$$

where

$$I_t^N = K_t - K_{t-1} \tag{C.8}$$

and K_t is the end-of-year-t stock of mortgages held by the federal government and its credit agencies.

Mortgage retirements were assumed to be the mean of acquisitions ten, eleven, twelve, thirteen, and fourteen years previously:

$$R_t = 0.2 \sum_{i=10}^{14} I_{t-i}^G \tag{C.9}$$

Thus, for gross investment in mortgages we have:

$$I_t^G = K_t - K_{t-1} + 0.2 \sum_{i=10}^{14} I_{t-i}^G \tag{C.10}$$

where K_t for $t = 1945$ to 1984 is taken directly from the Flow of Funds accounts. K_t for $t = 1932$ to 1944, required because of the assumed twelve-year life, is taken from the *Federal Reserve Bulletin* as the sum of holdings of the Home Owners Loan Corporation, the Federal Home Loan Banks (FHLB), the Reconstruction Finance Mortgage Companies (RFMC), the Federal National Mortgage Association (FNMA), the Federal Public Housing Agency, the Federal Land Banks, and the Federal Farm Mortgage Corporation. I_t^G for t prior to 1933 is assumed to be zero.

Other loans. These are the sum of other loans, loans to co-ops, loans to farmers, FHLB loans, and student loans, all taken at face value from the Flow of Funds accounts.

Taxes receivable. These are as shown, unadjusted, in the Flow of Funds.

Miscellaneous assets. These are a collection of items all taken at face value or par. They include special drawing rights and official foreign exchange, trade credits and the miscellaneous item in the Flow of Funds account for U.S. government, federal funds and security repos, open-market paper, and miscellaneous assets in the federally sponsored agencies accounts of the Flow of Funds; foreign exchange, Federal Reserve float, Federal Reserve loans to domestic banks, acceptances, bank loans not elsewhere classified, and miscellaneous assets in the Monetary Authority accounts of the Flow of Funds; and security RP's as listed in the state and local government's general funds accounts of the Flow of Funds.

LIABILITIES

The various liability items were taken at face value, or par, or converted to market by indices already described in connection with assets.

State and local obligations, short-term. Applied U.S. Treasury bill index. For state and local obligations, other, we applied the state and local bond index described in connection with assets.

Treasury issues. Applied Cox index for total U.S. government debt.

Agency issues. Applied a weighted average of Cox indexes of Treasury bonds and notes.

Savings bonds. Applied Cox index for U.S. Treasury notes.

U.S. government loans. Taken at face value.

Insurance and retirement reserves. Taken at face value.

Miscellaneous liabilities. These are a collection of items all taken at face value or par. They include, among U.S. government liabilities: loan participation, residential mortgages, trade debt, and "miscellaneous"; under federally sponsored credit agencies and mortgage pools, "miscellaneous liabilities"; and, under Monetary Authority, "miscellaneous liabilities."

C. *Price Effects: Nominal-to-Real Conversion*

Price effects are calculated as the change in the real market value of existing net debt, excluding gold, measured in average prices of the period. They may be described as:

$$PE_t = [(A - 1)DM_{t-1} + (B - 1)(DM_t - DM_{t-1})]/B \qquad (C.11)$$

where: PE = price effects,

$A = (P_t^e/P_{t-1}^e)$

$B = (P_t^e/P_t)$

P^e = end-of-period price deflator, equal to $(P_{t,4} + P_{t+1,1})/2$, where 1 and 4 refer to the first and fourth quarters, respectively,

P = annual GNP implicit price deflator, and

DM = end-of-year market value of net debt excluding gold.

Net revaluations on gold are calculated as

$$NR_t = GM_t - \left(\frac{P_t^e}{P_{t-1}^e}\right) GM_{t-1} - \left(\frac{P_t^e}{P_t}\right) IN_t \qquad \text{(C.12)}$$

where: NR = net revaluations,
         GM = end-of-year market value of the stock of gold, and
         IN_t = net investment in gold.

Net investment in gold is equal to the change in the physical stock of gold, multiplied by the average market price:

$$IN_t = 0.5(P_t^{GM} + P_{t-1}^{GM})\left(\frac{GO_t}{P_t^{GO}} - \frac{GO_{t-1}}{P_{t-1}^{GO}}\right) \qquad \text{(C.13)}$$

where: P_t^{GM} = market price of gold at the end of year t,
         P_t^{GO} = U.S. official price of gold at the end of year t, and
         GO_t = end-of-year official value of the stock of gold.

D.   Interest Effects

Interest effects equal the total change in par-to-market revaluations:

$$IE_t = \sum_{i=1}^{5} [(1 - MP_{i,t})PV_{i,t} - (1 - MP_{i,t-1})PV_{i,t-1}] \qquad \text{(C.14)}$$

where: $PV_{i,t}$ = par value of the ith financial instrument at the end
              of year t expressed as a positive quantity if it is a
              liability and a negative quantity if it is an asset, and

         $MP_{i,t}$ = market-to-par index for the ith financial instrument
              at the end of year t.

The five financial instruments are savings bonds, mortgages, agency issues, Treasury issues held by the Federal Reserve, and U.S. government and Treasury issues held by the public.

E.   High-Employment Budgets

The high-employment surplus is defined for a 4.0 percent level of unemployment in 1955, gradually increasing to 5.1 percent in 1975 and remaining constant thereafter, as indicated below.

	High-Employment
Year	Unemployment Rate
1955–58	4.0
1959	4.1
1960–62	4.2
1963–64	4.3
1965	4.4
1966	4.5
1967	4.4
1968	4.5
1969	4.6
1970	4.7
1971	4.8
1972–73	4.9
1974	5.0
1975–84	5.1

Data from 1955 to the third quarter of 1983 are taken from de Leeuw and Holloway (1982) and the *Survey of Current Business (SCB),* November 1983. The U.S. Department of Commerce now uses a 6 percent unemployment rate in estimating the high-employment surplus, which is presented periodically in the *SCB*. The series based on a 5.1 percent rate was extrapolated through 1984 on the basis of the following equation:

$$HES(5.1)_t = HES(6)_t$$
$$+ HEGNP_t \frac{(HES(5.1)_{83.3} - HES(6)_{83.3})}{HEGNP_{83.3}} \quad \text{(C.15)}$$
$$t = 83.3, \ldots, 84.4$$

where: $HES(5.1)$ = high-employment surplus estimated for 5.1 percent unemployment,

$HES(6)$ = high-employment surplus estimated for 6 percent unemployment,

$HEGNP$ = nominal high-employment GNP for 6 percent

and the numerical subscripts refer to year and quarter. Annual surpluses for 1983 and 1984 were calculated as the arithmetic means of the annual rates of quarterly surpluses. The same formulation was used for the projections from 1985 to 1990. High-employment GNP for those years was calculated as:

$$HEGNP_t = HEGNP_{84}(1 + g)^{t-84} \quad t = 85, \ldots, 90 \quad \text{(C.16)}$$

where g = rate of growth of nominal high-employment GNP. The growth rate g was calculated as $(1 + g) = (1 + r)(1 + p)$ where r = real rate of growth of high-employment GNP and p = rate of increase of GNP implicit price deflator. Following CBO projections, r was estimated as 0.032 and p as 0.042, thus yielding a value of 0.075344 for g.

"Base-line" (BL) no-deficit-reduction projections of $HES(6)$ were taken from the CBO, and correspond to their published actual surplus (AS) projections in *The Economic and Budget Outlook: An Update* (1985). Projections of $HES(6)$ on the assumption that the fiscal 1986 Congressional Budget Resolution (BR) or the Gramm–Rudman program (GR) is implemented were then calculated as

$$HES(6,X)_t = HES(BL)_t + AS(X)_t - AS(BL)_t$$

with the assumption that national income account *differences* in budget projections are the same as unified budget differences, and X = BR for fiscal 1986 Congressional Budget Resolution or X = GR for the Gramm–Rudman program.

Fiscal year unified budget annual projections (F) were converted to calendar years (C) as weighted averages:

$$C(t) \quad = 0.75F(t) + 0.25\,F(t + 1) \qquad t = 85, \ldots, 89 \quad (C.17)$$

$$C(90) = 0.75\,F(90) + 0.25\,F(90)\,[F(90)/F(89)], \qquad\qquad (C.18)$$

for the CBO baseline and budget resolution forecasts, and

$$C(t) = 0.75F(t) + 0.25F(t + 1) \qquad t = 85, \ldots, 90 \quad (C.19)$$

for Gramm–Rudman.

F. *Monetary Base*

The monetary base, seasonally adjusted and adjusted for changes in reserve requirements, is taken from the Federal Reserve Board's "Reserves of Depository Institutions." Annual observations were defined as the December monetary base divided by the end-of-year GNP implicit price deflator. Then,

$$MBCH_t = 100\left[\left(\frac{MB_t^e}{P_t^e} - \frac{MB_{t-1}^e}{P_{t-1}^e}\right)\bigg/ GNP72_{t-1}\right]$$

where: $MBCH$ = change in real monetary base as a percentage of
             real GNP,
       MB^e = monetary base at the end of the year t,

P^e = end-of-period GNP implicit price deflator, defined
as the average of the deflators for the fourth
quarter and the first quarters of the subsequent
year, and

GNP72 = gross national product in 1972 dollars.

G. *Gross National Product*

Data for GNP and its components are from *The National Income and Product Accounts, 1929–76,* the July 1982 *Survey of Current Business,* and the 1985 *Economic Report of the President.* The dependent variable in the GNP regressions is the percentage change in real GNP, which is defined as

$$GNPCH_t = 100 \left[\frac{GNP72_t - GNP72_{t-1}}{GNP72_{t-1}} \right]$$

H. *Unemployment*

The unemployment variable is the percentage point change in the unemployment rate, defined as

$$UNCH_t = 100 \left[\frac{UN_t}{UN_t + CIV_t} - \frac{UN_{t-1}}{UN_{t-1} + CIV_{t-1}} \right]$$

where: UNCH = percentage point change in the unemployment rate,
 UN = total unemployment, and
 CIV = total civilian employment.

Annual data are from the 1985 *Economic Report of the President.*

I. *Countries Other Than the United States*

Net debt is defined as total general government financial assets (excluding gold) minus financial liabilities, with basic data for France, Germany, and Italy for the 1970 to 1980 period and for the United Kingdom for the 1970 to 1978 period drawn from Cukierman and Mortensen (1983), Table 6. Data for Canada and Japan through 1980 were taken from the United Nations *Statistical Yearbook.* Net debt in 1981 and 1982 was calculated as the previous year's net debt plus the general government financial deficit for that year.

Bonds are recorded at market value in Germany, the United Kingdom, and the United States but at par elsewhere.

General government financial deficits include those of central, state, and local governments and social security funds. They exclude the net operating surplus of the public enterprise sector. Figures are taken from Price and Chouraqui (1983), Table 2.

For all countries other than the United States, price effects are calculated as the average amount of net debt during the year, multiplied by the December-to-December relative change in the consumer price index. Thus,

$$PE_t = (P^e_t - P^e_{t-1})D_t / P^e_{t-1} \qquad (C.20)$$

where: PE_t = price effects in year t,

P^e = December level of the consumer price index, and

D_t = average level of net debt in year t.

Cyclically adjusted budget deficits are OECD estimates, as re-printed in Price and Chouraqui (1983), Table 5. Cyclically and price-adjusted deficits are equal to the cyclically adjusted deficit plus price effects on the net debt.

Gross domestic product and consumer price statistics are from the International Monetary Fund's *International Financial Statistics*.

Notes

Chapter 1: *Debt and Deficits: Curse, or Blessing in Disguise?* (pp. 1–8)

1. Among those who have recently been addressing some of the critical conceptual issues of measurement of debt and deficits are Boskin (1982 and 1986), Buiter (1983), Cox (1985), Cox and Hirschhorn (1983), Cukierman and Mortensen (1983), Horrigan (1984), Horrigan and Protopadakis (1982), Penner (1982), Price and Chouraqui (1983), Ruggles and Ruggles (1982), and Seater (1981).

Chapter 2: *Tricks Played by Inflation* (pp. 9–25)

1. Economists must be repeatedly startled by a widespread lay confusion between debt and deficit. Network television newsmen, journalists, and others who should know better, refer to "debt" when they should mean "deficit." The page one headline in the *Chicago Tribune* on August 2, 1985, for example, read "Deficit-Denting Budget Passes— Plan Chips $55 billion off Debt." Of course, the Congressional agreement, claiming a deficit reduction of $55.5 billion in the 1986 fiscal

budget year, was projecting a remaining deficit of $171.9 billion which, creative accounting aside, would *add* $171.9 billion to the debt.

Debt and deficits, in principle, are simply related. If a person with no assets has a debt of $10 Monday night and runs a deficit of $2 on Tuesday, his debt Tuesday night is $12. As long as there are no assets to sell off, a deficit must be financed by borrowing.

Debt is thus increased by the amount of a deficit. The larger the deficit the greater the increase. A balanced budget leaves the debt unchanged. Only a budget surplus can reduce the debt.

2. See Table B.14 and Appendix C, "Sources and Methods," for details and derivation.
3. This makes no allowance, it should be acknowledged, for the probability that the true market value of various government agency low-interest, high-risk loans is considerably less than the values at which they are carried on the books. On this subject, see Weidenbaum (1972).

Chapter 3: *Capital Budgeting or Its Lack— and the Nation's Wealth* (pp. 26–32)

1. Prepared by the Mineral Management Service, Bureau of Land Management, and made available to me by David J. Rivait of the Office of the Administrator of the General Services Administration.
2. Estimates of the value of federal nonresidential structures and equipment by Boskin, Robinson, and Roberts (1985) are consistently higher than those we took from the Bureau of Economic Analysis. By 1984 their series would, on this count alone, raise our estimates of tangible assets and net worth by some $100 billion.

Chapter 4: *A Variety of Deficits* (pp. 33–40)

1. At this writing there are moves in Congress to accelerate to fiscal 1987 the removal of social security from the unified budget.
2. *Survey of Current Business,* April 1985, Table 2, p. 27. The fiscal 1985 deficit, as reported in November 1985, was actually $212 billion.
3. For a further discussion of issues raised in this chapter see Boskin (1982).

Chapter 5: *Deficit, Deficit, Who's Got the Surplus?* (pp. 41–46)

1. Domestic debt must be distinguished from foreign debt, and borrowing to finance government budget deficits must be distinguished from

borrowing to finance foreign trade deficits. Foreign holdings of our debt may only indirectly contribute to demand for our goods and services. And we suffer a loss of goods and services to foreigners to service the debt, unless we take care of interest and principal by further borrowing. Further, nations can always create their own money. Where they incur debt in foreign currencies, as have many Third World countries, there can be real dangers of default or bankruptcy. Nevertheless, with foreign debt and trade deficits, as with domestic deficits, it is important that they be measured correctly.

Chapter 6: *Deficits and the Economy: The Theory, Part I* (pp. 47–59)

1. The one exception in economic theory is the lump sum "head tax." This may be construed as a flat tax on all humans with heads and hence the only behavior that can avoid it is dying or refusing to be born. At that, head taxes can have effects by encouraging death and discouraging birth. And they may indeed encourage people to work harder and earn more in order to pay the tax and avoid the relative poverty it may induce.

2. Assuming only real interest income, and not nominal interest income, is taxed. Otherwise the required debt figure would be higher—and there is no debt that would be sufficient if the after-tax real return on government securities were not positive. If the gross public debt grew indefinitely at a rate 3 percent greater than GNP, as it did in 1984, it would take more than 150 years to reach the extreme situation described in the text.

3. Roughly in line with estimates of tangible wealth in 1981 presented in Eisner (1985), Table 13, p. 47.

Chapter 7: *Deficits and the Economy: The Theory, Part II* (pp. 60–77)

1. See Feldstein (1974) and a host of subsequent articles.

2. See Eisner (1983a) and the appendix to this chapter.

3. Peter Diamond (1965) has set forth conditions in an "overlapping generations model" where government debt would reduce the investment component of output. If the marginal net product of capital is positive, this would reduce future output.

Chapter 8: *Deficits and the Economy: The Facts*
(pp. 78–94)

1. Since we have accepted Bureau of Economic Analysis increases in the "high-employment" bench mark from 4.0 percent to 5.1 percent unemployment over the period of its "official" series, we may well understate the move to fiscal tightness. The high-employment surpluses would have been even greater in later years if calculated at 4.0 percent unemployment.

Chapter 9: *More Facts: A Statistical Analysis*
(pp. 95–113)

1. These are, of course, disequilibrium relations. We do not suggest on the basis of (9.2) that a balanced, price-adjusted high-employment budget would generate a permanent growth in real GNP of 4.421 percent or, on the basis of (9.4), permanent rates of decline in unemployment of 0.455 percentage points per year. Indeed, one might infer that it would prove impossible to maintain a balanced, adjusted high-employment budget indefinitely. For as unemployment reached truly full-employment levels, further stimuli to demand would increase the rate of inflation until the price-adjusted high-employment budget were sufficiently in surplus to be consistent with no further changes in the rate of unemployment. By way of illustration, without taking the specific numbers too seriously, equation (9.4) suggests that the rate of unemployment would be constant with a price-adjusted high-employment surplus equal to 0.419 percent of GNP. This would imply a 3.4 percent per annum growth in real GNP.

   Similarly, equation (9.3) indicates that zero change in unemployment would require an official high-employment deficit equal to 0.974 percent of GNP. This would also imply real per annum growth in GNP of 3.4 percent.

2. At least part of the explanation for the lower growth associated with a balanced price-adjusted budget in the later period is that the high-employment budget was defined finally for a 5.1 percent unemployment rate. A balance at this rate implied a surplus for the earlier 4.0 percent unemployment. A balanced budget at 4.0 percent would imply a greater rate of growth, closer to the 7.187 percent of the earlier period.

3. The monetary base consists essentially of legal reserves of depository institutions, held in the form of currency or federal revenue balances, and currency held outside depository institutions. The widely re-

garded but relatively narrow measure of "the money supply," M1, is the sum of: currency outside the Treasury and banks; demand deposits at commercial banks other than deposits due to domestic banks, the U.S. government, foreign banks, and official institutions; other checkable deposits at depository institutions, credit unions, and thrift institutions; and travelers' checks of nonbank issuers. A much broader measure, M2, consists of M1 plus savings and small time deposits, money market deposit accounts, most money market mutual fund balances, and overnight Eurodollars and "RPs."

4. The coefficient of determination is trivially higher in equation (9.13) with the price-adjusted surplus, and the improvement in fit is greater when the price-adjusted surplus variable is added to the monetary base equation than when the monetary base variable is added to the price-adjusted surplus equation.

5. Estimated parameters in component equations summed precisely to parameters of aggregate equations in ordinary least square regressions. The coefficients shown in Tables 9.8 and 9.9, however, are from regressions applying the Cochrane–Orcutt, first-order autoregressive correction. Since the autoregressive parameter, ρ, differed among component and aggregate equations, the sums of the estimated parameters of the component equations were not identically equal to the estimated parameters of the aggregate equations.

Chapter 10: *Deficits and the Rest of the World* (pp. 114–128)

1. Eisner and Pieper (1986). Much of the material of this chapter is also presented there.

2. The cyclically adjusted series are defined here for a somewhat lower (1972, actual) employment rate and, while similar, are not identical to those presented and used for the United States in Chapters 8 and 9.

Chapter 12: *Implications for Policy: Past, Present, and Future* (pp. 145–164)

1. While inflation rates are expected to be lower, the base of existing debt that is taxed by inflation will be much higher as a result of the last five years of large deficits.

2. *New York Times*, December 7, 1984, p. A46.

3. *New York Times,* December 14, 1985, p. A1.

4. *New York Times,* July 27, 1985, Op Ed page.

5. Further, of course, our results are dependent on the implementation of the deficit reductions specified. It has been charged that the Budget Resolution has in fact substantially overstated expenditure savings and that prospective deficit reductions are considerably less than indicated. On this see, for example, Sinai (1985).

6. In its final form, Gramm–Rudman accepts the $171.9 billion Budget Resolution target for fiscal 1986. It limits the permissible automatic cuts for 1986 to $11.7 billion, however. It is thus doubtful, given the very large fiscal 1986 deficit projections as of December 1985, that even the original $180 billion deficit target will be reached.

Appendix to Chapter 7 (pp. 182–184)

1. The reader should not confuse this comparative-static argument with questions of rates of actual or expected inflation, which are not part of the social security issue which has been raised.

References

ANDO, ALBERT K. and FRANCO MODIGLIANI. "The 'Life Cycle' Hypothesis of Saving: Aggregate Implications and Tests." *The American Economic Review* 53 (March 1963): 55–84.

BARRO, ROBERT J. "Are Government Bonds Net Wealth?" *Journal of Political Economy* 82 (Nov./Dec. 1974): 1095–1117.

———. *The Impact of Social Security on Private Savings: Evidence from the U.S. Time Series.* Washington, D.C.: American Enterprise Institute (1978).

———. "On the Determination of the Public Debt." *Journal of Political Economy* 87 (Oct. 1979): 940–971.

———. "The Behavior of U.S. Deficits." In Robert J. Gordon, ed., *The American Business Cycle: Continuity and Change.* Chicago: University of Chicago Press for the National Bureau of Economic Research, forthcoming (1986).

BARRO, ROBERT J. and GLENN M. MACDONALD. "Social Security and Consumer Spending in an International Cross Section." *Journal of Public Economics* 11 (June 1979): 275–289.

BARTH, JAMES R., GEORGE IDEN, and FRANK S. RUSSEK. "Do Federal Deficits Really Matter?" *Contemporary Policy Issues* 3 (Fall 1984–85): 79–95.

BOSKIN, MICHAEL J. "Federal Government Deficits: Some Myths and Realities." *The American Economic Review* 72 (May 1982): 296–303.

———. *The Real Federal Deficit*. Cambridge, Mass.: Harvard University Press, forthcoming (1986).

BOSKIN, MICHAEL J., MARC S. ROBINSON, TERRENCE O'REILLY, and PNAVEEN KUMAR. "New Estimates of the Value of Federal Mineral Rights and Land." *The American Economic Review* 75 (Dec. 1985): 923–936.

BOSKIN, MICHAEL J., MARC S. ROBINSON, and JOHN M. ROBERTS. "New Estimates of Federal Government Tangible Capital and Net Investment." Stanford University, Center for Economic Policy Research, unpublished manuscript (Nov. 1985).

BUCHANAN, JAMES M. "Barro on the Ricardian Equivalence Theorem." *Journal of Political Economy* 84 (April 1976): 337–342.

BUITER, WILLEM H. "The Theory of Optimum Deficits and Debt." In Federal Reserve Bank of Boston (1983): 46–69.

BUITER, WILLEM H. and JAMES TOBIN. "Debt Neutrality: A Brief Review of Doctrine and Evidence." In von Furstenberg (1979): 39–63.

CHIRINKO, ROBERT S. and ROBERT EISNER. "The Effects of Tax Policies in the Investment Equations in Macroeconomic Econometric Models." In Marshall E. Blume, Jean Crockett, and Paul Taubman, eds., *Saving, Investment and Capital Markets*. Cambridge, Mass.: Ballinger (1982).

———. "Tax Policy and Investment in Major U.S. Macroeconomic Econometric Models." *Journal of Public Economics* 20 (1983): 139–166.

COX, W. MICHAEL. "The Behavior of Treasury Securities: Monthly, 1942–1984." Federal Reserve Bank of Dallas (Feb. 1985).

COX, W. MICHAEL and ERIC HIRSCHHORN. "The Market Value of U.S. Government Debt: Monthly, 1942–1980." *Journal of Monetary Economics* 11 (March 1983): 261–272.

CUKIERMAN, ALEX and JORGEN MORTENSEN. "Monetary Assets and Inflation Induced Distortions of the National Accounts—Conceptual Issues and Correction of Sectoral Income Flows in 5 EEC Countries." *Economic Papers* 15. Commission of the European Communities, Directorate General for Economic and Financial Affairs, Internal Paper (June 1983).

DE LEEUW, FRANK and THOMAS M. HOLLOWAY. "The High-Employment Budget: Revised Estimates and Automatic Inflation Effects." *Survey of Current Business* 62 (April 1982): 21–33.

DIAMOND, PETER A. "National Debt in a Neoclassical Growth Model." *American Economic Review* 55 (Dec. 1965): 1125–1158.

EISNER, ROBERT. "Social Security, Saving and Investment." *Journal of Macroeconomics* 5 (Winter 1983): 1–19 (1983a).

―――. "Government Policy, Saving and Investment." *The Journal of Economic Education* (Spring 1983): 38–49 (1983b).

―――. "Which Budget Deficit? Some Issues of Measurement and Their Implications." *The American Economic Review* 74 (May 1984): 138–143.

―――. "The Total Incomes System of Accounts." *Survey of Current Business* 65 (Jan. 1985): 24–48.

EISNER, ROBERT and PAUL J. PIEPER. "A New View of the Federal Debt and Budget Deficits." *The American Economic Review* 74 (March 1984): 11–29.

―――. "How to Make Sense of the Deficit." *The Public Interest*, No. 78 (Winter 1985): 101–118.

―――. "Measurement and Effects of Government Debt and Deficits." In *Economic Policy and National Accounting in Inflationary Conditions, Studies in Banking and Finance*. Amsterdam: North Holland, Division of Elsevier Science Publishers (1986).

FELDSTEIN, MARTIN. "Social Security, Induced Retirement, and Aggregate Accumulation." *Journal of Political Economy* 82 (Sept.-Oct. 1974): 905–925.

―――. "Social Security and Private Saving: Reply." *Journal of Political Economy* 90 (June 1982): 630–642.

FRIEDMAN, MILTON. *A Theory of the Consumption Function*. Princeton University Press for NBER (1957).

―――. "The Role of Monetary Policy." *The American Economic Review* 58 (March 1968): 1–17.

GOLDSMITH, RAYMOND W. *Institutional Investors and Corporate Stock—A Background Study*. New York: National Bureau of Economic Research (1973).

GORDON, ROBERT J. "Output Fluctuations and Gradual Price Adjustment." *Journal of Economic Literature* 19 (June 1981): 493–530.

―――. "Price Inertia and Policy Ineffectiveness in the United States, 1890–1980." *Journal of Political Economy* 90 (Dec. 1982): 1087–1117.

HABERLER, GOTTFRIED. *Prosperity and Depression*. Third edition. Geneva: League of Nations (1941).

HORRIGAN, BRYAN R. "Sizing Up the Deficit: An Efficient Tax Perspective." In Federal Reserve Bank of Philadelphia, *Business Review*, (May/June 1984): 15–24.

HORRIGAN, BRYAN R. and ARIS A. PROTOPAPADAKIS. "Federal Deficits: A Faulty Gauge of Government's Impact on Financial Markets." In Federal Reserve Bank of Philadelphia, *Business Review* (March/April 1982): 3–16.

KEYNES, JOHN M. *The General Theory of Employment, Interest, and Money.* New York: Harcourt Brace (1936).

LEIMER, DEAN R. and SELIG D. LESNOY. "Social Security and Private Saving: New Time-Series Evidence." *Journal of Political Economy* 90 (June 1982): 606–629.

LERNER, ABBA P. "Functional Finance and the Federal Debt." *Social Research* 10 (Feb. 1943): 38–51.

————. *The Economics of Control.* New York: Macmillan (1946).

LUCAS, ROBERT E., JR. *Studies in Business Cycle Theory.* Cambridge, Mass.: MIT Press (1981).

LUCAS, ROBERT E., JR. and THOMAS J. SARGENT. "After Keynesian Economics." In *After the Phillips Curve: Persistence of High Inflation and High Unemployment.* Federal Reserve Bank of Boston Conference Series 19 (1978). Reprinted in *Rational Expectations and Economic Practice.* Edited by Robert E. Lucas Jr. and Thomas J. Sargent. Minneapolis: University of Minnesota Press (1981): 295–319.

MILGRAM, GRACE. "Estimates of the Value of Land in the United States Held by Various Sectors of the Economy, Annually, 1952 to 1968." In Goldsmith (1973): 343–377.

MODIGLIANI, FRANCO and RICHARD BRUMBERG. "Utility Analysis and the Consumption Function: An Interpretation of Cross-Section Data." In *Post-Keynesian Economics.* Edited by Kenneth J. Kurihara. New Brunswick, N.J.: Rutgers University Press (1954): 388–436.

MUNDELL, ROBERT. "Inflation and Real Interest." *Journal of Political Economy* 71 (June 1963): 280–283.

MUSGRAVE, JOHN. "Fixed Reproducible Tangible Wealth in the United States, 1980–83." *Survey of Current Business* 64 (Aug. 1984): 54–57.

PATINKIN, DON. "Price Flexibility and Full Employment." *The American Economic Review* 38 (Sept. 1948): 543–564.

————. *Money, Interest and Prices.* Second edition. New York: Harper & Row (1965).

PENNER, RUDOLPH G. "How Much Is Owed by the Federal Government?" *Carnegie-Rochester Conference Series on Public Policy: Monetary Regimes and Protectionism* 16 (Spring 1982): 233–256.

PIGOU, ARTHUR C. "The Classical Stationary State." *Economic Journal* 53 (Dec. 1943): 343–351.

————. "Economic Progress in a Stable Environment." *Economica* 14 (Aug. 1947): 180–188.

PRICE, ROBERT W. and JEAN-CLAUDE CHOURAQUI. "Public Sector Deficits: Problems and Policy Implications." *OECD Occasional Studies* (June 1983): 13–44.

RICARDO, DAVID. "On the Principles of Political Economy and Taxation." In *The Works of David Ricardo*. Edited by J. R. McCulloch. London: John Murray (1871).

———. "Funding System." In *The Works and Correspondence of David Ricardo*. Vol. IV. Edited by Piero Sraffa. Cambridge, England: Cambridge University Press (1951).

RUGGLES, RICHARD and NANCY D. RUGGLES. "Integrated Economic Accounts for the United States, 1947–1980." *Survey of Current Business* 62 (May 1982): 1–53.

SALANT, WILLIAM A. "Taxes, Income Determination and the Balanced Budget Theorem." *The Review of Economics and Statistics* 39 (May 1957). Reprinted in *Readings in Business Cycles*. Edited by R. A. Gordon and L. R. Klein. Published for the American Economic Association. Homewood, Ill.: Irwin (1965), pp. 680–695.

SEATER, JOHN J. "The Market Value of Outstanding Government Debt, 1919–1975." *Journal of Monetary Economics* 8 (July 1981): 85–101.

SINAI, ALLEN. "The Budget, Crisis Management, and the Economic Outlook." *Economic Policy Studies Series* 11 (October 16, 1985). (Statement prepared for the House Budget Committee, Hearings on the Economic and Budget Outlook, October 10, 1985, Washington, D.C.) New York: Shearson Lehman Brothers (1985).

TOBIN, JAMES. *National Economic Policy*. New Haven: Yale University Press (1946).

———. "Money and Economic Growth." *Econometrica* 33(4) (Oct. 3 1965): 671–684.

TOBIN, JAMES and WILLEM BUITER. "Fiscal and Monetary Policies, Capital Formation, and Economic Activity." In von Furstenberg (1980), pp. 73–151.

VON FURSTENBERG, GEORGE M., ED. *Social Security Versus Private Saving*. Cambridge, Mass.: Ballinger (1979).

———. *The Government and Capital Formation*. Cambridge, Mass.: Ballinger (1980).

VON FURSTENBERG, GEORGE M., R. JEFFERY GREEN, and JIN-HO JEONG. "Tax and Spend, or Spend and Tax?" *Review of Economics and Statistics* (forthcoming). Manuscript copy (1985).

WAKEFIELD, JOSEPH C. "Federal Budget Developments." *Survey of Current Business* 65 (April 1985): 27, Table 2.

WEIDENBAUM, MURRAY L. "Subsidies in Federal Credit Programs." In Congress of the United States, Joint Economic Committee, *The Economics of Federal Credit Programs: Part 1—General Study Papers* (May 1972). Reprinted by American Enterprise Institute, Reprint 4. Washington, D.C. (September 1972).

Reports and Documents

Budget of the United States, Fiscal Year 1986, Special Analyses. Office of Management and Budget. Washington, D.C.: USGPO (1985b).

Business Statistics, 1979. Bureau of Economic Analysis. Washington, D.C.: USGPO (1980).

The Economic and Budget Outlook: An Update. Washington, D.C.: Congressional Budget Office (Aug. 1985).

Economic Indicators (Nov. 1985). Council of Economic Advisers. Washington, D.C.: USGPO (1985c).

Economic Report of the President February 1985. Council of Economic Advisers. Washington, D.C.: USGPO (1985a).

Federal Reserve Bank of Boston. *The Economics of Large Government Deficits.* Federal Reserve Bank of Boston Conference Series 27. Boston (1983).

Federal Reserve System Board of Governors. "Reserves of Depository Institutions," mimeo (July 1985).

———. *Banking and Monetary Statistics 1941–1970.* Washington, D.C. (1976).

———. Flow of Funds. *Balance Sheets for the U.S. Economy 1945–83.* Washington, D.C. (1985).

———. Flow of Funds. "Summary of Credit Market Debt Outstanding and Credit Market Debt Owed by Nonfinancial Sectors," mimeo Washington, D.C. (Feb. 1985).

Fixed Reproducible Tangible Wealth in the United States, 1925–79. Bureau of Economic Analysis. Washington, D.C.: USGPO (1982).

International Financial Statistics (1983 yearbook). Washington, D.C.: International Monetary Fund (1983).

The National Income and Product Accounts of the United States 1929–1976. Bureau of Economic Analysis. Washington, D.C.: USGPO (1981).

Report of the Director of the Mint (annual, 1968–80). U.S. Treasury Dept., Bureau of the Mint.

Statement of Liabilities and Other Financial Commitments of the United States Government as of September 30, 1982. U.S. Treasury Dept., Bureau of Government Financial Operations, Financial Reports Branch.

Treasury Bulletin (various issues, 1945–84). U.S. Treasury Dept.

The United States Budget in Brief, Fiscal Year 1986. Office of Management and Budget. Washington, D.C.: USGPO (1985a).

Yearbook of National Accounts Statistics 1981. New York: United Nations (1983).

Index